Edexcel International GCSE
Biology

Edexcel International GCSE Biology is no picnic, but this brilliant CGP book explains everything you need to know — facts, theory, practical skills... the lot.

What's more, we've included plenty of exam-style questions to put your knowledge to the test. There's even a set of realistic practice papers in the back. Amazing!

It's great for Biology parts of Edexcel's International GCSE Science Double Award too — if you're studying this course, you'll only need to learn the Paper 1 topics.

How to access your free Online Edition

This book includes a free Online Edition to read on your PC, Mac or tablet.
You'll just need to go to **cgpbooks.co.uk/extras** and enter this code:

4039 0721 1059 9870

By the way, this code only works for one person. If somebody else has used this book before you, they might have already claimed the Online Edition.

Complete
Revision & Practice
<u>Everything</u> you need to pass the exams!

Contents

Throughout this book you'll see grade stamps like these:

These grade stamps help to show how difficult the questions are.

Remember — to get a top grade you need to be able to answer **all** the questions, not just the hardest ones.

Section 6 — Coordination and Response

Section 7 — Reproduction and Inheritance

Section 8 — Ecology and the Environment

Edexcel International GCSE Exam Information

1) For the Edexcel International GCSE in Biology, you'll sit two exam papers at the end of your course.

2) Paper 1 is 2 hours long and worth 110 marks. Paper 2 is 1 hour 15 minutes long and worth 70 marks.

3) Some material in the specification will only be tested in Paper 2. The Paper 2 material in this book is marked with a green 'Paper 2' box. The 'Warm-Up' and Revision Summary questions that cover Paper 2 material are printed in green, and the 'Exam Questions' are marked with this stamp: | PAPER 2 |

If you're doing a Science (Double Award) qualification you don't need to learn the Paper 2 material.

Published by CGP

From original material by Paddy Gannon.

Editors: Ellen Burton, Laura Collins, Katherine Faudemer.

ISBN: 978 1 78908 082 7

With thanks to Rachel Kordan for the proofreading.
With thanks to Ana Pungartnik for the copyright research.

DDT diagram on page 133 from Biological Science Combined Volume Hardback, 1990, Soper, Green, Stout, Taylor. Cambridge University Press

Data used to construct the graph on page 185 from R. Doll, R. Peto, J. Boreham, I Sutherland. Mortality in relation to smoking: 50 years' observations on male British doctors. BMJ 2004; 328: 1519. With permission from BMJ Publishing Group Ltd.

Printed by Elanders Ltd, Newcastle upon Tyne.
Clipart from Corel®
Illustrations by: Sandy Gardner Artist, email sandy@sandygardner.co.uk

Based on the classic CGP style created by Richard Parsons.

Characteristics of Living Organisms

Welcome to the wonderful world of Biology. It's wonderful because it's all about living organisms — which includes you. You may not think you have much in common with a slug or a mushroom, but you'd be wrong. You see, all living organisms share the same eight basic characteristics...

1) They Need **Nutrition**

Living organisms need nutrients to provide them with energy and the raw materials for growth and repair. Nutrients include things like proteins, fats and carbohydrates, as well as vitamins and minerals. See pages 23 and 25.

2) They **Respire**

Organisms release energy from their food by a process called respiration. See page 49.

3) They **Excrete** Their **Waste**

Waste products such as carbon dioxide and urine have to be removed. The removal of waste is called excretion. See page 72.

4) They **Respond** to Their Surroundings

Living organisms can react to changes in their surroundings. See page 77.

5) They **Move**

Organisms move towards things like water and food, and away from things like predators and poisons. Even plants can move a bit.

6) They Can **Control** Their **Internal Conditions**

Internal conditions include temperature and water content. See page 85.

7) They **Reproduce**

Organisms have to produce offspring (children) in order for their species to survive. See p.96-98.

8) They **Grow** and **Develop**

Yup, even the smallest organisms have to grow and develop into their adult form.

Levels of Organisation

Organisms are made up of <u>cells</u> — these are like <u>tiny building blocks</u>.

Cells Contain Organelles

1) Cells can be <u>eukaryotic</u> or <u>prokaryotic</u>. Eukaryotic cells are <u>complex</u>, and include all <u>animal</u> and <u>plant</u> cells. Prokaryotic cells are <u>smaller</u> and <u>simpler</u>, e.g. bacteria.

2) <u>Organelles</u> are tiny structures <u>within</u> cells. You can only see them using a powerful <u>microscope</u>.

A Typical Animal Cell Looks Like This...

Here are some of the organelles found in a <u>typical animal cell</u>:

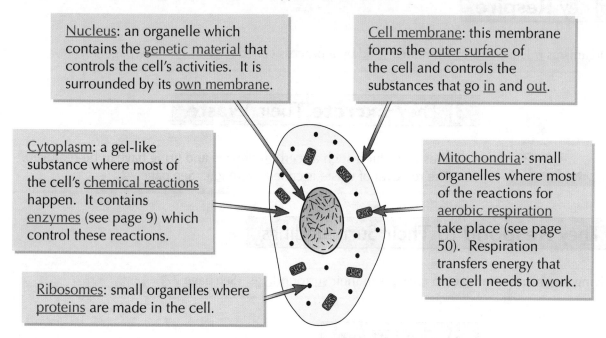

<u>Nucleus</u>: an organelle which contains the <u>genetic material</u> that controls the cell's activities. It is surrounded by its <u>own membrane</u>.

<u>Cell membrane</u>: this membrane forms the <u>outer surface</u> of the cell and controls the substances that go <u>in</u> and <u>out</u>.

<u>Cytoplasm</u>: a gel-like substance where most of the cell's <u>chemical reactions</u> happen. It contains <u>enzymes</u> (see page 9) which control these reactions.

<u>Mitochondria</u>: small organelles where most of the reactions for <u>aerobic respiration</u> take place (see page 50). Respiration transfers energy that the cell needs to work.

<u>Ribosomes</u>: small organelles where <u>proteins</u> are made in the cell.

A Typical Plant Cell Looks Like This...

<u>Plant cells</u> usually have all the organelles that animal cells have, plus a <u>few extra</u>:

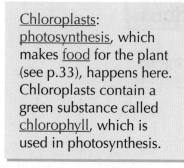

<u>Chloroplasts</u>: <u>photosynthesis</u>, which makes <u>food</u> for the plant (see p.33), happens here. Chloroplasts contain a green substance called <u>chlorophyll</u>, which is used in photosynthesis.

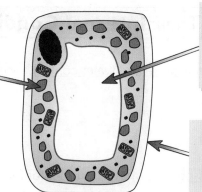

<u>Vacuole</u>: a large organelle that contains <u>cell sap</u> (a weak solution of sugars and salts). It helps to <u>support</u> the cell.

<u>Cell wall</u>: a rigid structure made of <u>cellulose</u>, which surrounds the cell membrane. It <u>supports</u> the cell and <u>strengthens</u> it.

REVISION TIP

There's quite a bit to learn in biology — but that's life, I guess...

On this page are a <u>typical animal cell</u> and <u>plant cell</u>. A good way to check that you know what all the bits and pieces are is to <u>copy out</u> the diagrams and see if you can remember all the labels.

Levels of Organisation

Some organisms consist of a <u>single cell</u>. Some organisms are <u>multicellular</u> —
they contain <u>lots</u> of cells, which need some form of <u>organisation</u>.

Cells are **Specialised**

Most cells don't look exactly like the ones shown on the previous page.
They're <u>specialised</u> to carry out a <u>particular function</u>, so their structures can vary.

For example, in humans, <u>red blood cells</u> are specialised for carrying oxygen
and <u>white blood cells</u> are specialised for defending the body against disease.

red blood cells   white blood cell

Similar Cells are Organised into **Tissues**

1) A <u>tissue</u> is a group of similar cells that <u>work together</u> to carry out a <u>particular function</u>.

> For example, plants have <u>xylem tissue</u> (for transporting water and mineral salts)
> and <u>phloem tissue</u> (for transporting sucrose and amino acids).

2) A tissue can contain <u>more than one</u> cell type (see next page).

Tissues are Organised into **Organs**

An <u>organ</u> is a group
of different <u>tissues</u>
that <u>work together</u> to
perform a function.

Lungs in mammals and
leaves on plants are two
examples of <u>organs</u> —
they're both made up of
several <u>different tissue types</u>.

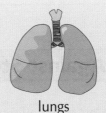

lungs

leaves

Organs Make Up **Organ Systems**

Organs work together
to form <u>organ systems</u>.
Each system does a <u>different job</u>.

For example, in mammals, the <u>digestive system</u> is made up of
organs including the stomach, intestines, pancreas and liver.

Stem Cells

Your body is made up of all sorts of cells — this page tells you where they all came from.

Embryonic Stem Cells Can Turn into ANY Type of Cell

1) Cell differentiation is the process by which a cell changes to become specialised for its job.

2) As cells change, they develop different organelles and turn into different types of cells. This allows them to carry out specific functions.

3) Undifferentiated cells, called stem cells, can divide to produce lots more undifferentiated cells. They can differentiate into different types of cell, depending on what instructions they're given.

4) Stem cells are found in early human embryos. They're exciting to doctors and medical researchers because they have the potential to turn into any kind of cell at all. This makes sense if you think about it — all the different types of cell found in a human being have to come from those few cells in the early embryo.

5) Adults also have stem cells, but they're only found in certain places, like bone marrow. Unlike embryonic stem cells, they can't turn into any cell type at all, only certain ones, such as blood cells.

6) Stem cells from embryos and bone marrow can be grown in a lab to produce clones (genetically identical cells) and made to differentiate into specialised cells to use in medicine or research.

Stem Cells May Be Able to Cure Many Diseases

1) Medicine already uses adult stem cells to cure disease. For example, stem cells transferred from the bone marrow of a healthy person can replace faulty blood cells in the patient who receives them.

2) Embryonic stem cells could also be used to replace faulty cells in sick people — you could make insulin-producing cells for people with diabetes, nerve cells for people paralysed by spinal injuries, and so on.

3) However, there are risks involved in using stem cells in medicine.

> For example, stem cells grown in the lab may become contaminated with a virus which could be passed on to the patient and so make them sicker.

Some People Are Against Stem Cell Research

1) Some people are against stem cell research because they feel that human embryos shouldn't be used for experiments since each one is a potential human life.

2) Others think that curing existing patients who are suffering is more important than the rights of embryos.

3) One fairly convincing argument in favour of this point of view is that the embryos used in the research are usually unwanted ones from fertility clinics which, if they weren't used for research, would probably just be destroyed. But of course, campaigners for the rights of embryos usually want this banned too.

4) These campaigners feel that scientists should concentrate more on finding and developing other sources of stem cells, so people could be helped without having to use embryos.

Paper 2

Plants, Animals and Fungi

Living organisms can be arranged into groups, according to the features they have in common.
Three of these groups are plants, animals and fungi...

Learn the Features of Plants, Animals and Fungi

Plants, animals and fungi are eukaryotic organisms —
they are made up of eukaryotic cells (see page 2). If you've
ever wondered what features you share with a housefly,
then this table is for you. Read on to find out more...

*Plants, animals and fungi
have different cell structures.
For more on the structure of plant
and animal cells, see page 2.*

Organisms		Description	Examples
Plants		1) Plants are multicellular. 2) They have chloroplasts (see p.2) which means they can photosynthesise (see p.33). 3) Their cells have cell walls, which are made of cellulose. 4) Plants store carbohydrates as sucrose or starch.	Flowering plants like: • cereals (e.g. maize). • herbaceous legumes (e.g. peas and beans).
Animals		1) Animals are also multicellular. 2) They don't have chloroplasts and they can't photosynthesise. 3) Their cells don't have cell walls. 4) Most have some kind of nervous coordination (see p.77). This means that they can respond rapidly to changes in their environment. 5) They can usually move around from one place to another. 6) They often store carbohydrate in the form of glycogen.	• Mammals (e.g. humans). • Insects (e.g. houseflies and mosquitoes).
Fungi		1) Some are single-celled. 2) Others have a body called a mycelium, which is made up of hyphae (thread-like structures). The hyphae contain lots of nuclei. 3) They can't photosynthesise. 4) Their cells have cell walls made of chitin. 5) Most feed by saprotrophic nutrition — they secrete extracellular enzymes into the area outside their body to dissolve their food, so they can then absorb the nutrients. 6) They can store carbohydrate as glycogen.	• Yeast — this is a single-celled fungus. • Mucor — this is multicellular and has a mycelium and hyphae.

Protoctists, Bacteria and Viruses

Just when you thought you'd mastered all the groups — here's a few more you need to know about...

Learn the Features of Protoctists, Bacteria and Viruses

Protoctists are eukaryotic organisms (see p.5). Bacteria are prokaryotic organisms (single prokaryotic cells).

Organism		Description	Examples
Protoctists	nucleus	1) These are single-celled and microscopic (really tiny). 2) Some have chloroplasts and are similar to plant cells. 3) Others are more like animal cells.	• Chlorella (plant-cell-like) • Amoeba (animal-cell-like) — lives in pond water.
Bacteria	cell wall, cytoplasm, circular chromosome, cell membrane, plasmids (extra bits of DNA)	1) These are also single-celled and microscopic. 2) They don't have a nucleus. 3) They have a circular chromosome of DNA. 4) Some can photosynthesise. 5) Most bacteria feed off other organisms — both living and dead.	• Lactobacillus bulgaricus — can be used to make milk go sour and turn into yoghurt. It's rod-shaped. • Pneumococcus — spherical (round) in shape.
Viruses	protein coat, DNA or RNA. There's more on DNA on p.93. DNA and RNA are both nucleic acids, so they're fairly similar.	1) These are particles, rather than cells, and are smaller than bacteria. 2) They can only reproduce inside living cells. A virus is an example of a parasite — it depends on another organism to grow and reproduce. 3) They infect all types of living organisms. 4) They come in loads of different shapes and sizes. 5) They don't have a cellular structure — they have a protein coat around some genetic material (either DNA or RNA).	• Influenza virus • Tobacco mosaic virus — this makes the leaves of tobacco plants discoloured by stopping them from producing chloroplasts. • HIV

Some Organisms Are Pathogens

Pathogens are organisms that cause disease. They include some fungi, protoctists and bacteria. Viruses are also pathogens (even though they're not living organisms).

E.g.

PROTOCTIST: Plasmodium, which causes malaria.

BACTERIUM: Pneumococcus, which causes pneumonia.

VIRUSES: Influenza virus (which causes 'flu') and HIV (which causes AIDS).

Bacteria is the plural of bacterium.

Warm-Up & Exam Questions

It's easy to think you've learnt everything in the section until you try the questions.
Don't panic if there's a bit you've forgotten, just go back over that bit until it's firmly fixed in your brain.

Warm-Up Questions

1) Give two similarities and two differences between the structure
   of an animal cell and the structure of a plant cell.
2) Describe the structure of a mycelium.
3) Name a protoctist with a structure similar to: a) a plant cell   b) an animal cell.
4) Name the organism that causes malaria. Is it a bacterium, virus, protoctist or fungus?

Exam Questions

1   A bean plant produces carbohydrate during photosynthesis.   *Grade 3-4*
     Which of the following organelles allows the cells of a bean plant to photosynthesise?

     ☐ **A** ribosome   ☐ **B** chloroplast   ☐ **C** cytoplasm   ☐ **D** mitochondrion

     [1 mark]

2   All living organisms are made up of cells, which contain organelles.   *Grade 4-6*

     (a) The cell nucleus is an organelle. Describe the structure of a cell nucleus.

     [2 marks]

     (b) Describe the function of:
          (i) chloroplasts

     [1 mark]

          (ii) the vacuole

     [1 mark]

     (c) Organelles and cells are the two smallest levels of organisation in multicellular organisms.
          List the next three levels in order of increasing size.

     [2 marks]

3   The diagrams show the bacteria   *Grade 4-6*
     Lactobacillus bulgaricus and *Pneumococcus*.

     (a) (i) Which diagram (**A** or **B**) shows
              Lactobacillus bulgaricus? Explain your answer.

     A   B

     [1 mark]

          (ii) Describe how *Lactobacillus bulgaricus* can be used by the food industry.

     [1 mark]

     (b) *Pneumococcus* is a pathogen. Explain what is meant by the term pathogen.

     [1 mark]

Exam Questions

(c) *Lactobacillus bulgaricus* and *Pneumococcus* do not photosynthesise.
Suggest how these bacteria obtain the nutrients they need.

[1 mark]

(d) Give **three** structural features of a typical bacterial cell.

[3 marks]

4 *Mucor* and yeast are both fungi.

(a) Describe the structure of the mycelium of *Mucor*.

[2 marks]

(b) Which row of the table correctly shows two features of yeast?

		Feature 1	Feature 2
☐	A	Can store carbohydrate	Is multi-celled
☐	B	Is single-celled	Has cell walls containing chitin
☐	C	Can photosynthesise	Is single-celled
☐	D	Has cell walls containing chitin	Can photosynthesise

[1 mark]

5 Viruses can infect every type of living organism.

(a) The leaves of a tobacco plant can become discoloured if it is infected by a particular virus.
Name the virus that affects tobacco plants in this way and explain its effect.

[2 marks]

(b) Name **two** viruses that may infect humans and state the disease that each can cause.

[4 marks]

6 Read the information below and answer the question that follows.

The picture on the right shows an adult starfish.
Starfish are found in oceans around the world.
On the undersides of their arms they have small
structures called 'tube feet', which are very
sensitive to chemicals in the water, helping them
to detect food. When they detect food, they move
their arms to travel in the right direction.
Each of their arms contains two gonads, which
release eggs or sperm into the water.

Suggest and explain **three** pieces of evidence from the passage that show starfish are
living organisms.

[3 marks]

Enzymes

Chemical reactions are what make you work. And enzymes are what make them work.

Enzymes are Catalysts Produced by Living Things

1) Living things have thousands of different chemical reactions going on inside them all the time. These reactions need to be carefully controlled — to get the right amounts of substances in the cells.

2) You can usually make a reaction happen more quickly by raising the temperature. This would speed up the useful reactions but also the unwanted ones too... not good. There's also a limit to how far you can raise the temperature inside a living creature before its cells start getting damaged.

3) So living things produce enzymes that act as biological catalysts.

> A catalyst is a substance which increases the speed of a reaction, without being changed or used up in the reaction.

4) Enzymes reduce the need for high temperatures and we only have enzymes to speed up the useful chemical reactions in the body. These reactions are called metabolic reactions.

5) Enzymes are all proteins and all proteins are made up of chains of amino acids. These chains are folded into unique shapes, which enzymes need to do their jobs (see below).

Enzymes are Very Specific

1) Chemical reactions usually involve things either being split apart or joined together.

2) A substrate is a molecule that is changed in a reaction.

3) Every enzyme molecule has an active site — the part where a substrate joins on to the enzyme.

4) Enzymes are really picky — they usually only speed up one reaction. This is because, for an enzyme to work, a substrate has to be the correct shape to fit into the active site.

5) This is called the 'lock and key' model, because the substrate fits into the enzyme just like a key fits into a lock.

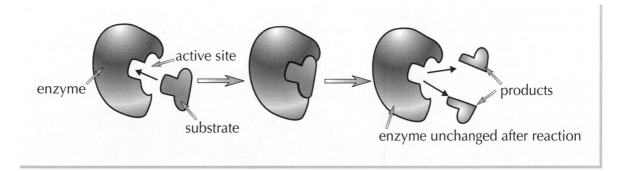

enzyme · active site · substrate · enzyme unchanged after reaction · products

Enzymes speed up chemical reactions

Just like you've got to have the correct key for a lock, you've got to have the right substrate for an enzyme. If the substrate doesn't fit, the enzyme won't catalyse the reaction.

More on Enzymes

Enzymes are clearly very clever, but they're <u>not</u> very versatile.
They need just the right <u>conditions</u> if they're going to work properly.

Enzymes Like it **Warm** but **Not Too Hot**

1) Changing the <u>temperature</u> changes the <u>rate</u> of an enzyme-catalysed reaction.

2) Like with any reaction, a higher temperature <u>increases</u> the rate at first. The enzymes and substrate have <u>more energy</u>, so they <u>move about more</u> and are <u>more likely</u> to <u>collide</u> and form <u>enzyme-substrate complexes</u>.

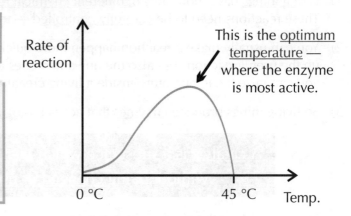

Rate of reaction

This is the <u>optimum temperature</u> — where the enzyme is most active.

0 °C   45 °C   Temp.

3) But if it gets <u>too hot</u>, some of the <u>bonds</u> holding the enzyme together <u>break</u>.

4) This changes the shape of the enzyme's <u>active site</u>, so the substrate <u>won't fit</u> any more. The enzyme is said to be <u>denatured</u>.

5) All enzymes have an <u>optimum temperature</u> that they work best at.

Enzymes Also Need the **Right pH**

1) The <u>pH</u> also affects enzymes. If it's too high or too low, the pH interferes with the <u>bonds</u> holding the enzyme together. This changes the <u>shape</u> of the <u>active site</u> and <u>denatures</u> the enzyme.

2) All enzymes have an <u>optimum pH</u> that they work best at. It's often <u>neutral pH 7</u>, but <u>not always</u>.

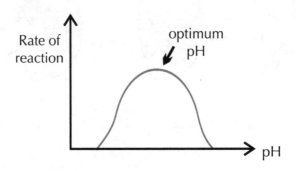

Rate of reaction

optimum pH

pH

If only enzymes could speed up revision...

Scientists have caught on to the idea that enzymes are <u>really useful</u>. They're used in biological <u>detergents</u> (to break down nasty stains) and in some <u>baby foods</u> (to predigest the food).

Investigating Enzyme Activity

I bet you've been asked countless times how you would <u>investigate</u> the <u>effect of temperature on enzyme activity</u>. Well if you read these pages, you'll finally have the answers...

You Can Investigate How **Temperature** Affects **Enzyme Activity**

There are a couple of different ways to investigate how <u>temperature</u> affects enzyme activity.

You Can **Measure How Fast** a **Product Appears**...

1) The enzyme <u>catalase</u> catalyses the <u>breakdown</u> of <u>hydrogen peroxide</u> into <u>water</u> and <u>oxygen</u>.

2) You can collect the <u>oxygen</u> and measure <u>how much</u> is produced in a <u>set time</u>.

3) Use a <u>pipette</u> to add a set amount of <u>hydrogen peroxide</u> to a <u>boiling tube</u>. Put the tube in a <u>water bath</u> at 10 °C.

4) <u>Set up</u> the rest of the apparatus as shown. Add a source of <u>catalase</u> (e.g. 1 cm³ of potato) to the <u>hydrogen peroxide</u> and quickly <u>attach the bung</u>.

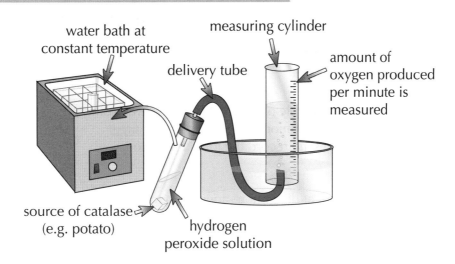

water bath at constant temperature

measuring cylinder

delivery tube

amount of oxygen produced per minute is measured

source of catalase (e.g. potato)

hydrogen peroxide solution

5) Record how much <u>oxygen</u> is produced in the <u>first minute</u>. <u>Repeat three times</u> and calculate the <u>mean</u>.

6) <u>Repeat</u> at 20 °C, 30 °C and 40 °C.

7) <u>Control any variables</u> (e.g. pH, the potato used, the size of potato pieces, etc.) to make it a <u>fair test</u>.

If the temperature is increased too much, no product will appear...

...because the enzyme is denatured. Measuring how fast a product appears is just one option for investigating the effect of temperature on enzyme activity — turn the page for another way...

PRACTICAL Investigating Enzyme Activity

...and You Can Also Measure How Fast a Substrate Disappears

1) The enzyme amylase catalyses the breakdown of starch to maltose.

2) It's easy to detect starch using iodine solution — if starch is present, the iodine solution will change from browny-orange to blue-black.

3) Set up the apparatus as shown in the diagram. Put a drop of iodine solution into each well on the spotting tile.

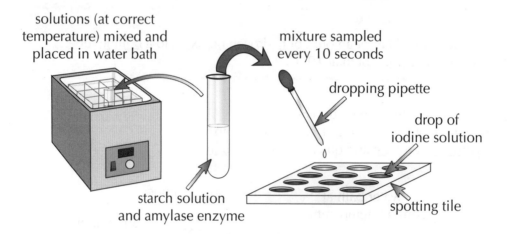

solutions (at correct temperature) mixed and placed in water bath

mixture sampled every 10 seconds

dropping pipette

drop of iodine solution

starch solution and amylase enzyme

spotting tile

4) Every ten seconds, drop a sample of the mixture into a well using a pipette. When the iodine solution remains browny-orange (i.e. starch is no longer present) record the total time taken.

5) Repeat with the water bath at different temperatures to see how it affects the time taken for the starch to be broken down. Remember to control all of the variables each time.

You Can Also Investigate How pH Affects Enzyme Activity

1) You can adapt these experiments to investigate the effect of pH on enzyme activity.

2) Follow the same method, but add a buffer solution with a different pH level to a series of different tubes containing the enzyme-substrate mixture.

3) As before, control any variables — use the water bath to keep the temperature of the reaction mixture the same for each pH, and make sure volumes and concentrations are kept the same.

PRACTICAL TIP A water bath helps to keep the temperature constant

You can make one with a beaker and a Bunsen burner, but an electric water bath can be more easily controlled. Whichever you use, make sure you're careful when you're around hot water.

Warm-Up & Exam Questions

The best way to check whether you've learnt something is to test yourself. Have a go at these questions.

Warm-Up Questions

1) What is the name for the part of an enzyme that a substrate joins onto?
2) Describe the lock and key model of enzyme activity.
3) Why don't enzymes work well at cold temperatures?

Exam Questions

1 Which row in the following table best describes enzymes?

	are affected by pH	speed up reactions	get used up during reactions	all have the same shape
☐ **A**	✓	✓		
☐ **B**			✓	
☐ **C**	✓	✓		✓
☐ **D**		✓	✓	✓

[1 mark]

PRACTICAL

2 The enzyme amylase is involved in the breakdown of starch into simple sugars.

A student investigated the effect of temperature on the activity of amylase in starch solution. Amylase and starch solution were added to test tubes X, Y and Z. The test tubes were placed in water baths of different temperatures, as shown in the table on the right. Spotting tiles were prepared with a drop of iodine solution in each well. Iodine solution is a browny-orange colour but it turns blue-black in the presence of starch.

Test tube	Temp (°C)
X	32
Y	36
Z	48

Every 30 seconds, a drop of the solution from each of the test tubes was added to a separate well on a spotting tile. The resulting colour of the solution in the well was recorded in the table below.

Time (s)	30	60	90	120	150
Tube **X**	Blue-black	Blue-black	Blue-black	Browny-orange	Browny-orange
Tube **Y**	Blue-black	Browny-orange	Browny-orange	Browny-orange	Browny-orange
Tube **Z**	Blue-black	Blue-black	Blue-black	Blue-black	Blue-black

(a) State the temperature at which the rate of reaction was greatest. Explain your answer.

[2 marks]

(b) Suggest an explanation for the results in tube **Z**.

[1 mark]

(c) Suggest two variables that should be controlled in this experiment.

[2 marks]

(d) The student repeated her experiment at 37 °C and got the same results as she got for her experiment at 36 °C. Suggest one way in which she could determine whether the rate of reaction is greatest at 36 °C or 37 °C.

[1 mark]

Diffusion

Diffusion is <u>really important</u> in living organisms — it's how a lot of <u>substances</u> get <u>in</u> and <u>out</u> of cells. Basically particles <u>move about randomly</u>, and after a bit they end up <u>evenly spaced</u>.

Diffusion — Don't be Put Off by the **Fancy Word**

1) <u>Diffusion</u> is simple. It's just the <u>gradual movement</u> of particles from places where there are <u>lots</u> of them to places where there are <u>fewer</u> of them.

2) That's all it is — just the <u>natural tendency</u> for stuff to <u>spread out</u>.

3) Here's the fancy <u>definition</u>:

> <u>Diffusion</u> is the <u>net movement</u> of <u>particles</u> from an area of <u>higher concentration</u> to an area of <u>lower concentration</u>.

The particles are said to move down the concentration gradient.

4) Diffusion is a <u>passive</u> process — it <u>doesn't</u> require <u>energy</u>.

5) Diffusion happens in both <u>liquids</u> and <u>gases</u> — that's because the particles in these substances are free to <u>move about</u> randomly.

6) The <u>simplest type</u> is when different <u>gases</u> diffuse through each other. This is what's happening when the smell of perfume diffuses through a room:

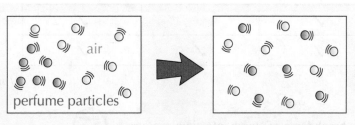

perfume particles diffused in the air

The <u>bigger</u> the <u>difference</u> in concentration, the <u>faster</u> the diffusion rate.

Cell Membranes are Pretty **Clever**...

1) They're clever because they <u>hold</u> the cell together <u>but</u> they let stuff <u>in and out</u> as well.

2) Substances can move in and out of cells by <u>diffusion</u>, <u>osmosis</u> (see next page) and <u>active transport</u> (see page 18).

3) Only very <u>small</u> molecules can <u>diffuse</u> through cell membranes though — things like <u>glucose</u>, <u>amino acids</u>, <u>water</u> and <u>oxygen</u>. <u>Big</u> molecules like <u>starch</u> and <u>proteins</u> can't fit through the membrane.

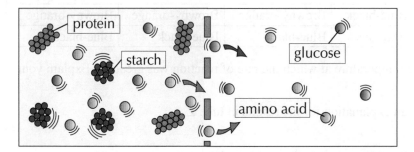

1) Just like with diffusion in air, particles flow through the cell membrane from where there's a <u>higher concentration</u> (more of them) to where there's a <u>lower concentration</u> (not such a lot of them).

2) They're only moving about <u>randomly</u> of course, so they go <u>both</u> ways — but if there are a lot <u>more</u> particles on one side of the membrane, there's a <u>net</u> (overall) movement <u>from</u> that side.

Osmosis

If you've got your head round <u>diffusion</u>, osmosis will be a <u>breeze</u>.
If not, you need to read the previous page...

Osmosis is a **Special Case** of **Diffusion**, That's All

Osmosis is the <u>net movement of water molecules</u> across
a <u>partially permeable membrane</u> from a region of
<u>higher water concentration</u> to a region of <u>lower water concentration</u>.

You could also describe osmosis as the net movement of water molecules across a partially permeable
membrane from a region of lower solute concentration to a region of higher solute concentration.

1) A <u>partially permeable</u> membrane is just one with very small holes in it. So small, in fact, only
tiny <u>molecules</u> (like water) can pass through them, and bigger molecules (e.g. <u>sucrose</u>) can't.
A <u>cell membrane</u> is a <u>partially permeable</u> membrane.

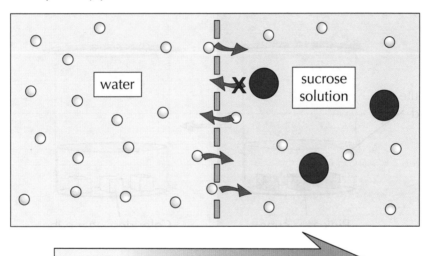

Net movement of water molecules

2) The water molecules actually pass <u>both ways</u> through the membrane during osmosis.
This happens because water molecules <u>move about randomly</u> all the time.

3) But because there are <u>more</u> water molecules on one side than on the other, there's a steady
<u>net flow</u> of water into the region with <u>fewer</u> water molecules, e.g. into the <u>sucrose</u> solution.

4) This means the <u>sucrose</u> solution gets more <u>dilute</u>. The water acts like it's trying to "<u>even up</u>"
the concentration either side of the membrane.

Water Moves **Into** and **Out** of **Cells** by **Osmosis**

1) <u>Tissue fluid</u> surrounds the cells in the body — it's basically just <u>water</u> with <u>oxygen</u>, <u>glucose</u> and stuff
dissolved in it. It's squeezed out of the <u>blood capillaries</u> to supply the cells with everything they need.

2) The tissue fluid will usually have a <u>different concentration</u> to the fluid <u>inside</u> a cell. This means
that water will either move <u>into the cell</u> from the tissue fluid, or <u>out of the cell</u>, by <u>osmosis</u>.

3) If a cell is <u>short of water</u>, the solution inside it will become quite <u>concentrated</u>. This usually
means the solution <u>outside</u> is more <u>dilute</u>, and so water will move <u>into</u> the cell by osmosis.

4) If a cell has <u>lots of water</u>, the solution inside it will be <u>more dilute</u>, and
water will be <u>drawn out</u> of the cell and into the fluid outside by osmosis.

 **Diffusion Experiments**

For all you non-believers — here's an experiment you can do to see diffusion in action.

You Can **Investigate Diffusion** in a **Non-Living System**

Phenolphthalein is a pH indicator — it's pink in alkaline solutions and colourless in acidic solutions. You can use it to investigate diffusion in agar jelly:

1) First, make up some agar jelly with phenolphthalein and dilute sodium hydroxide. This will make the jelly a lovely shade of pink.

2) Put some dilute hydrochloric acid in a beaker.

3) Cut out a few cubes from the jelly and put them in the beaker of acid.

4) If you leave the cubes for a while they'll eventually turn colourless as the acid diffuses into the agar jelly and neutralises the sodium hydroxide.

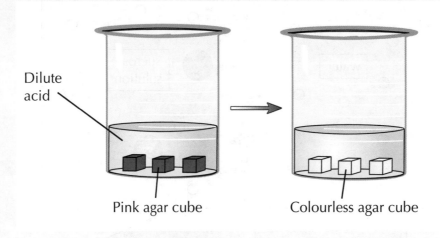

Dilute acid

Pink agar cube   Colourless agar cube

Investigating the **Rate** of Diffusion

1) You can investigate the rate of diffusion by using different sized cubes of agar jelly and timing how long it takes for each cube to go colourless.

2) The cube with the largest surface area to volume ratio (see page 19) will lose its colour quickest.

 You might have to describe a diffusion experiment in the exam

If you're asked to describe an experiment, make sure you do it step-by-step, as if you're guiding someone who's never done it before through how to carry it out.

Osmosis Experiments

Well what do you know — there are experiments that show <u>osmosis</u> in action too.

You Can **Investigate Osmosis** in **Living** and **Non-Living Systems**

Living System — Potato Cylinders

1) Cut up a <u>potato</u> into identical cylinders, and get some beakers with <u>different sugar solutions</u> in them. One should be <u>pure water</u>, another should be a <u>very concentrated sugar solution</u>. Then you can have a few others with concentrations <u>in between</u>.

2) You measure the <u>length</u> of the cylinders, then leave a few cylinders in each beaker for half an hour or so. Then you take them out and measure their lengths <u>again</u>.

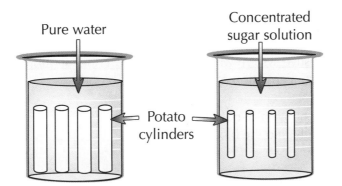

Pure water

Concentrated sugar solution

Potato cylinders

The only thing that you should change is the <u>concentration</u> of the <u>sugar solution</u>. Everything else (e.g. the volume of solution and the time the experiment runs for) must be kept the <u>same</u> in each case or the experiment won't be a <u>fair test</u>.

3) If the cylinders have drawn in water by osmosis, they'll be a bit <u>longer</u>. If water has been drawn out, they'll have <u>shrunk</u> a bit. Then you can plot a few <u>graphs</u> and things.

Non-living System — Visking Tubing

1) Fix some <u>Visking tubing</u> over the end of a <u>thistle funnel</u>. Then <u>pour</u> some <u>sugar solution</u> down the glass tube into the thistle funnel.

2) Put the thistle funnel into a <u>beaker</u> of <u>pure water</u> — <u>measure</u> where the sugar solution comes up to on the <u>glass tube</u>.

3) Leave the apparatus <u>overnight</u>, then <u>measure</u> where the solution is in the glass tube. <u>Water</u> should be <u>drawn through</u> the Visking tubing by osmosis and this will <u>force</u> the solution <u>up</u> the glass tube.

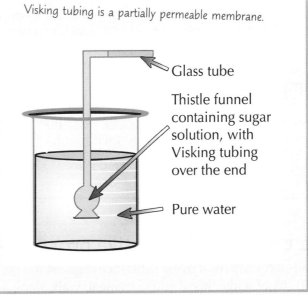

Visking tubing is a partially permeable membrane.

Glass tube

Thistle funnel containing sugar solution, with Visking tubing over the end

Pure water

Active Transport

The movement of substances has been too passive for my liking. It's time to get active.

Active Transport Works Against a Concentration Gradient

Here's what you need to know:

> Active Transport is the movement of particles
> against a concentration gradient (i.e. from an area of
> lower concentration to an area of higher concentration)
> using energy released during respiration.

Active transport, like diffusion and osmosis, is used to move substances in and out of cells.

Example 1:

Active transport is used in the digestive system when there is a low concentration of nutrients in the gut, but a high concentration of nutrients in the blood:

1) When there's a higher concentration of nutrients in the gut they diffuse naturally into the blood.

2) BUT — sometimes there's a lower concentration of nutrients in the gut than there is in the blood.

3) This means that the concentration gradient is the wrong way. The nutrients should go the other way if they followed the rules of diffusion.

4) Active transport allows nutrients to be taken into the blood, despite the fact that the concentration gradient is the wrong way. This is essential to stop us starving. But active transport needs ENERGY from respiration to make it work.

Example 2:

Active transport is also used by plants — it's how they get minerals from the soil (lower mineral concentration) into their root hair cells (higher mineral concentration).

Active transport is an active process — it requires energy

Active transport involves moving substances against the concentration gradient, so it needs energy to make it work. Think of it like this: if you're trying to walk along a crowded street, it's hard to walk in the opposite direction to the one most people are travelling in. You have to push your way through — and that requires energy. The energy for active transport comes from respiration.

Movement of Substances

This page is all about the factors that affect the movement of substances <u>in and out of cells</u>. It might not be fun, but it will be <u>useful</u>. Read on...

Four Factors Affect The Movement of Substances

The <u>rates</u> of diffusion, osmosis and active transport <u>vary</u> — they're affected by <u>several factors</u>:

1) Surface Area to Volume Ratio

1) This can be a bit <u>tricky</u> to get your head around, but it's easier if you think of cells as <u>cubes</u> for now.

2) The <u>rate</u> of diffusion, osmosis and active transport is <u>higher</u> in cells (or cubes) with a <u>larger surface area to volume ratio</u>.

3) The <u>smaller</u> cube has a <u>larger</u> surface area to volume ratio — this means <u>substances</u> would <u>move</u> into and out of this cube <u>faster</u>.

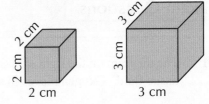

Surface area (cm²)	2 × 2 × 6 = 24	3 × 3 × 6 = 54
Volume (cm³)	2 × 2 × 2 = 8	3 × 3 × 3 = 27
Surface area to volume ratio	24 : 8 = <u>3 : 1</u>	54 : 27 = <u>2 : 1</u>

2) Distance

If substances only have a <u>short distance</u> to move, then they'll move in and out of cells faster. For example, cell membranes are very thin.

3) Temperature

As the particles in a substance get <u>warmer</u> they have <u>more energy</u> — so they <u>move faster</u>. This means as <u>temperature increases</u>, substances move in and out of cells <u>faster</u>.

4) Concentration Gradient

1) Substances move in and out of a cell <u>faster</u> if there's a <u>big difference</u> in <u>concentration</u> between the inside and outside of the cell (see page 14).

2) If there are <u>lots more</u> particles on one side, there are more there to <u>move across</u>.

3) This <u>only</u> increases the rate of <u>diffusion</u> and <u>osmosis</u> though — concentration gradients <u>don't affect</u> the rate of <u>active transport</u>.

Surface area to volume ratios crop up a lot in Biology...

...so it's a good idea to try to understand them now. To make it easy to compare ratios, it's best to <u>simplify</u> them so that there's a <u>1 on one side</u>. To do this, just divide both sides by the <u>same number</u> until you've got 1 on one side. For example, divide 24 : 8 by 8 to get 3 : 1.

Warm-Up & Exam Questions

More questions I'm afraid. There are quite a few of them, but that's because they're pretty important...

Warm-Up Questions

1) What is meant by the term osmosis?
2) Explain how water moves into and out of human body cells.
3) What process releases the energy needed for active transport?

Exam Questions

1   The diagram on the right shows a cell and the surrounding tissue fluid. Oxygen moves in and out of the cell by diffusion.

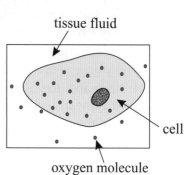
tissue fluid

cell

oxygen molecule

(a)   In which direction is the net movement of particles during diffusion?

☐   **A**   From an area of low concentration to another area of low concentration.

☐   **B**   From an area of low concentration to an area of high concentration.

☐   **C**   From an area of high concentration to another area of high concentration.

☐   **D**   From an area of high concentration to an area of low concentration.

[1 mark]

(b)   Describe the effect that diffusion will have on the oxygen concentration inside this cell.

[1 mark]

2   The diagram below shows a tank divided in two by the structure labelled **X**. Osmosis will occur between the two sides of the tank.

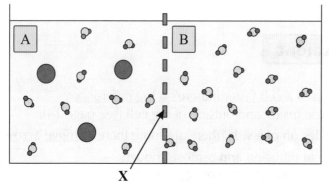

X

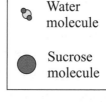

Water molecule

Sucrose molecule

(a)   Name the structure labelled **X** on the diagram.

[1 mark]

(b)   Explain what will happen to the level of liquid on side **B**.

[2 marks]

Exam Questions

PRACTICAL

3 A student made up some gelatine with cresol red solution and ammonium hydroxide.
Cresol red solution is a pH indicator that is red in alkaline solutions and yellow in acidic
solutions. He cut the gelatine into cubes of different sizes, and placed the cubes in a beaker
of dilute hydrochloric acid. He measured how long it took for the cubes to change from red
to yellow as the acid moved into the gelatine and neutralised the ammonium hydroxide.
His results are shown in the table.

Size (mm)	Time taken for cube to become yellow (s)			
	Trial 1	Trial 2	Trial 3	Trial 4
$5 \times 5 \times 5$	174	167	177	182
$7 \times 7 \times 7$	274	290	284	292
$10 \times 10 \times 10$	835	825	842	838

a) Name the process by which hydrochloric acid moves into the gelatine cubes in this experiment.

[1 mark]

b) Calculate the average time for a $10 \times 10 \times 10$ mm gelatine cube to become yellow in this
experiment. Show your working.

[2 marks]

c) Explain the relationship between the size of the gelatine cube and the time taken for the cube to
become yellow.

[3 marks]

4 Two germinating barley seedlings were placed in solutions that contained a known
concentration of potassium ions, as shown in the diagram below. Each seedling was
grown at a different temperature. The uptake of potassium ions was measured.

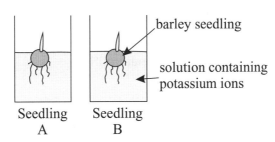

barley seedling

solution containing
potassium ions

Seedling   Seedling
   A   B

Barley seedlings take up potassium ions by active transport.
The graph shows the uptake of potassium ions by the barley seedlings.

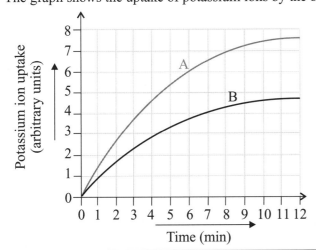

(a) Suggest which seedling was grown
at the higher temperature.
Explain your answer.

[2 marks]

(b) What effect would increasing the
concentration of the potassium
ion solution have on the uptake of
potassium ions via active transport?

[1 mark]

Revision Summary for Section 1

Well, that's it for <u>Section 1</u> — it's time to see what you've learnt so far.
- Try these questions and <u>tick off each one</u> when you <u>get it right</u>.
- When you've done <u>all the questions</u> for a topic and are <u>completely happy</u> with it, tick off the topic.

Characteristics of Living Organisms and Levels of Organisation (p.1-3) ☑

1) What are the eight basic characteristics that all living organisms share?
2) Name three organelles that are found in both animal and plant cells. Describe their functions.
3) What is a tissue?
4) What is an organ? And an organ system?

Specialised Cells and Stem Cells (p.4) ☑

5) What is cell differentiation?
6) Give two ways that embryonic stem cells could be used to cure diseases.

Groups of Living Organisms (p.5-6) ☑

7) What are plant cell walls made of?
8) How do most animals store carbohydrate?
9) Explain what is meant by the term 'saprotrophic nutrition'.
10) Give two examples of protoctists.
11) Give three features of viruses.
12) What are pathogens? Name two pathogens.

Enzymes and Investigating Enzyme Activity (p.9-12) ☑

13) What name is given to biological catalysts?
14) What is a catalyst?
15) What does it mean when an enzyme has been 'denatured'?
16) Briefly describe an experiment to show how temperature can affect enzyme activity.
17) In an experiment to investigate how pH can affect enzyme activity, outline how you could vary the pH of the reaction mixture.

Diffusion, Osmosis and Active Transport (p.14-19) ☑

18) What is diffusion?
19) A solution of pure water is separated from a concentrated sucrose solution by a partially permeable membrane. In which direction will molecules flow, and what substance will these molecules be?
20) Describe an experiment using a non-living system that shows diffusion taking place. Then do the same for osmosis.
21) How is active transport different from diffusion in terms of:
   a) energy requirements,
   b) concentration gradients?
22) Describe how surface area to volume ratio affects the movement of substances in and out of cells.

Biological Molecules

Biological molecules are things like <u>carbohydrates</u>, <u>lipids</u> and <u>proteins</u>. They're generally <u>long</u>, <u>complex molecules</u> made up from <u>smaller basic units</u>. And, unsurprisingly, they're what this page is all about...

Learn the **Structure** of **Carbohydrates**, **Lipids** and **Proteins**

Carbohydrates are Made Up of Simple Sugars

- <u>Carbohydrate</u> molecules contain the elements <u>carbon</u>, <u>hydrogen</u> and <u>oxygen</u>.
- <u>Starch</u> and <u>glycogen</u> are <u>large</u>, <u>complex carbohydrates</u>, which are made up of many <u>smaller units</u> (e.g. <u>glucose</u> or <u>maltose</u> molecules) joined together in a <u>long chain</u>.

maltose → starch

and other simple sugars, e.g. glucose

Proteins are Made Up of Amino Acids

- <u>Proteins</u> are made up of <u>long chains</u> of <u>amino acids</u>.
- They all contain <u>carbon</u>, <u>nitrogen</u>, <u>hydrogen</u> and <u>oxygen</u> atoms.

amino acids → proteins

Lipids are Made Up of Fatty Acids and Glycerol

- <u>Lipids</u> (fats and oils) are built from <u>fatty acids</u> and <u>glycerol</u>.
- Lipids contain <u>carbon</u>, <u>hydrogen</u> and <u>oxygen</u> atoms.

Glycerol & fatty acids → Lipid

Before a **Food Test**, You Need to Make a **Food Sample**

1) There are some clever ways to <u>identify</u> what type of <u>biological molecule</u> a sample contains.
2) The <u>methods</u> for carrying out these tests are coming up on the next page.
3) However, before you can carry out the tests, you need to prepare a <u>food sample</u>.
4) Here's what you'd do:

1) Get a piece of food and <u>break it up</u> using a <u>pestle and mortar</u>.
2) Transfer the ground up food to a <u>beaker</u> and add some <u>distilled water</u>.
3) Give the mixture a good <u>stir</u> with a glass rod to <u>dissolve</u> some of the food.
4) <u>Filter</u> the solution using a funnel lined with filter paper to <u>get rid</u> of the <u>solid</u> bits of food.

You'll need to make food samples for the food tests on the next page

It's also important that you remember what carbohydrates, proteins and lipids are made up from — it's going to come up again when you read about digestion so you might as well get it stuck in your brain now.

 **PRACTICAL** # Food Tests

Before you get going with this, make sure you can remember how to prepare a <u>food sample</u>.
If you can't, have a look back to the previous page before you go any further...

Use the **Benedict's Test** to Test for **Glucose**

The tests on this page can be used to test other types of samples too, not just food samples.

<u>Glucose</u> is found in all sorts of foods such as <u>biscuits</u>, <u>cereal</u> and <u>bread</u>.
You can test for <u>glucose</u> in foods using the <u>Benedict's test</u>:

1) Prepare a <u>food sample</u> and transfer <u>5 cm³</u> to a test tube.
2) Prepare a <u>water bath</u> so that it's set to <u>75 °C</u>.
3) Add some <u>Benedict's solution</u> to the test tube (about <u>10 drops</u>) using a pipette.
4) Place the test tube in the water bath using a test tube holder and leave it in there for <u>5 minutes</u>. Make sure the tube is <u>pointing away</u> from you.

Always use an excess of Benedict's solution — this makes sure that all the glucose reacts.

5) If the food sample contains <u>glucose</u>, the solution in the test tube will change from its normal <u>blue</u> colour. It will become <u>green</u> or <u>yellow</u> in <u>low concentrations</u> of glucose, or <u>brick-red</u> in <u>high concentrations</u> of glucose.

Use **Iodine Solution** to Test for **Starch**

You can also check food samples for the presence of <u>starch</u>. Foods like <u>pasta</u>, <u>rice</u> and <u>potatoes</u> contain a lot of starch. Here's how to do the test:

1) Make a <u>food sample</u> and transfer <u>5 cm³</u> of your sample to a test tube.
2) Then add a few drops of <u>iodine solution</u> and <u>gently shake</u> the tube to mix the contents. If the sample contains starch, the colour of the solution will change from <u>browny-orange</u> to <u>black</u> or <u>blue-black</u>.

Use the **Biuret Test** to Test for **Proteins**

You can use the <u>biuret test</u> to see if a type of food contains <u>protein</u>.
<u>Meat</u> and <u>cheese</u> are protein rich and good foods to use in this test. Here's how it's done:

1) Prepare a <u>sample</u> of your food and transfer <u>2 cm³</u> of your sample to a test tube.
2) Add 2 cm³ of <u>biuret solution</u> to the sample and mix the contents of the tube by <u>gently shaking</u> it.
3) If the food sample contains protein, the solution will change from <u>blue</u> to <u>pink</u> or <u>purple</u>. If no protein is present, the solution will stay blue.

Use the **Sudan III Test** to Test for **Lipids**

<u>Lipids</u> are found in foods such as <u>olive oil</u>, <u>margarine</u> and <u>milk</u>.
You can test for the presence of lipids in a food using <u>Sudan III stain solution</u>.

1) Prepare a <u>sample</u> of the food you're testing (but you don't need to filter it). Transfer about <u>5 cm³</u> into a test tube.
2) Use a pipette to add <u>3 drops</u> of <u>Sudan III stain solution</u> to the test tube and <u>gently shake</u> the tube.
3) Sudan III stain solution <u>stains</u> lipids. If the sample contains lipids, the mixture will separate out into <u>two layers</u>. The top layer will be <u>bright red</u>. If no lipids are present, no separate red layer will form at the top of the liquid.

A Balanced Diet

Your body needs the <u>right fuel</u> or it won't work properly — that means <u>cutting down</u> on the lard.

You Need to **Eat Different Foods** to Get **Different Nutrients**

Nutrient		Found in...	Function(s)
<u>Carbohydrates</u>		Pasta, rice, sugar	Provide <u>energy</u>.
<u>Lipids</u> (fats and oils)		Butter, oily fish	Provide <u>energy</u>, act as an <u>energy store</u> and provide <u>insulation</u>.
<u>Proteins</u>		Meat, fish	Needed for <u>growth</u> and <u>repair</u> of tissue, and to provide energy in emergencies.
<u>Vitamins</u>	A	Liver (yum...)	Helps to <u>improve vision</u> and keep your <u>skin</u> and <u>hair</u> <u>healthy</u>.
	C	Fruit, e.g. oranges	Needed to <u>prevent scurvy</u>.
	D	Eggs	Needed for <u>calcium absorption</u>. *Vitamin D is also made by your body when your skin is exposed to sunlight.*
<u>Mineral ions</u>	Calcium	Milk, cheese	Needed to make <u>bones</u> and <u>teeth</u>.
	Iron	Red meat	Needed to make <u>haemoglobin</u> for healthy <u>blood</u>.
<u>Water</u>		Food and drink	Just about <u>every bodily function</u> relies on water — we need a constant supply to <u>replace</u> water lost through urinating, breathing and sweating.
<u>Dietary fibre</u>		Wholemeal bread, fruit	Aids the <u>movement</u> of food through the <u>gut</u>.

A **Balanced Diet** Supplies **All** Your **Essential Nutrients**

1) A balanced diet gives you all the <u>essential nutrients</u> you need — in the <u>right proportions</u>.
2) The <u>six</u> essential nutrients are <u>carbohydrates</u>, <u>proteins</u>, <u>lipids</u>, <u>vitamins</u>, <u>minerals</u> and <u>water</u>.
3) You also need <u>fibre</u> (to keep the gut in good working order).

Energy Requirements Vary in Different People

You get <u>energy</u> from the food you eat, but the <u>amount</u> of energy you need <u>isn't</u> a set thing — it's <u>different</u> for everyone. The energy a person needs depends on things like...

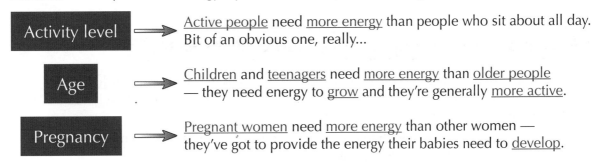

Activity level ➡ <u>Active people</u> need <u>more energy</u> than people who sit about all day. Bit of an obvious one, really...

Age ➡ <u>Children</u> and <u>teenagers</u> need <u>more energy</u> than <u>older people</u> — they need energy to <u>grow</u> and they're generally <u>more active</u>.

Pregnancy ➡ <u>Pregnant women</u> need <u>more energy</u> than other women — they've got to provide the energy their babies need to <u>develop</u>.

Energy From Food

Food Can be Burnt to See How Much Energy it Contains

The posh name for this is <u>calorimetry</u>. You need to know how to do it with a <u>simple experiment</u>:

First You Need a Dry Food, Water and a Flame...

1) You need a <u>food</u> that'll <u>burn easily</u> — something that's <u>dry</u>, e.g. dried beans or pasta, will work best.

2) <u>Weigh</u> a small amount of the food and then <u>skewer</u> it on a <u>mounted needle</u>.

3) Next, add <u>a set volume</u> of <u>water</u> to a boiling tube (held with a clamp) — this will be used to <u>measure</u> the amount of <u>energy</u> that's released when the food is burnt.

4) <u>Measure</u> the <u>temperature</u> of the water, then <u>set fire</u> to the food using a <u>Bunsen burner flame</u>. Make sure the Bunsen isn't near the water or your results might be a bit wonky.

5) Time for the exciting bit — immediately <u>hold</u> the burning food <u>under</u> the boiling tube until it <u>goes out</u>. Then <u>relight</u> the food and <u>hold</u> it under the tube — <u>keep doing this</u> until the food <u>won't</u> catch fire again.

6) The last thing to do is <u>measure</u> the <u>temperature</u> of the water <u>again</u>. Then you're ready for a bit of <u>maths</u>...

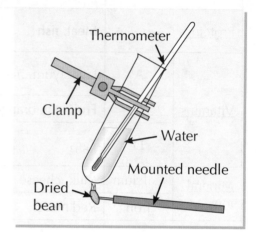

Thermometer

Clamp

Water

Mounted needle

Dried bean

...Then You Can Calculate the Amount of Energy in the Food

1) Calculate the Amount of Energy in Joules

$$\text{ENERGY IN FOOD (in J)} = \text{MASS OF WATER (in g)} \times \text{TEMPERATURE CHANGE OF WATER (in °C)} \times 4.2$$

1) <u>1 cm³</u> of water is the same as <u>1 g</u> of water.

2) The <u>4.2</u> in the formula is the <u>amount of energy</u> (in joules) needed to <u>raise</u> the temperature of <u>1 g</u> of water by <u>1 °C</u>.

⬅ This is the specific heat capacity of water, otherwise known as a calorie.

2) Calculate the Amount of Energy in Joules per Gram

$$\text{ENERGY PER GRAM OF FOOD (in J/g)} = \frac{\text{ENERGY IN FOOD (in J)}}{\text{MASS OF FOOD (in g)}}$$

You need to do this calculation so you can <u>compare</u> the energy values of different foods <u>fairly</u>.

The Accuracy of the Experiment Can be Increased

1) The experiment <u>isn't perfect</u> — quite a bit of the <u>energy</u> released from burning is <u>lost</u> to the surroundings. It's why the energy value on the <u>packet</u> of the food you used is likely to be <u>much higher</u> than your own.

2) <u>Insulating</u> the boiling tube, e.g. with foil, would minimise heat loss and keep <u>more energy</u> in the water — making your results <u>more accurate</u>.

Enzymes and Digestion

Remember <u>enzymes</u> from page 9? (If not go and have a look.) Various enzymes are used in <u>digestion</u> — they're produced by specialised cells and then <u>released</u> into the <u>gut</u> to help break down the food.

Digestive Enzymes Break Down **Big Molecules** into **Smaller Ones**

1) <u>Starch</u>, <u>proteins</u> and <u>fats</u> are <u>BIG molecules</u>. They're <u>too big</u> to pass through the <u>walls</u> of the digestive system. They're also <u>insoluble</u>.
2) <u>Sugars</u>, <u>amino acids</u>, <u>glycerol</u> and <u>fatty acids</u> are much <u>smaller molecules</u>. They're <u>soluble</u> and can <u>pass easily</u> through the walls of the digestive system.
3) The <u>digestive enzymes</u> break down the BIG molecules into the smaller ones.

Amylase Converts **Starch** into **Maltose**...

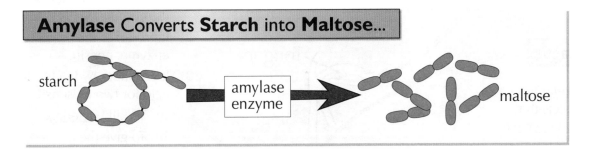

...and **Maltase** Converts **Maltose** into **Glucose**

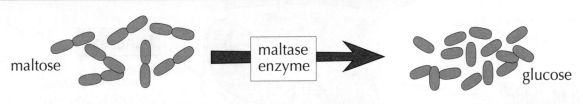

Proteases convert **Proteins** into **Amino Acids**

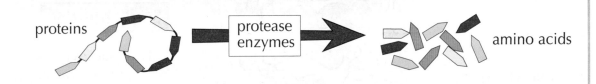

Lipases convert **Lipids** into **Glycerol** and **Fatty Acids**

Enzymes break down BIG molecules into LITTLE molecules...

...which lets them pass through the gut wall <u>more easily</u>. You need to know the <u>enzymes</u> on this page, including which <u>big molecules</u> they break down, and which <u>little molecules</u> the big molecules break into. Scribble them out again and again until you can do it in your sleep...

The Alimentary Canal

So, now you know what the enzymes do, here's a nice big picture of the whole of your gut.

Your Alimentary Canal Runs Through Your Body

The alimentary canal is another name for the gut.

You need to know the names and functions of the alimentary canal's main parts, plus a few of the organs associated with it.

Mouth

1) Salivary glands in the mouth produce amylase enzyme in the saliva.
2) Teeth break down food.

Oesophagus

The muscular tube that connects the mouth and stomach.

Liver

Where bile is produced (see next page).

Gall bladder

Where bile is stored (see next page).

Large intestine

1) Also called the colon.
2) Where excess water is absorbed from the food.

Rectum

1) The last part of the large intestine.
2) Where the faeces (made up mainly of indigestible food) are stored before they bid you a fond farewell through the anus.

Tongue

Stomach

1) It pummels the food with its muscular walls.
2) It produces the protease enzyme, pepsin.
3) It produces hydrochloric acid for two reasons:
   a) To kill bacteria.
   b) To give the optimum pH for the protease enzyme to work (pH 2 — acidic).

Pancreas

Produces protease, amylase and lipase enzymes. It releases these into the small intestine.

Small intestine

1) Produces protease, amylase and lipase enzymes to complete digestion.
2) This is also where the nutrients are absorbed out of the alimentary canal into the body.
3) The first part is the duodenum and the last part is the ileum.

There's more to eating a sandwich than meets the eye...

Did you know that the whole of your alimentary canal is actually a big hole that goes right through your body? Think about it. It just gets loads of food, digestive juices and enzymes piled into it...

More on Digestion

The digestive system is well <u>adapted</u> to its function of <u>breaking down</u> and <u>absorbing food</u>.
Here are three examples that show what a clever system it is...

Bile Neutralises the Stomach Acid and Emulsifies Fats

1) Bile is <u>produced</u> in the <u>liver</u>. It's <u>stored</u> in the <u>gall bladder</u> before it's released into the <u>small intestine</u>.

2) The <u>hydrochloric acid</u> in the stomach makes the pH <u>too acidic</u> for enzymes in the small intestine to work properly. Bile is <u>alkaline</u> — it <u>neutralises</u> the acid and makes conditions <u>alkaline</u>. The enzymes in the small intestine <u>work best</u> in these alkaline conditions.

3) Bile also <u>emulsifies</u> fats. In other words it breaks the fat into <u>tiny droplets</u>. This gives a much <u>bigger surface area</u> of fat for the enzyme lipase to work on — which makes its digestion <u>faster</u>.

Food is Moved Through The Gut by Peristalsis

1) There's <u>muscular</u> tissue all the way down the alimentary canal (see previous page).

2) Its job is to <u>squeeze</u> balls of food (called boluses) through your gut — <u>otherwise</u> it would get <u>clogged up</u> with bits of old food.

3) This squeezing action, which is <u>waves</u> of <u>circular muscle contractions</u>, is called <u>peristalsis</u>.

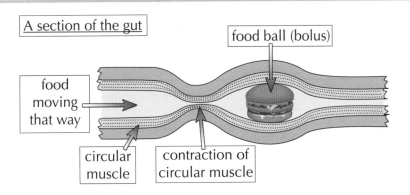

A section of the gut

food ball (bolus)

food moving that way

circular muscle

contraction of circular muscle

Villi in the Small Intestine Help with Absorption

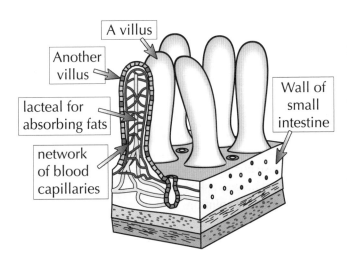

A villus

Another villus

lacteal for absorbing fats

network of blood capillaries

Wall of small intestine

1) The <u>small intestine</u> is <u>adapted</u> for absorption of food.

2) It's very <u>long</u>, so there's time to break down and absorb <u>all</u> the food before it reaches the end.

3) There's a really <u>big surface area</u> for absorption, because the walls of the small intestine are covered in <u>millions and millions</u> of tiny little projections called <u>villi</u>.

4) Each <u>cell</u> on the surface of a villus also has its own <u>microvilli</u> — little projections that increase the surface area even more.

5) Villi have a <u>single permeable</u> layer of surface cells and a very <u>good blood supply</u> to assist <u>quick absorption</u>.

Warm-Up & Exam Questions

That section should have given you plenty of food for thought. Ha ha. Ok — you can stop rolling around on the floor laughing now. It's time to power your way through these questions.

Warm-Up Questions

1) Name the smaller basic units that make up the following molecules: a) a lipid, b) a protein.

2) Describe how you would test for lipids in a food sample.

3) Some iodine is added to a sample and the colour changes from browny-orange to blue-black. What does this indicate?

Exam Questions

1   There are a number of digestive enzymes found in the human body.

Use the words from the box to complete the table, showing the correct enzyme or function in each space provided.

| amylase | lipases | glycerol | maltase | amino acids |

Enzyme	Function
proteases	convert proteins into ....
	converts starch into maltose
	converts maltose into glucose
	convert lipids into fatty acids and ....

[5 marks]

2   The elements below make up different biological molecules.
1. carbon
2. hydrogen
3. nitrogen
4. oxygen

Which of these elements make up lipids?

☐ **A**   2, 3 and 4 only   ☐ **C**   1 and 4 only

☐ **B**   1, 2 and 4 only   ☐ **D**   1 and 2 only

[1 mark]

PRACTICAL

3   A student was given test tubes containing the following glucose concentrations: 0 M, 0.02 M, 0.1 M, 1 M. The test tubes were not labelled and he was asked to perform tests to determine which test tube contained which glucose solution.

(a)   Describe the test he could carry out to try and distinguish between the glucose solutions.

[3 marks]

Section 2 — Human Nutrition

(b) The table shows the substance observed in the test tubes following his tests. Complete the table to show which glucose solution (0 M, 0.02 M, 0.1 M, 1 M) each test tube contained.

	Tube 1	Tube 2	Tube 3	Tube 4
substance observed	yellow precipitate	blue solution	red precipitate	green precipitate
glucose concentration (M)				

[1 mark]

PAPER 2   **PRACTICAL**

4   A student is carrying out an experiment to find out how much energy there is in a dried bean.

The bean is held over a Bunsen burner until it ignites, and is then held under a test tube of water, as shown in the diagram on the right.

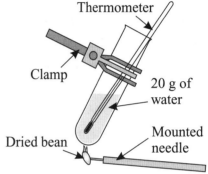

(a) Give **two** measurements that the student should make and record before starting the experiment.

[2 marks]

(b) Give the dependent variable in this experiment.

[1 mark]

(c) At the end of the experiment, the temperature of the water has risen by 21 °C. Using the formula below, calculate the amount of energy in the dried bean.

Energy in food (J) = mass of water (g) × temperature change of water (°C) × 4.2

[1 mark]

(d) If the dried bean weighed 0.7 g, calculate the energy (in joules) per g of dried beans.

[1 mark]

(e) The packet the student took the dried bean from stated that the energy content of the dried beans is 4600 J/g. Suggest why the value she measured in her experiment is different from this value.

[2 marks]

(f) Suggest **one** way that the student could improve the accuracy of her results.

[1 mark]

5   Some bacterial species produce lipase (an enzyme that breaks down lipids). Two different species of bacteria were placed separately on an agar plate. The agar contained a lipid which made it cloudy. The plate was then left overnight. The results are shown in the diagram.

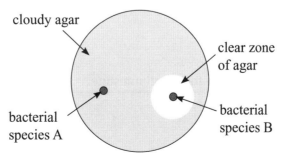

Use the diagram to suggest which species of bacteria contains lipase. Explain your answer.

[2 marks]

Revision Summary for Section 2

That's <u>Section 2</u> done and dusted. Well, nearly — have a go at these questions before you go for a cuppa.
- Try these questions and <u>tick off each one</u> when you <u>get it right</u>.
- When you've done <u>all the questions</u> for a topic and are <u>completely happy</u> with it, tick off the topic.

Biological Molecules and Food Tests (p.23-24) ☑

1) Name the three main chemical elements that are found in carbohydrates. ☑

2) What type of biological molecules are made up of:
   a) fatty acids and glycerol?
   b) amino acids? ☑

3) Describe how you could use biuret solution to test for proteins. ☑

4) What solution could you use to see if there's starch in a sample? ☑

A Balanced Diet and Energy from Food (p.25-26) ☑

5) What nutrients does the body get energy from? ☑

6) Why does the body need proteins? What foods contain proteins? ☑

7) Eric has just been to see his doctor. He has been told that he needs to increase the amount of vitamin D in his diet. What foods can Eric get this nutrient from? Why does Eric need vitamin D? ☑

8) Explain fully what is meant by the term 'a balanced diet'. ☑

9) Explain the difference in energy requirements between:
   a) children and older people.
   b) a woman who's pregnant and one who isn't. ☑

10) a) Describe a simple experiment to measure the amount of energy in a food.
    b) Give one way you could make the experiment more accurate. ☑

Enzymes, Digestion and the Alimentary Canal (p.27-29) ☑

11) What is the main role of digestive enzymes? ☑

12) Name the enzymes that convert starch into glucose. ☑

13) What do proteases do? ☑

14) When lipids are digested, what molecules are they broken down into? ☑

15) Describe the function(s) of the:
    a) mouth,
    b) oesophagus,
    c) small intestine. ☑

16) Where in the body is bile:
    a) produced?   b) stored?   c) used? ☑

17) What are the two functions of bile? ☑

18) Explain how villi help with absorption in the small intestine. ☑

Photosynthesis

Plants can make their own food — it's ace. Here's how...

Photosynthesis Produces Glucose Using Sunlight

1) Photosynthesis is the process that produces 'food' in plants. The 'food' it produces is glucose.

2) Photosynthesis happens in the leaves of all green plants — this is largely what the leaves are for.

3) Photosynthesis happens inside the chloroplasts, which are found in leaf cells and in other green parts of a plant. Chloroplasts contain a pigment called chlorophyll, which absorbs sunlight and uses its energy to convert carbon dioxide and water into glucose. Oxygen is also produced.

4) Photosynthesis is an important process because it converts light energy to chemical energy, which is stored in the glucose. This chemical energy is released when glucose is broken down during respiration (see pages 49-50).

Learn the Word and Symbol Equations for Photosynthesis:

$$\text{carbon dioxide} + \text{water} \xrightarrow[\text{chlorophyll}]{\text{LIGHT}} \text{glucose} + \text{oxygen}$$

$$6CO_2 + 6H_2O \xrightarrow[\text{chlorophyll}]{\text{LIGHT}} C_6H_{12}O_6 + 6O_2$$

Limiting Factors Affect the Rate of Photosynthesis

The rate of photosynthesis varies. It all depends on what the limiting factor is at that moment in time.

1) A limiting factor is something which stops photosynthesis from happening any faster. Light intensity, CO_2 concentration and temperature can all be the limiting factor.

2) The limiting factor depends on the environmental conditions. E.g. in winter low temperatures might be the limiting factor. At night, light is likely to be the limiting factor.

Not Enough LIGHT Slows Down the Rate of Photosynthesis

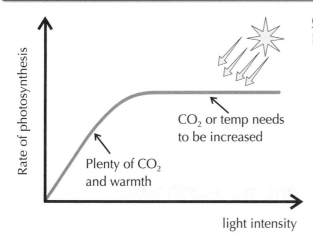

CO₂ or temp needs to be increased

Plenty of CO₂ and warmth

Rate of photosynthesis

light intensity

Chlorophyll uses light energy to perform photosynthesis. It can only do it as quickly as the light energy is arriving.

1) If the light intensity is increased, the rate of photosynthesis will increase steadily, but only up to a certain point.

2) Beyond that, it won't make any difference because then it'll be either the temperature or the CO_2 level which is now the limiting factor.

Photosynthesis

Too Little CO₂ Slows Down the Rate of Photosynthesis

CO_2 is one of the <u>raw materials</u> needed for photosynthesis — only <u>0.04%</u> of the air is CO_2, so it's <u>pretty scarce</u> as far as plants are concerned.

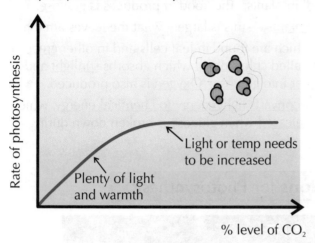

Plenty of light and warmth

Light or temp needs to be increased

Rate of photosynthesis

% level of CO₂

1) As with light intensity, increasing the concentration of CO_2 will only <u>increase</u> the rate of photosynthesis up to a point. After this the graph <u>flattens out</u>, showing that CO_2 is no longer the limiting factor.

2) As long as <u>light</u> and <u>CO_2</u> are in plentiful supply then the factor limiting photosynthesis must be <u>temperature</u>.

The TEMPERATURE Has to be Just Right

Temperature affects the rate of photosynthesis — because it affects the <u>enzymes</u> involved.

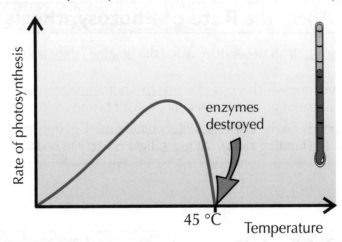

Rate of photosynthesis

enzymes destroyed

45 °C   Temperature

1) As the <u>temperature increases</u>, so does the <u>rate</u> of photosynthesis — up to a point.

2) If the temperature is <u>too high</u> (over about 45 °C), the plant's <u>enzymes</u> will be <u>denatured</u> (destroyed), so the rate of photosynthesis rapidly decreases.

3) <u>Usually</u> though, if the temperature is the <u>limiting factor</u> it's because it's too low, and things need <u>warming up a bit</u>.

You can control the growing environment in a glasshouse

You can create the <u>optimum conditions</u> for photosynthesis if you keep the <u>three limiting factors</u> in balance — plenty of <u>light</u> and <u>CO_2</u> and nice, <u>warm temperatures</u> (but not too hot). You can control all three factors in a glasshouse. This'll help you to grow some monstrous tomatoes.

Adaptations for Photosynthesis

Most photosynthesis takes place in the leaves, so leaves have
a few tricks up their sleeves to make sure it all goes well.

Leaves are Designed for **Making Food** by **Photosynthesis**

The whole structure of leaves is geared towards that.
You need to know all the different parts of a typical leaf shown on the diagram:

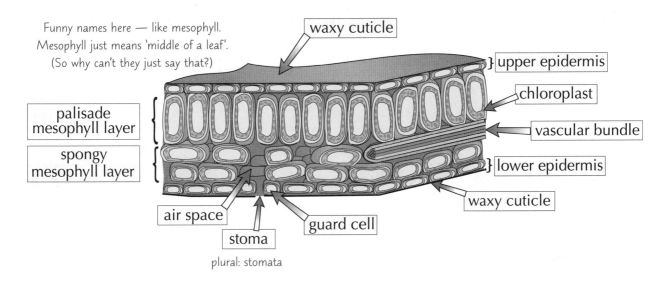

Funny names here — like mesophyll.
Mesophyll just means 'middle of a leaf'.
(So why can't they just say that?)

waxy cuticle

upper epidermis

chloroplast

palisade
mesophyll layer

vascular bundle

spongy
mesophyll layer

lower epidermis

waxy cuticle

air space

stoma

guard cell

plural: stomata

Leaves are **Adapted** for **Efficient Photosynthesis**

1) Leaves are broad, so there's a large surface area exposed to light.

2) Most of the chloroplasts are found in the palisade layer.
   This is so that they're near the top of the leaf where they can get the most light.

3) The upper epidermis is transparent so that light can pass through it to the palisade layer.

4) Leaves have a network of vascular bundles — these are the transport vessels xylem and phloem
   (see page 41). They deliver water and other nutrients to every part of the leaf and take away
   the glucose produced by photosynthesis. They also help to support the leaf structure.

5) The waxy cuticle helps to reduce water loss by evaporation.

6) The adaptations of leaves for efficient gas exchange (see page 53) also make photosynthesis
   more efficient. E.g. the lower surface is full of little holes called stomata, which let CO_2 diffuse
   directly into the leaf.

Efficient photosynthesis means maximum 'food' production

Think back to the photosynthesis equation on page 33. Plants need three main things from their
environment in order to photosynthesise: carbon dioxide, water and light. So leaves are adapted
to make sure a plant gets as much of them as possible. Pretty straightforward really.

PRACTICAL Photosynthesis Experiments

The <u>two products</u> from photosynthesis are <u>glucose</u> and <u>oxygen</u> (see page 33). Glucose is stored by plants as <u>starch</u>. You can test for starch (see below) and oxygen (see next page) to <u>investigate photosynthesis</u>.

You Need to Know How to **Test a Leaf** for **Starch**

1) Start by dunking the leaf in boiling water (hold it with tweezers or forceps). This <u>stops</u> any <u>chemical reactions</u> happening inside the leaf.

2) Now put the leaf in a boiling tube with some <u>ethanol</u> and heat it in an electric water bath until it boils — this gets rid of any <u>chlorophyll</u> and makes the leaf a <u>white-ish</u> colour.

3) Finally, <u>rinse</u> the leaf in <u>cold water</u> and add a few drops of <u>iodine solution</u> — if <u>starch</u> is <u>present</u> the leaf will turn <u>blue-black</u>.

The **Starch Test** Shows Whether **Photosynthesis** is **Taking Place**

If a plant can't <u>photosynthesise</u>, it can't make <u>starch</u>. You can use this principle to show that <u>chlorophyll</u> and <u>CO$_2$</u> are <u>needed for photosynthesis</u>. Here's how...

Chlorophyll

You can show that <u>chlorophyll</u> is needed for photosynthesis using <u>variegated</u> (green and white) <u>leaves</u>. Only the <u>green parts</u> of the leaf contain <u>chlorophyll</u>.

1) Take a variegated leaf from a plant that's been <u>exposed to light</u> for a bit. Make sure you <u>record</u> which bits are <u>green</u> and which bits <u>aren't</u>.

2) Test the leaf for starch as above — you'll see that only the bits that were <u>green</u> turn <u>blue-black</u>.

3) This suggests that only the parts of the leaf that <u>contained chlorophyll</u> are able to <u>photosynthesise</u> and <u>produce starch</u>.

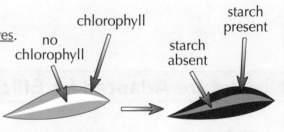

no chlorophyll | chlorophyll | starch present

starch absent

Variegated leaf before testing

Variegated leaf after testing

The white parts of the leaf go yellow/orange because the brown iodine solution stains them.

CO$_2$

1) You can show that <u>CO$_2$</u> is needed for photosynthesis with the apparatus shown on the right.

2) The soda lime will <u>absorb CO$_2$</u> out of the air in the jar.

3) If you leave the plant in the jar for a while and then <u>test</u> a leaf for starch, it <u>won't</u> turn blue-black.

4) This shows that <u>no starch</u> has been made in the leaf, which means that <u>CO$_2$ is needed</u> for photosynthesis.

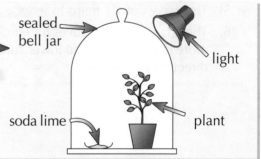

sealed bell jar

light

soda lime

plant

For both tests, control variables that could affect the results

For example, the <u>temperature</u> should be kept constant. Make sure you stay safe too — <u>ethanol</u> is highly <u>flammable</u>, so keep it away from naked flames, e.g. Bunsen burners.

More Photosynthesis Experiments  PRACTICAL

More starch testing on this page I'm afraid. But there's also a bit about how oxygen production can show the rate of photosynthesis. Don't say I don't mix things up a bit for you...

The **Starch Test** Shows Whether **Photosynthesis** is **Taking Place**

Remember, if a plant can't photosynthesise, it can't make starch. You can use this principle to show that light is needed for photosynthesis. Here's how:

1) To show that light is needed for photosynthesis you need a plant that's been grown without any light, e.g. in a cupboard for 48 hours. This will mean that it has used up its starch stores.

2) Cut a leaf from the plant and test it for starch using iodine solution (see previous page) — the leaf won't turn blue-black.

3) This shows that light is needed for photosynthesis, as no starch has been made.

Even though the plant is kept in the dark, you need to make sure it's warm enough to photosynthesise and that there's plenty of CO_2 — or it won't be a fair test.

Oxygen Production Shows the Rate of Photosynthesis

Canadian pondweed can be used to measure the effect of light intensity on the rate of photosynthesis. The rate at which the pondweed produces oxygen corresponds to the rate at which it's photosynthesising — the faster the rate of oxygen production, the faster the rate of photosynthesis.

Here's how the experiment works:

1) The apparatus is set up according to the diagram. The gas syringe should be empty to start with. Sodium hydrogencarbonate may be added to the water to make sure the plant has enough carbon dioxide (it releases CO_2 in solution).

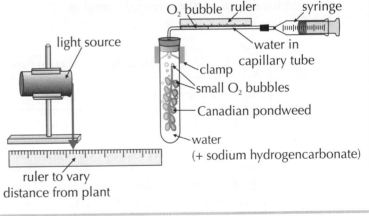

O₂ bubble   ruler   syringe
water in capillary tube
light source
clamp
small O₂ bubbles
Canadian pondweed
water (+ sodium hydrogencarbonate)
ruler to vary distance from plant

2) A source of white light is placed at a specific distance from the pondweed.

3) The pondweed is left to photosynthesise for a set amount of time. As it photosynthesises, the oxygen released will collect in the capillary tube.

4) At the end of the experiment, the syringe is used to draw the gas bubble in the tube up alongside a ruler and the length of the gas bubble is measured. This is proportional to the volume of O_2 produced.

5) For this experiment, any variables that could affect the results should be controlled, e.g. the temperature and time the pondweed is left to photosynthesise.

6) The experiment is then repeated with the light source placed at different distances from the pondweed.

The apparatus above can be altered to measure the effect of temperature and CO_2 on photosynthesis, e.g. the test tube of pondweed is put into a beaker of water at a set temperature and CO_2 is bubbled into the test tube (then the experiment's repeated with different temperatures of water or concentrations of CO_2).

Warm-Up & Exam Questions

So, here we go again — another set of questions to test your knowledge. But don't roll your eyes, I promise they'll be really, really enjoyable. OK, don't hold me to that, but make sure you do them...

Warm-Up Questions

1) What is meant by a limiting factor for the rate of photosynthesis?
2) Explain why the rate of photosynthesis decreases if the temperature is too high.
3) Outline an experiment you could do to show that carbon dioxide is needed for photosynthesis.
4) What can you measure to show the rate of photosynthesis?

Exam Questions

1 The diagram shows a cross-section through a typical leaf. Some of the structures in the leaf are labelled **A** to **E**.

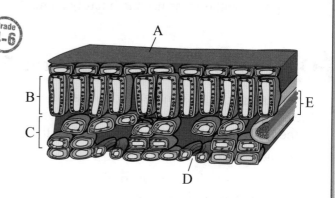

The table below contains descriptions of how the structures labelled in the diagram make the leaf well-adapted for efficient photosynthesis.

Copy and complete the table by matching the letters in the diagram to the correct description. The first one has been done for you.

Description of structure	Letter
contains air spaces to aid gas exchange	C
delivers water and nutrients to every part of the leaf	
helps to reduce water loss by evaporation	
where most of the chloroplasts in the leaf are located, to maximise the amount of light they receive	
allows carbon dioxide to diffuse directly into the leaf	

[4 marks]

2 Photosynthesis is an important process in plants.

(a) Explain how photosynthesis is involved in creating a store of chemical energy for the plant.

[2 marks]

(b) (i) Write down the word equation for photosynthesis.

[2 marks]

(ii) Write down the balanced symbol equation for photosynthesis.

[2 marks]

Exam Questions

3 A student investigated the effect of different concentrations of carbon dioxide on the rate of photosynthesis of a Swiss cheese plant. The results are shown on the graph below.

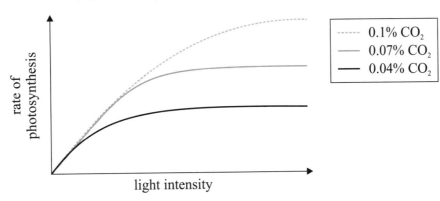

(a) Describe the effect that increasing the concentration of carbon dioxide has on the rate of photosynthesis as light intensity increases.

[2 marks]

(b) Explain why all the lines on the graph level off eventually.

[1 mark]

PRACTICAL

4 A green leaf was boiled in water to soften it, and then boiled in ethanol.
It was washed with water and some brown iodine solution was dropped onto it.
The extra iodine solution was washed away.

(a) The ethanol in the experiment turned green and the leaf went white.
Suggest why this happened.

[1 mark]

(b) When the iodine was added to the leaf, it turned blue-black.
Explain what this result shows.

[1 mark]

The method above was repeated with the leaf shown below.

white part of the leaf
(does not contain chlorophyll)

green parts of the leaf
(contain chlorophyll)

(c) Describe the result you would expect to see when the leaf was tested with iodine solution.
Explain your answer.

[4 marks]

PRACTICAL

5 Describe an investigation to show that light is a requirement of photosynthesis.

[6 marks]

Minerals for Healthy Growth

Plants are important in <u>food chains</u> and <u>nutrient cycles</u> because they can take <u>minerals</u> from the soil and <u>energy</u> from the Sun and turn it into food. And then, after all that hard work, we eat them.

Plants Need **Three** Main **Mineral Ions** For **Growth**

1) Plants need certain <u>elements</u> so they can produce important compounds.
2) They get these elements from <u>mineral ions</u> in the <u>soil</u>.
3) If there aren't enough of these mineral ions in the soil, plants suffer <u>deficiency symptoms</u>.

1) **Nitrates**

Contain nitrogen for making <u>amino acids</u> and <u>proteins</u>. These are needed for <u>cell growth</u>. If a plant can't get enough nitrates it will be <u>stunted</u> and <u>older leaves</u> will turn <u>yellow</u>.

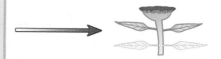

2) **Phosphates**

Contain phosphorus for making <u>DNA</u> and <u>cell membranes</u> and they're needed for <u>respiration</u> and <u>growth</u>. Plants without enough phosphate have <u>poor root growth</u> and their <u>older leaves</u> are <u>purple</u>.

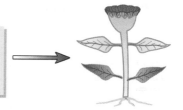

3) **Potassium**

To help the <u>enzymes</u> needed for <u>photosynthesis</u> and <u>respiration</u>. If there's not enough potassium in the soil, plants have <u>poor flower and fruit growth</u> and <u>discoloured leaves</u>.

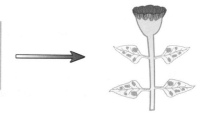

Magnesium is Also Needed in **Small Amounts**

1) The three main mineral ions are needed in fairly <u>large amounts</u>, but there are other elements which are needed in much <u>smaller</u> amounts.
2) <u>Magnesium</u> is one of the most significant as it's required for making <u>chlorophyll</u> (needed for <u>photosynthesis</u>).
3) Plants without enough magnesium have <u>yellow leaves</u>.

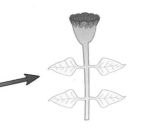

Plants can't make minerals — they get them from the soil

When a farmer or a gardener buys fertiliser, that's pretty much what he or she is buying — <u>nitrates</u>, <u>phosphates</u> and <u>potassium</u>. A fertiliser's <u>NPK label</u> tells you the relative proportions of nitrogen (<u>N</u>), phosphorus (<u>P</u>) and potassium (<u>K</u>) it contains, so you can choose the <u>right one</u> for your plants and soil. Don't forget about <u>magnesium</u>, though — it's dead important for making <u>chlorophyll</u>.

Transport in Plants

Like all multicellular organisms, plants need a way of transporting substances from A to B.

Multicellular Organisms Need Transport Systems

1) The cells in all living organisms need a variety of substances to live, e.g. plant cells need things like water, minerals and sugars. They also need to get rid of waste substances.

2) In unicellular organisms, these substances can diffuse directly into and out of the cell across the cell membrane. The diffusion rate is quick because of the short distances substances have to travel.

3) But in multicellular organisms (like animals and plants) direct diffusion from the outer surface would be too slow — that's because substances would have to travel large distances to reach every single cell.

4) So multicellular organisms need transport systems to move substances to and from individual cells quickly.

However, carbon dioxide diffuses into plants at the leaves (where it's needed).

Plants Have Two Main Transport Systems

Plants have two systems transporting stuff around.
Both go to every part of the plant, but they're totally separate.

Xylem tubes transport water and minerals

The xylem carry water and mineral salts from the roots up the shoot to the leaves in the transpiration stream (see next page).

Water and minerals

Phloem tubes transport food

1) The phloem transport sugars, like sucrose, and amino acids from where they're made in the leaves to other parts of the plant.

2) This movement of food substances around the plant is known as translocation.

Sucrose and amino acids

Root Hairs Take In Water

1) The cells on plant roots grow into long 'hairs' which stick out into the soil.

2) Each branch of a root will be covered in millions of these microscopic hairs.

3) This gives the plant a big surface area for absorbing water from the soil.

Root hair cells also take in minerals — this is done by active transport (see page 18).

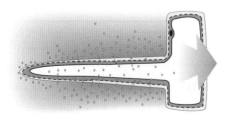

Water is taken in by osmosis (see page 15).

There's usually a higher concentration of water in the soil than there is inside the plant, so the water is drawn into the root hair cell by osmosis.

Transpiration

If you don't water a house plant for a few days it starts to go all droopy. Then it dies. Plants need water.

Transpiration is the **Loss of Water** from the Plant

1) Transpiration is caused by the evaporation and diffusion (see page 14) of water from a plant's surface.

2) Most transpiration happens at the leaves.

3) This evaporation creates a slight shortage of water in the leaf, and so more water is drawn up from the rest of the plant through the xylem vessels (see previous page) to replace it.

4) This in turn means more water is drawn up from the roots, and so there's a constant transpiration stream of water through the plant.

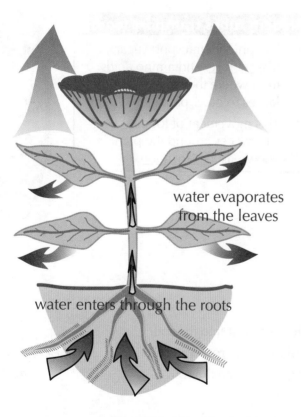

water evaporates from the leaves

water enters through the roots

- Transpiration is just a side-effect of the way leaves are adapted for photosynthesis.

- They have to have stomata in them so that gases can be exchanged easily (see page 53).

- Because there's more water inside the plant than in the air outside, the water escapes from the leaves through the stomata by diffusion.

Transpiration involves evaporation and diffusion

A big tree loses about a thousand litres of water from its leaves every single day — it's a fact. That's as much water as the average person drinks in a whole year, so the roots have to be very effective at drawing in water from the soil. Which is why they have all those root hairs, you see.

Transpiration

The rate of transpiration varies according to the environmental conditions...

Transpiration Rate is Affected by Four Main Things

Light Intensity

1) The <u>brighter</u> the light, the <u>greater</u> the transpiration rate.
2) <u>Stomata</u> begin to <u>close</u> as it gets darker. Photosynthesis can't happen in the dark, so they don't need to be open to let <u>CO_2</u> in. When the stomata are closed, very little water can escape.

Temperature

1) The <u>warmer</u> it is, the <u>faster</u> transpiration happens.
2) When it's warm the water particles have <u>more energy</u> to evaporate and diffuse out of the stomata.

Wind Speed

1) The <u>higher</u> the wind speed around a leaf, the <u>greater</u> the transpiration rate.
2) If wind speed around a leaf is <u>low</u>, the water vapour just <u>surrounds the leaf</u> and doesn't move away. This means there's a <u>high concentration</u> of water particles outside the leaf as well as inside it, so <u>diffusion</u> doesn't happen as quickly.
3) If it's windy, the water vapour is <u>swept away</u>, maintaining a <u>low concentration</u> of water in the air outside the leaf. Diffusion then happens quickly, from an area of high concentration to an area of low concentration.

Humidity

1) The <u>drier</u> the air around a leaf, the <u>faster</u> transpiration happens.
2) This is like what happens with air movement. If the air is <u>humid</u> there's a lot of water in it already, so there's not much of a <u>difference</u> between the inside and the outside of the leaf.
3) Diffusion happens <u>fastest</u> if there's a <u>really high concentration</u> in one place, and a <u>really low concentration</u> in the other.

Paper 2

Thinking about drying washing might help you remember these

The four factors that affect the rate of transpiration are the same as the ones that affect how quickly your laundry dries — it's quickest when it's <u>sunny</u>, <u>warm</u>, <u>windy</u> and <u>dry</u>.

 **PRACTICAL**

Measuring Transpiration

It's time for another <u>experiment</u> — you get to use a piece of equipment you've probably never heard of...

A **Potometer** can be Used to **Estimate Transpiration Rate**

A <u>potometer</u> is a special piece of apparatus used to <u>estimate transpiration rates</u>. It actually <u>measures water uptake</u> by a plant, but it's <u>assumed</u> that water uptake by the plant is <u>directly related</u> to water loss by the leaves (transpiration). Here's how to use a potometer:

1) <u>Cut</u> a shoot <u>underwater</u> to prevent air from entering the xylem.
   Cut it at a <u>slant</u> to increase the surface area available for water uptake.

2) <u>Assemble</u> the potometer <u>in water</u> and insert the shoot <u>under water</u>, so no <u>air</u> can enter.

3) Remove the apparatus from the water but keep the end
   of the capillary tube <u>submerged</u> in a beaker of water.

   Setting up a potometer is tough — if there are air bubbles in the apparatus or the plant's xylem it will affect your results.

4) Check that the apparatus is <u>watertight</u> and <u>airtight</u>.

5) <u>Dry</u> the leaves, allow time for the shoot to <u>acclimatise</u> and then <u>shut</u> the tap.

6) Remove the end of the capillary tube from the beaker of water until <u>one air bubble</u>
   has formed, then put the end of the tube <u>back into the water</u>.

7) Record the <u>starting position</u> of the air bubble.

8) Start a <u>stopwatch</u> and record the <u>distance moved</u> by
   the bubble per unit time, e.g. per hour.

9) Keep the <u>conditions constant</u> throughout the experiment,
   e.g. the <u>temperature</u> and <u>air humidity</u>.

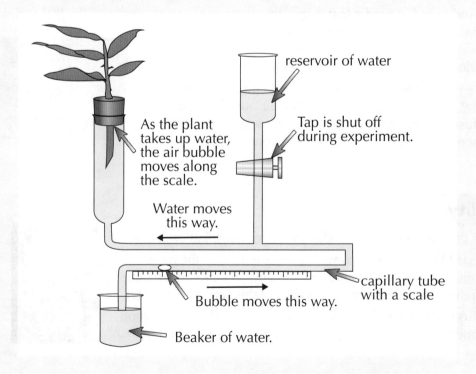

reservoir of water

Tap is shut off during experiment.

As the plant takes up water, the air bubble moves along the scale.

Water moves this way.

Bubble moves this way.

capillary tube with a scale

Beaker of water.

Measuring Transpiration

Now you know how to use a potometer, you can start to mix things up a bit.
Here's your chance to find out exactly how much the four factors on p.43 affect transpiration rate.

See How **Environmental Conditions** Affect Transpiration Rates

You can use a potometer to <u>estimate</u> how different factors affect the transpiration rate. The set up on the previous page will be your <u>control</u> — you can <u>vary</u> an <u>environmental condition</u>, run the experiment again and <u>compare</u> the results to the <u>control</u> to see how the change <u>affected</u> the transpiration rate.

Light Intensity

You could use a <u>lamp</u> to <u>increase</u> the <u>intensity of light</u> that hits the plant — this should <u>increase</u> the transpiration rate. To <u>decrease</u> the light intensity, put the potometer in a <u>cupboard</u> (this should <u>decrease</u> the transpiration rate).

Temperature

You could increase or decrease the temperature by putting the potometer in a <u>room</u> that's <u>warmer</u> or <u>colder</u> than where you did the control experiment. An <u>increase</u> in temperature should <u>increase</u> the transpiration rate and a <u>decrease</u> in temperature should <u>lower</u> it.

Humidity

You could <u>increase</u> the humidity of the air around the plant by <u>spraying a little water</u> into a clear <u>plastic bag</u> before <u>sealing</u> it around the plant. This should <u>decrease</u> the rate of transpiration.

Wind Speed

You could use a <u>fan</u> to <u>increase</u> the wind speed around the plant — this should <u>increase</u> the transpiration rate.

Make sure you know how to use a potometer

The <u>tricky bit</u> is setting up the apparatus — keeping air out and water in is harder than it sounds, but if you're only writing about the experiment in an exam, you <u>don't</u> have to worry about that. Phew. Only the questions to go, then it's the end of Section 3. What a relief.

Warm-Up & Exam Questions

Just a few simple warm-up questions and a few slightly harder exam questions stand between you and mastering transport in plants...

Warm-Up Questions

1) What do plants need nitrates for?
2) Explain why small, unicellular organisms do not need a transport system, but large, multicellular organisms (such as plants) do.
3) State the four main factors that affect the rate of transpiration in plants.

Exam Questions

1   Aphids are insects that feed on plant sap. Sap is the name given to the liquids carried around a plant in transport vessels. It contains nutrients, such as sucrose.

Which of the following statements about the sucrose-containing sap is correct?

☐   **A** The sap also contains amino acids and is transported in xylem vessels.

☐   **B** The sap also contains mineral ions and is transported in xylem vessels.

☐   **C** The sap also contains amino acids and is transported in phloem vessels.

☐   **D** The sap also contains mineral ions and is transported in phloem vessels.

[1 mark]

PAPER 2

2   Plants absorb water and mineral ions through their root hair cells.

(a)   Name and describe the process by which water is drawn into a root hair cell from the soil.

[2 marks]

(b)   Describe how root hair cells are adapted for absorbing lots of water from the soil.

[1 marks]

3   A scientist planted 10 seedlings of the same variety in a growth medium containing a complete supply of minerals. He then planted a further 10 seedlings in a growth medium deficient in magnesium. The seedlings were left to grow under carefully controlled conditions.

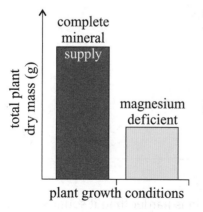

(a)   At the end of the investigation, the seedlings grown without magnesium had yellow leaves. The seedlings grown in a complete supply of minerals did not.
Suggest why the magnesium-deficient plants had yellow leaves.

[1 mark]

(b)   At the end of the investigation, the scientist measured the total dry mass of each group of plants. His results are shown in the graph.

(i) Describe the results shown in the graph.

[1 mark]

(ii) Suggest a possible explanation for the scientist's results.

[3 marks]

Exam Questions

PAPER 2

4 A scientist measured the rate of transpiration in two plants over 48 hours. The results are shown in the graph.

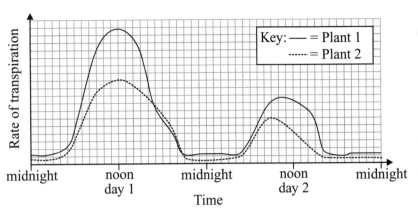

(a) What is meant by the term **transpiration**?

[1 mark]

(b) At what time on **day 2** was the rate of transpiration highest for **plant 2**?

[1 mark]

(c) The rate of transpiration for both plants was slower on **day 2** than on **day 1**. Suggest and explain **one** reason for this.

[2 marks]

(d) Suggest why the rate of transpiration for both plants was very low at night. Explain your answer.

[2 marks]

PAPER 2   PRACTICAL

5 A student was investigating transpiration in basil plants under different conditions. She used twelve plants, three plants in each of the four different conditions. The plants were weighed before and after the experiment. She calculated the % loss in the mass per day and recorded her results in the table.

plant	in a room (% loss in mass)	next to a fan (% loss in mass)	by a lamp (% loss in mass)	next to a fan and by a lamp (% loss in mass)
1	5	8	10	13
2	5	9	11	15
3	4	11	9	13
mean	4.7	9.3		13.6

(a) Calculate the mean % loss in plant mass for the three plants by a lamp. Show your working.

[2 marks]

(b) Explain why the plants located next to a fan lost more mass than those in a still room.

[3 marks]

(c) The student then covered the undersides of the leaves with petroleum jelly. Explain how this would affect the rate of transpiration from the leaves.

[2 marks]

(d) Suggest how you could alter the student's experiment to investigate the effects of humidity on the rate of transpiration in basil plants.

[2 marks]

Revision Summary for Section 3

That's <u>Section 3</u> sorted. Before you stride on to the next section though, have a go at these questions.
- Try these questions and <u>tick off each one</u> when you <u>get it right</u>.
- When you've done <u>all the questions</u> for a topic and are <u>completely happy</u> with it, tick off the topic.

Photosynthesis and the Rate of Photosynthesis (p.33-35) ☑
1) Where in a leaf does photosynthesis take place?
2) What effect would a low carbon dioxide concentration have on the rate of photosynthesis?
3) How does being broad help a leaf to photosynthesise?
4) Describe one other way that leaves are adapted for efficient photosynthesis.

Photosynthesis Experiments (p.36-37) ☑
5) Briefly describe an experiment to show that chlorophyll is required for photosynthesis.
6) Describe an experiment that you could carry out to see how light intensity affects the rate of photosynthesis.

Minerals for Healthy Growth (p.40) ☑
7) Name the three main mineral ions plants need for healthy growth.
8) Which mineral ion is needed by plants to make chlorophyll?
9) How can you tell by looking at a plant that it isn't getting enough magnesium?

Transport in Plants and Transpiration (p.41-45) ☑
10) What is the function of xylem vessels in plants?
11) What is the function of phloem vessels in plants?
12) How does water get into a plant through its root hair cells?
13) Where does water escape from a plant during transpiration?
14) How is the transpiration rate affected by:
    a) increased temperature,
    b) increased humidity?
15) Describe an experiment that you could do to measure how temperature affects the transpiration rate of a plant.

Respiration

You need <u>energy</u> to keep your body going. Energy comes from <u>food</u>, and it's <u>released</u> by <u>respiration</u>.

Respiration is NOT "Breathing In and Out"

1) <u>Respiration</u> is the process of transferring energy from <u>glucose</u>. It goes on in <u>every cell</u> in your body.

2) Some of the energy is transferred by <u>heat</u>.

3) The energy transferred by respiration <u>can't</u> be used directly by cells — so it's used to make a substance called <u>ATP</u>. ATP <u>stores the energy</u> needed for many <u>cell processes</u>.

4) When a cell <u>needs energy</u>, ATP molecules are <u>broken down</u> and energy is <u>released</u>.

5) There are <u>two types</u> of respiration, <u>aerobic</u> and <u>anaerobic</u>.

> Respiration is the process of <u>transferring energy</u> from <u>glucose</u>, which happens constantly <u>in every living cell</u>.

The **Temperature Change** Produced can be **Measured**

You saw above that <u>respiration</u> transfers some energy by <u>heat</u> (that's why <u>running</u> makes you get <u>hot</u>) — well here's an experiment to show that.

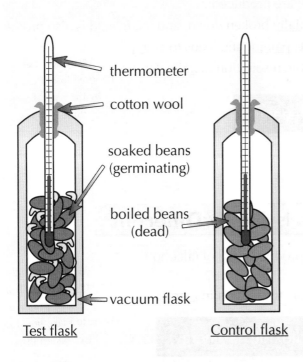

thermometer

cotton wool

soaked beans (germinating)

boiled beans (dead)

vacuum flask

Test flask   Control flask

- First, <u>soak</u> some <u>dried beans</u> in <u>water</u> for a day or two. They will start to <u>germinate</u> (you should see little sprouts coming out of them). Germinating beans will <u>respire</u>.

- <u>Boil</u> a <u>similar-sized</u>, second bunch of dried beans. This will <u>kill the beans</u> and make sure they <u>can't respire</u>. The dead beans will act as your <u>control</u>.

- Add each set of beans to a <u>vacuum flask</u>, making sure there's some <u>air</u> left in the flasks (so the beans can <u>respire aerobically</u>).

- Place a <u>thermometer</u> into each flask and seal the top with <u>cotton wool</u>.

- Record the <u>temperature</u> of each flask daily for a week.

- <u>Repeats</u> should be carried out, using the same mass of beans each time.

- The beans are well-insulated in the flasks, so when the germinating beans <u>respire</u>, the <u>test flask's temperature</u> will <u>increase</u> compared to the control flask.

Respiration releases energy from glucose

Make sure you understand what the two flasks of beans show. The <u>control</u> flask of boiled beans is there to show that it's the <u>respiring, germinating beans</u> in the test flask that are causing the <u>temperature to rise</u>.

Respiration

You need to know all about <u>aerobic respiration</u> and <u>anaerobic respiration</u>...

Aerobic Respiration Needs Plenty of Oxygen

1) <u>Aerobic respiration</u> is what happens when there's <u>plenty of oxygen</u> available.

2) <u>Aerobic</u> just means "<u>with oxygen</u>" and it's the most efficient way to transfer <u>energy</u> from <u>glucose</u>. It produces <u>lots</u> of <u>ATP</u> — <u>32 molecules</u> per molecule of glucose.

3) This is the type of respiration that you're using <u>most of the time</u>. You need to learn the <u>word equation</u> and the <u>balanced chemical equation</u>:

glucose + oxygen $\longrightarrow$ carbon dioxide + water (+ energy)
$$C_6H_{12}O_6 + 6O_2 \longrightarrow 6CO_2 + 6H_2O$$

This is the reverse of the photosynthesis equation (see page 33).

Anaerobic Respiration Doesn't Use Oxygen At All

1) When you do really <u>vigorous exercise</u> your body can't supply enough <u>oxygen</u> to your muscles for aerobic respiration — even though your <u>heart rate</u> and <u>breathing rate</u> increase as much as they can. Your muscles have to start <u>respiring anaerobically</u> as well.

2) <u>Anaerobic</u> just means "<u>without</u> oxygen". It's <u>NOT</u> the best way to convert glucose into energy — it releases much <u>less energy</u> per glucose molecule than aerobic respiration (just <u>2 molecules</u> of ATP are produced).

3) In anaerobic respiration, the glucose is only <u>partially</u> broken down, and <u>lactic acid</u> is also produced.

4) The <u>lactic acid</u> builds up in the muscles — it gets <u>painful</u> and leads to <u>cramp</u>. You need to learn the <u>word equation</u> for anaerobic respiration in <u>animals</u>:

Lactic acid can be removed from the muscles by the blood flowing through them.

glucose $\longrightarrow$ lactic acid (+ energy)

Anaerobic Respiration in Plants is Slightly Different

1) <u>Plants</u> can respire <u>without oxygen</u> too, but they produce <u>ethanol</u> (alcohol) and CO_2 <u>instead</u> of lactic acid.

2) You need to learn the <u>word equation</u> for anaerobic respiration in <u>plants</u>:

Fungi, like yeast, also respire anaerobically like this — and people use yeast to make bread rise (see page 148).

glucose $\longrightarrow$ ethanol + carbon dioxide (+ energy)

Only aerobic respiration uses oxygen...

So when you're just sitting about, you use <u>aerobic respiration</u> to get all your energy — but when you do hard exercise, you can't get enough oxygen to your muscles, so you use <u>anaerobic respiration</u> too.

Investigating Respiration

Not convinced about <u>carbon dioxide</u> being produced by <u>respiration</u>?
Well here's how to <u>detect</u> it yourself...

Carbon Dioxide Production can be Detected using an Indicator

1) You can use <u>hydrogen-carbonate indicator</u> to show that living organisms produce <u>CO_2</u> as they respire.
2) Normally this solution is <u>orange</u>, but it <u>changes colour</u> to a <u>lovely yellow</u> in the presence of <u>carbon dioxide</u>.
3) Here's how you can set up an experiment to demonstrate <u>carbon dioxide production</u> by some <u>beans</u>:

Firstly, prepare one set of <u>germinating beans</u> and one set of <u>boiled beans</u> (the control) as described in the experiment on page 49.

Now, set up the experiment as shown in the diagrams below:
- Put the same amount of <u>hydrogen-carbonate indicator</u> into two <u>test tubes</u>.
- Place a <u>platform</u> made of <u>gauze</u> into each test tube and place the beans on this.
- <u>Seal</u> the test tubes with a <u>rubber bung</u>.
- Leave the apparatus for a <u>set period</u> of <u>time</u> (e.g. an hour).

Results:

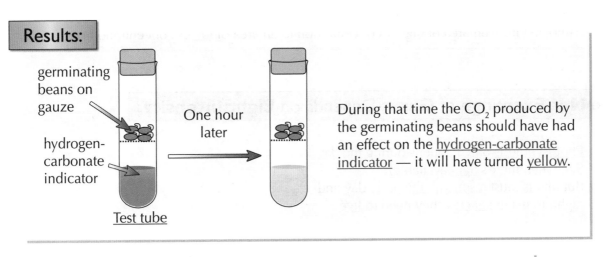

germinating beans on gauze

hydrogen-carbonate indicator

Test tube

One hour later

During that time the CO_2 produced by the germinating beans should have had an effect on the <u>hydrogen-carbonate indicator</u> — it will have turned <u>yellow</u>.

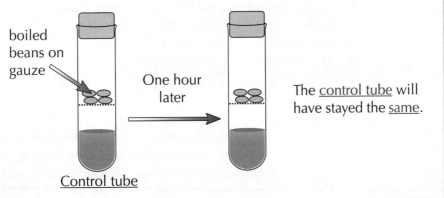

boiled beans on gauze

One hour later

The <u>control tube</u> will have stayed the <u>same</u>.

Control tube

You don't always have to use beans...

You can also do this experiment with <u>small organisms</u> like woodlice or maggots (the control for these would be glass beads though). Make sure you treat any animals ethically (see p.161).

Gas Exchange — Flowering Plants

Diffusion is the net movement of particles from an area of higher concentration to an area of lower concentration. Now's a good time to flick back to page 14 if you don't have a clue what I'm on about...

Plants Exchange Carbon Dioxide and Oxygen

1) When plants photosynthesise they use up CO_2 from the atmosphere and produce O_2 as a waste product.
2) When plants respire they use up O_2 and produce CO_2 as a waste product.
3) These waste products are lost through little holes in the undersides of leaves called stomata.

Plants Exchange Gases By Diffusion

So there are lots of gases moving to and fro in plants, and this movement happens by diffusion. E.g.

1) When a plant is photosynthesising it uses up lots of CO_2, so there's hardly any inside the leaf. Luckily this makes more CO_2 move into the leaf by diffusion (from an area of higher concentration to an area of lower concentration).

2) At the same time lots of O_2 is being made as a waste product of photosynthesis. Some is used in respiration, and the rest diffuses out through the stomata (moving from an area of higher concentration to an area of lower concentration).

The Net Exchange of Gases Depends on Light Intensity

1) Photosynthesis only happens during the day (i.e. when there's light available). But plants must respire all the time, day and night, to get the energy they need to live.

2) During the day (when light intensity is high) plants make more oxygen by photosynthesis than they use in respiration. So in daylight, they release oxygen. They also use up more carbon dioxide than they produce, so they take in carbon dioxide.

3) At night though (or when light intensity is low) plants only respire — there's not enough light for photosynthesis. This means they take in oxygen and release carbon dioxide — just like us.

Gases move in and out of plants by diffusion...

Which gases move in or out depends on the time of day. Just remember, plants photosynthesise when the Sun is shining, so in the day they'll be taking in lots of carbon dioxide and giving out oxygen.

Gas Exchange — Flowering Plants

Gas exchange in plants takes place in the leaves...

Leaves are Adapted for Efficient Gas Exchange

1) Leaves are <u>broad</u>, so there's a large surface area for <u>diffusion</u>.
2) They're also <u>thin</u>, so <u>gases</u> only have to travel a <u>short distance</u> to reach the cells where they're needed.
3) There are <u>air spaces</u> inside the leaf. This lets gases like carbon dioxide and oxygen move easily between cells. It also increases the surface area for <u>gas exchange</u>.
4) The lower surface is full of little holes called <u>stomata</u>. They're there to let gases like <u>CO_2</u> and <u>O_2</u> diffuse in and out. They also allow <u>water</u> to escape — which is known as <u>transpiration</u> (see page 42).

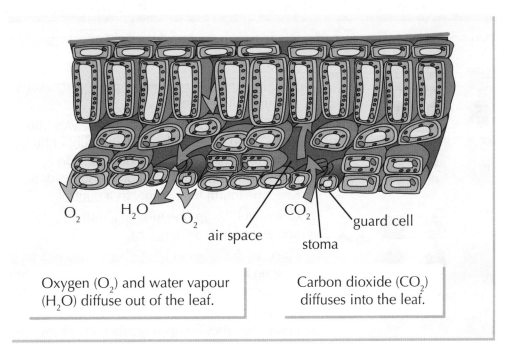

Oxygen (O_2) and water vapour (H_2O) diffuse out of the leaf.

Carbon dioxide (CO_2) diffuses into the leaf.

Stomata can be Opened and Closed

1) <u>Stomata</u> begin to <u>close</u> as it gets dark. Photosynthesis can't happen in the dark, so they don't need to be open to let <u>CO_2</u> in. When the stomata are <u>closed</u>, water <u>can't escape</u>. This stops the plant <u>drying out</u>.

2) Stomata also <u>close</u> when supplies of <u>water</u> from the <u>roots</u> start to <u>dry up</u>. This <u>stops</u> the plant from <u>photosynthesising</u> (bad), but if they <u>didn't close</u>, the plant might dry out and <u>die</u> (worse).

3) The <u>opening</u> and <u>closing</u> of stomata is <u>controlled</u> by the cells that surround them (called <u>guard cells</u>). Guard cells do this by changing their <u>shape</u> and <u>volume</u>. Guard cells <u>increase in volume</u> to <u>open</u> stomata and <u>decrease in volume</u> to <u>close</u> stomata.

Interesting fact — stomata is the plural of stoma

If you're asked to <u>explain</u> how leaves are adapted for gas exchange, don't just <u>describe</u> the <u>features</u> of the leaves. You also need to go on to say <u>how</u> these features make gas exchange efficient.

PRACTICAL — Investigating Gas Exchange in Plants

Hydrogen-carbonate Indicator Shows CO₂ Concentration...

You might remember from p.51 that a solution of hydrogen-carbonate indicator in air with a normal CO₂ concentration is orange.

Well if the CO₂ concentration of the air increases, more CO₂ will dissolve in it, and it becomes more yellow.

And if the CO₂ concentration of the air decreases, CO₂ will come out of the solution, and it becomes purple.

...So You Can Show Differences in Net Gas Exchange in Plants

Here's an experiment using hydrogen-carbonate indicator to show how light affects gas exchange:

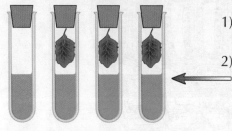

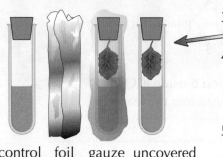

control   foil   gauze   uncovered

1) Add the same volume of hydrogen-carbonate indicator to four boiling tubes.

2) Put similar-sized, healthy-looking leaves into three of the tubes and seal with a rubber bung. Trap the leaf stem with the bung to stop it falling down into the solution if you need to. Keep the fourth tube empty as a control.

3) Completely wrap one tube in aluminium foil, and a second tube in gauze.

4) Place all the tubes in bright light. This will let plenty of light on to the uncovered leaf, and a little light onto the leaf covered in gauze. The leaf covered in foil will get no light — assuming you've wrapped it up properly.

5) Leave the tubes for an hour, then check the colour of the indicator.

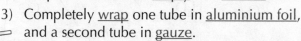

Results

1) There shouldn't be any change in the colour of the control tube.

2) You'd expect the indicator in the darkened tube to go yellow. Respiration will still take place but there will be no photosynthesis, so the CO₂ concentration in the tube will increase.

3) You'd expect the indicator in the shaded tube to stay a similar colour. With a little photosynthesis and some respiration taking place, roughly equal amounts of CO₂ will be taken up and produced by the leaf, so the CO₂ concentration in the tube won't change very much.

4) You'd expect the indicator in the well-lit tube to go purple. There will be some respiration, but lots of photosynthesis, leading to net uptake of CO₂ by the leaf. This will lower the CO₂ concentration in the tube.

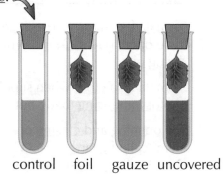

control   foil   gauze   uncovered

Give it a go, then draw a nice colour-picture of it...

This experiment might sound like a long-winded way to get some coloured tubes, but CO₂ is pretty hard to measure (being generally like the rest of the air), so this is actually a neat way to show it.

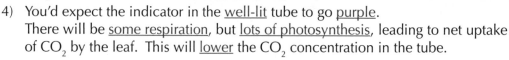

Paper 2

Paper 2

Warm-Up & Exam Questions

Right, question time. Give these your best shot...

Exam Questions

1   Respiration is a process carried out by all living cells.
    It can take place aerobically or anaerobically.

(a) State the purpose of respiration.

[1 mark]

(b) Give **two** differences between aerobic and anaerobic respiration.

[2 marks]

(c) Which of the following is the balanced symbol equation for aerobic respiration?

☐ **A** $C_6H_{12}O_6 + 6CO_2 \rightarrow 6O_2 + 6H_2O$ ☐ **C** $6O_2 + 6H_2O \rightarrow C_6H_{12}O_6 + 6CO_2$

☐ **B** $C_6H_{12}O_6 + 6O_2 \rightarrow 6CO_2 + 6H_2O$ ☐ **D** $6CO_2 + 6H_2O \rightarrow C_6H_{12}O_6 + 6O_2$

[1 mark]

PAPER 2

2   Plants exchange gases with the atmosphere. The diagram below shows a cross section through
    part of a leaf, with arrows indicating the movement of two different gases during daylight hours.

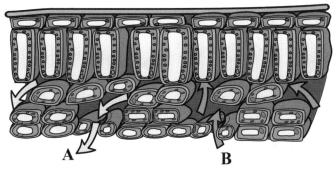

A   B

(a) (i) Suggest the gas that is most likely to be represented by each of the letters on the diagram.

[2 marks]

(ii) Name the process by which gases move into and out of leaves.

[1 mark]

(b) (i) Which process in leaves produces oxygen as a waste product?

[1 mark]

(ii) Which process in leaves produces carbon dioxide as a waste product?

[1 mark]

Exam Questions

3 A student investigating respiration prepared a neutral solution of bromothymol blue indicator and added it to two test tubes. She put gauze platforms in both tubes and placed a living beetle in one tube and glass beads in the other (see below). She then sealed the tubes and left them for two hours.

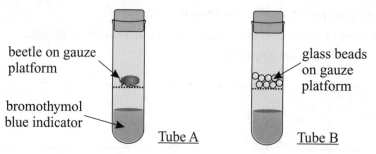

beetle on gauze platform

bromothymol blue indicator

Tube A

glass beads on gauze platform

Tube B

Bromothymol blue indicator is green in neutral solutions and yellow in acidic solutions. Carbon dioxide forms an acid when it dissolves in solution.

(a) Describe and explain the appearance of each tube after the two hour period.

[4 marks]

(b) Explain why the student put glass beads into one of the tubes.

[1 mark]

PAPER 2

4 A student has designed an experiment to investigate the effect of light intensity on net gas exchange in plants. He places healthy beech leaves into three tubes containing orange hydrogen-carbonate indicator and seals the tubes with rubber bungs. He prepares a fourth tube containing only indicator as a control.

In order to vary the amount of light reaching the three leaves, the student wraps tube **A** in gauze to block out some light, and tube **B** in foil to block out all light. He leaves tubes **C** and **D** (the control) unwrapped. His apparatus is shown below.

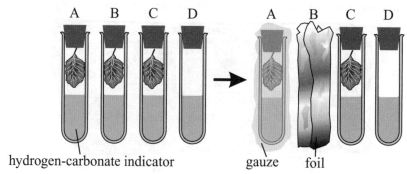

A B C D → A B C D

hydrogen-carbonate indicator

gauze foil

(a) Suggest why the student sealed the tubes with rubber bungs.

[1 mark]

(b) Explain why the student included a control tube.

[1 mark]

(c) The student left the tubes near a bright light for two hours. After this time there was no change in the colour of the indicator solution in tube D. Explain the changes he saw in the indicator solution in the other three tubes, A, B and C, after the two hour period.

[6 marks]

The Respiratory System

The respiratory system lets you breathe in and out. Pretty important. But before we get into the breathing stuff, we need to look more closely at the structure of the thorax...

The **Lungs** Are in the **Thorax**

1) The thorax is the top part of your body.

2) It's separated from the lower part of the body by a muscle called the diaphragm.

3) The lungs are like big pink sponges and are surrounded by the pleural membranes.

4) The lungs are protected by the ribcage.
   The intercostal muscles run between the ribs.

5) The air that you breathe in goes through the trachea. This splits into two tubes called bronchi (each one is a bronchus), one going to each lung.

6) The bronchi split into progressively smaller tubes called bronchioles.

7) The bronchioles finally end at small bags called alveoli where the gas exchange takes place (see page 60).

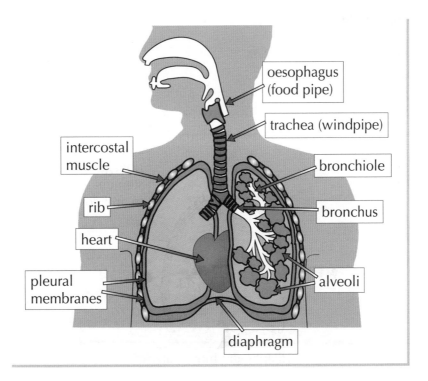

Take a deep breath...

...scribble out a picture of the thorax and label it. It doesn't have to be pretty — you just need to make sure you're getting the labels in the right place. Learning the structure of the thorax will make the next few pages about ventilation and gas exchange make a lot more sense. Believe me.

Ventilation

You need to get <u>oxygen</u> into your bloodstream to supply your cells for <u>respiration</u>.
You also need to get rid of <u>carbon dioxide</u> from your blood.
This all happens in your <u>lungs</u> when you breathe air <u>in and out</u>...

Breathing **In**...

1) <u>Intercostal muscles</u> and <u>diaphragm contract</u>.
2) Thorax volume <u>increases</u>.
3) This decreases the pressure, drawing air <u>in</u>.

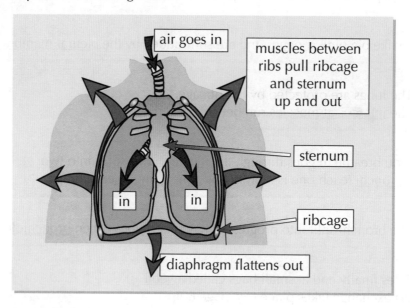

...and Breathing **Out**

1) <u>Intercostal muscles</u> and <u>diaphragm relax</u>.
2) Thorax volume <u>decreases</u>.
3) Air is forced <u>out</u>.

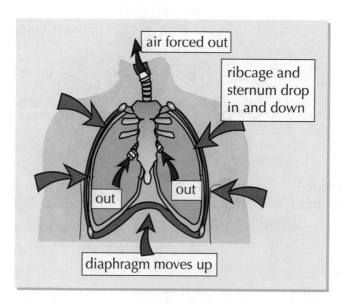

Breathing — changing the size of the space in your lungs

So when you breathe in, you don't have to suck the air in. You just make the <u>space in your lungs</u>
<u>bigger</u> and the <u>air rushes in to fill it</u>. Once you've got this page learned, flip over and carry on...

Investigating Breathing

When you exercise, your muscle cells respire more — they need more O_2 and more CO_2 is produced. So an increase in your breathing rate helps to deliver more oxygen to the cells and to remove the waste CO_2.

You Can Investigate the **Effect** of **Exercise** on **Breathing Rate**

1) There's a really simple experiment you can do to see what happens to breathing rate when you exercise:

- Firstly, sit still for five minutes.
  Then, for one minute, count the number of breaths you take.
- Now do four minutes of exercise (running, skipping...) and as soon as you stop count your breaths for a minute.
- Repeat the steps above, and work out your mean (average) results for resting and after exercise.
- You could also pester two other people to do the same so you get three sets of results to compare.

2) Your results should show that exercise increases breathing rate.

3) This is because your muscles respire more during exercise. They need to be supplied with more O_2 and have more CO_2 removed (see p.50, so your breathing rate increases.

4) During this experiment you need to control all the variables that might affect your results — e.g. you can control the time spent exercising using a stopwatch and the temperature of the room using air conditioning or a thermostat.

You Can Investigate the **Release** of **Carbon Dioxide** in Your Breath

1) You can do an experiment with limewater to show that carbon dioxide is released when we breathe out.

2) Limewater is a colourless solution which turns cloudy in the presence of carbon dioxide.

- Set up two boiling tubes as in the diagram on the right. Put the same amount of limewater in each.
- Put your mouth around the mouthpiece and breathe in and out several times.
- As you breathe in, air from the room is drawn in through boiling tube A. This air contains very little carbon dioxide so the limewater in this boiling tube remains colourless.

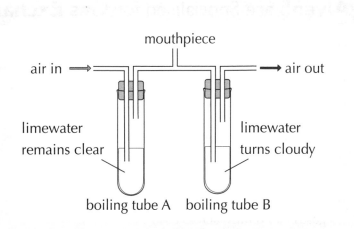

- When you breathe out, the air you exhale bubbles through the limewater in boiling tube B. This air contains CO_2 produced during respiration, so the limewater in this boiling tube turns cloudy.

3) Since the limewater in boiling tube A remains clear, you can tell that the carbon dioxide in the exhaled air was from respiration — it wasn't inhaled through boiling tube A. If you'd inhaled in the carbon dioxide, the limewater in boiling tube A would've turned cloudy too.

Gas Exchange — Humans

Gas exchange doesn't only happen in plants — it happens in humans too.
Oxygen goes into your bloodstream and you offload carbon dioxide...

Alveoli Carry Out Gas Exchange in the Body

1) The lungs contain millions and millions of little air sacs called alveoli where gas exchange happens.

2) The blood passing next to the alveoli has just returned to the lungs from the rest of the body, so it contains lots of carbon dioxide and very little oxygen. Oxygen diffuses out of the alveolus (high concentration) into the blood (low concentration). Carbon dioxide diffuses out of the blood (high concentration) into the alveolus (low concentration) to be breathed out.

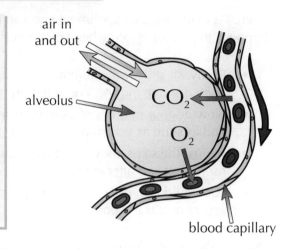

3) When the blood reaches body cells, oxygen is released from the red blood cells (where there's a high concentration) and diffuses into the body cells (where the concentration is low).

4) At the same time, carbon dioxide diffuses out of the body cells (where there's a high concentration) into the blood (where there's a low concentration). It's then carried back to the lungs.

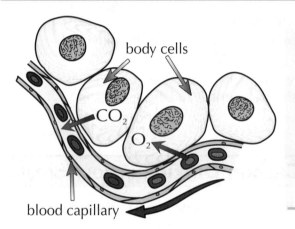

Alveoli are Specialised for Gas Exchange

1) The huge number of microscopic alveoli gives the lungs an enormous surface area.

2) There's a moist lining for gases to dissolve in.

3) The alveoli have very thin walls — only one cell thick, so the gases don't have far to diffuse.

4) They have a great blood supply to maintain a high concentration gradient.

5) The walls are permeable — so gases can diffuse across easily.

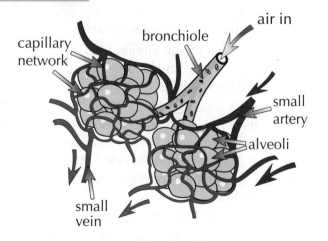

Alveoli are exchange surfaces

A large surface area is a key way that organisms' exchange surfaces are made more effective — molecules can only diffuse through a membrane when they're right next to it, and a large surface area means that a lot more molecules are close to the membrane. Make sure you're clear on this, and the other ways that alveoli are adapted for their function. If you know it, it'll be easy marks in the exam.

Gas Exchange — Humans

Everyone knows smoking's <u>bad for you</u>, but you need to learn about these specific consequences.

Smoking Tobacco Can Cause Quite a Few Problems

Smoking can severely affect your <u>lungs</u> and <u>circulatory system</u>. Here's how:

1) Emphysema, Smoker's Cough and Bronchitis

1) Smoking <u>damages</u> the walls inside the <u>alveoli</u>, <u>reducing</u> the <u>surface area</u> for gas exchange and leading to diseases like <u>emphysema</u>.

2) The <u>tar</u> in cigarettes damages the <u>cilia</u> (little hairs) in your lungs and trachea. These hairs, along with <u>mucus</u>, catch a load of <u>dust</u> and <u>bacteria</u> before they reach the lungs. The cilia also help to keep the <u>trachea clear</u> by sweeping mucus <u>back towards the mouth</u>. When these cilia are damaged, <u>chest infections</u> are more likely.

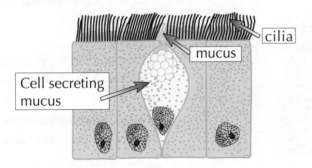

3) Tar also <u>irritates</u> the <u>bronchi</u> and <u>bronchioles</u>, encouraging mucus to be produced which can't be cleared very well by damaged cilia — this causes <u>smoker's cough</u> and <u>chronic bronchitis</u>.

2) Coronary Heart Disease

1) The <u>carbon monoxide</u> in cigarette smoke <u>reduces</u> the amount of <u>oxygen</u> the blood can carry. To make up for this, <u>heart rate increases</u> — which leads to an increase in <u>blood pressure</u>.

2) High blood pressure <u>damages</u> the <u>artery walls</u>, making the formation of <u>blood clots</u> more likely. This increases the risk of <u>coronary heart disease</u> (e.g. heart attacks).

3) Cancer

Tobacco smoke also contains <u>carcinogens</u> — chemicals that can lead to <u>cancer</u>.

Fancy a smoke? Probably not after reading this little lot...

<u>Emphysema</u>, a <u>smoker's cough</u>, <u>bronchitis</u>, <u>coronary heart disease</u> and <u>cancer</u>... it's quite the list. Make sure you know how smoking tobacco causes these problems.

Warm-Up & Exam Questions

The questions on this page are great practice for the exam. I'd give them a go if I were you...

Warm-Up Questions

1) Where in the thorax are the pleural membranes found?
2) True or False? After air enters the body through the nose and mouth, it passes into the trachea.
3) Which muscles contract to increase the volume of the thorax when breathing in?

Exam Questions

1 The respiratory system is found in the thorax.

(a) A diagram of the human thorax is shown on the left. Label the diaphragm and ribcage on the diagram.

[2 marks]

(b) A structure of the respiratory system is labelled **X** in the diagram. Name structure **X**.

[1 mark]

(c) Name the structures in the respiratory system where gas exchange takes place.

[1 mark]

2 The statements below describe the events that take place when you breathe in. Put them in the correct order by writing the numbers **1** to **4** in the boxes, where **1** represents the first event.

Event	Order
Pressure in lungs decreases	
Intercostal muscles and diaphragm contract	
Air enters the lungs	
Thorax volume increases	

[3 marks]

PRACTICAL

3 Describe an investigation to find the effect of exercise on a person's breathing rate.

[6 marks]

4 Gas exchange in humans occurs in the alveoli.

(a) Explain the exchange of oxygen between an alveolus and a capillary.

[3 marks]

(b) Explain **two** ways that alveoli are adapted for gas exchange.

[4 marks]

Revision Questions for Section 4

Well, that's <u>Section 4</u> complete — take a deep breath and crack on with these questions.

- Try these questions and <u>tick off each one</u> when you <u>get it right</u>.
- When you've done <u>all the questions</u> for a topic and are <u>completely happy</u> with it, tick off the topic.

Respiration (p.49-51) ☑

1) What is the role of ATP? ☑
2) Describe an experiment used to monitor the temperature change produced by respiration. ☑
3) What is aerobic respiration? ☑
4) Give the word and symbol equations for aerobic respiration. ☑
5) What is anaerobic respiration? ☑
6) What are two drawbacks of anaerobic respiration compared to aerobic respiration? ☑
7) Give the word equation for anaerobic respiration in plants. ☑
8) Name an indicator solution that can be used to detect carbon dioxide. ☑

Gas Exchange — Flowering Plants (p.52-54) ☑

9) What are the little holes on the lower surface of leaves called? ☑
10) Why do plants need to exchange gases with their surroundings? ☑
11) a) At night, there's a lot of O_2 inside the leaf and not a lot of CO_2. True or false?
    b) Explain your answer to part a). ☑
12) Explain how leaves are adapted for efficient gas exchange. ☑
13) Describe an experiment you could use to show the effect of light on gas exchange in leaves. What would you use as a control? ☑

The Respiratory System and Ventilation (p.57-59) ☐

14) Name the key structures of the respiratory system. ☑
15) What causes air to be forced out of the lungs when you breathe out? ☑
16) Explain why exercise increases your breathing rate. ☑
17) Name a solution that you can use to show the presence of carbon dioxide in your breath. ☐

Gas Exchange — Humans (p.60-61) ☑

18) Why do the alveoli have very thin walls? ☑
19) How does smoking contribute to coronary heart disease? ☑
20) Name two other diseases linked to smoking tobacco. ☑

Functions of the Blood

All multicellular organisms need a transport system (see page 41) and in humans, it's the blood.

Blood has **Four Main Components**

They are:

| Plasma | Platelets | Red Blood Cells | White Blood Cells |

Plasma is the **Liquid Bit** of **Blood**

It's basically blood minus the blood cells (see below and on the next page). Plasma is a
pale yellow liquid which carries just about everything that needs transporting around your body:

1) Red and white blood cells and platelets.
2) Digested food products (like glucose and amino acids) from the gut to all the body cells.
3) Carbon dioxide from the body cells to the lungs.
4) Urea from the liver to the kidneys (where it's removed in the urine, see page 72).
5) Hormones, which act as chemical messengers (see page 83).
6) Heat energy.

Paper 2

Platelets are **Small Fragments** of Cells that **Help Blood Clot**

1) When you damage a blood vessel, platelets clump together to 'plug' the damaged area.

2) This is known as blood clotting. Blood clots stop you losing too much blood
    and prevent microorganisms from entering the wound.

3) In a clot, platelets are held together by a mesh of a protein called fibrin (though
    this process also needs other proteins called clotting factors to work properly).

Paper 2

Red Blood Cells Have the Job of Carrying **Oxygen**

They transport oxygen from the lungs to all the cells in the body.
A red blood cell is well adapted to its function:

1) Red blood cells are small and have a biconcave shape (which is a posh way of saying they look a little
    bit like doughnuts, see diagram below) to give a large surface area for absorbing and releasing oxygen.

2) They contain haemoglobin, which is what gives blood
    its colour — it contains a lot of iron. In the lungs,
    haemoglobin reacts with oxygen to become
    oxyhaemoglobin. In body tissues the reverse
    reaction happens to release oxygen to the cells.

3) Red blood cells don't have a nucleus — this frees up space
    for more haemoglobin, so they can carry more oxygen.

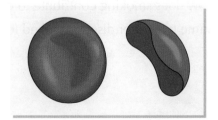

Blood — red blood cells, white blood cells, platelets and plasma

Sometimes, when you're ill, you might have a sample of your blood taken so that it can be analysed. Blood
tests can be used to diagnose loads of things — not just disorders of the blood. This is because the blood
transports so many chemicals produced by so many organs... and it's easy to take a sample of blood.

White Blood Cells and Immunity

Your body is <u>constantly</u> fighting off attack from all sorts of <u>nasties</u> — yep, things really are out to get you.

Your **Immune System** Deals with **Pathogens**

1) <u>Pathogens</u> are microorganisms that <u>cause disease</u>, e.g. certain types of bacteria and viruses (see p.6).

2) Once pathogens have entered your body they'll reproduce rapidly unless they're <u>destroyed</u>. That's the job of your <u>immune system</u>, and <u>white blood cells</u> are the <u>most important part</u> of it.

3) There are two different types of white blood cell you need to know about: <u>phagocytes</u> and <u>lymphocytes</u>.

Phagocytes Ingest **Pathogens**

1) <u>Phagocytes</u> detect things that are '<u>foreign</u>' to the body, e.g. pathogens. They then <u>engulf</u> the pathogens and <u>digest them</u>.

2) Phagocytes are <u>non-specific</u> — they attack anything that's not meant to be there.

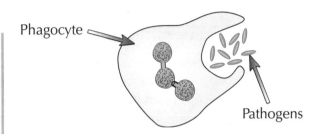

Phagocyte

Pathogens

Lymphocytes Produce **Antibodies**

1) Every pathogen has unique molecules (called <u>antigens</u>) on its surface.

2) When certain white blood cells, called <u>lymphocytes</u>, come across a <u>foreign antigen</u>, they will start to produce <u>proteins</u> called <u>antibodies</u> — these lock on to the invading pathogens and mark them out for destruction by other white blood cells. The antibodies produced are <u>specific</u> to that type of antigen — they won't lock on to any others.

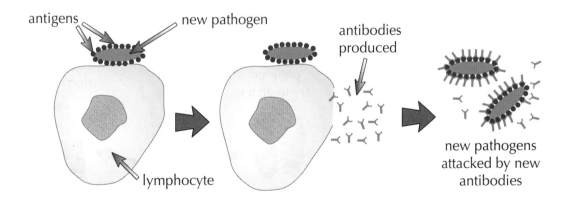

antigens   new pathogen   antibodies produced

lymphocyte

new pathogens attacked by new antibodies

3) Antibodies are then produced <u>rapidly</u> and flow round the body to mark all similar pathogens.

4) <u>Memory cells</u> are also produced in response to a foreign antigen. These remain in the body and <u>remember</u> a <u>specific</u> antigen. They can reproduce very fast if the <u>same</u> antigen enters the body again. That's why you're <u>immune</u> to <u>most</u> diseases if you've already had them — the body carries a "<u>memory</u>" of what the antigen was like, and can quickly produce loads of antibodies if you get infected again.

Vaccination

Vaccinations have changed the way we fight disease. We don't always have to deal with the problem once it's happened — we can prevent it happening in the first place.

Vaccination — Protects from Future Infections

1) When you're infected with a new pathogen it can take your lymphocytes a while to produce the antibodies to deal with it. In that time you can get very ill, or maybe even die.

2) To avoid this you can be vaccinated against some diseases, e.g. polio or measles.

3) Vaccination usually involves injecting dead or inactive pathogens into the body. These carry antigens, so even though they're harmless they still trigger an immune response — your lymphocytes produce antibodies to attack them.

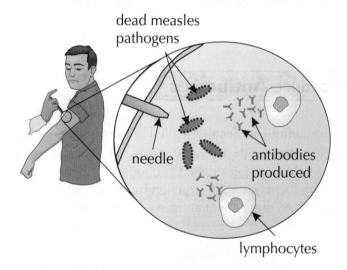

dead measles pathogens

needle

antibodies produced

lymphocytes

4) Memory cells will also be produced and will remain in the blood, so if live pathogens of the same type ever appear, the antibodies to kill them will be produced much faster and in greater numbers.

If live measles pathogens try to attack...

... so you don't get ill.

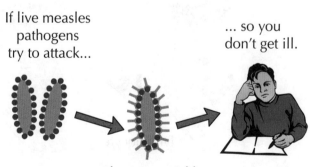

... they are quickly recognised by memory cells and attacked by antibodies...

Practice exam questions are a lot like vaccinations...

We expose you to some harmless questions (the vaccine) that you learn how to recognise and answer, then when you're confronted with the real exam (the full strength pathogen), you've got the necessary knowledge (antibodies) to answer (kill) them. Gosh, you'd best get revising...

Paper 2

Paper 2

Blood Vessels

Blood needs a good set of 'tubes' to carry it round the body. Here's a page on the different types:

Blood Vessels are Designed for Their Function

There are three different types of blood vessel:

1) ARTERIES — these carry the blood away from the heart.
2) CAPILLARIES — these are involved in the exchange of materials at the tissues.
3) VEINS — these carry the blood to the heart.

Arteries Carry Blood Under Pressure

1) The heart pumps the blood out at high pressure so the artery walls are strong and elastic.

2) The elastic fibres allow arteries to expand.

3) The walls are thick compared to the size of the hole down the middle (the "lumen"). They contain thick layers of muscle to make them strong.

4) The largest artery in the body is the aorta (see next page).

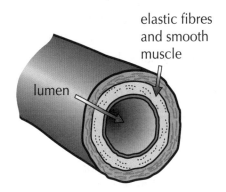

elastic fibres and smooth muscle

lumen

Capillaries are Really Small

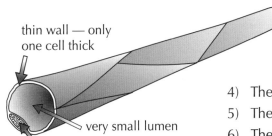

thin wall — only one cell thick

very small lumen

nucleus of cell

1) Arteries branch into capillaries.

2) Capillaries are really tiny — too small to see.

3) They carry the blood really close to every cell in the body to exchange substances with them.

4) They have permeable walls, so substances can diffuse in and out.

5) They supply food and oxygen, and take away wastes like CO_2.

6) Their walls are usually only one cell thick. This increases the rate of diffusion by decreasing the distance over which it happens.

Veins Take Blood Back to the Heart

1) Capillaries eventually join up to form veins.

2) The blood is at lower pressure in the veins so the walls don't need to be as thick as artery walls.

3) They have a bigger lumen than arteries to help the blood flow despite the lower pressure.

4) They also have valves to help keep the blood flowing in the right direction.

5) The largest vein in the body is the vena cava (see next page).

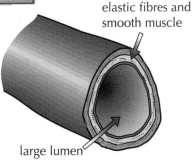

elastic fibres and smooth muscle

large lumen

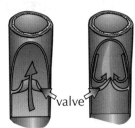

valve

The Heart

Blood doesn't just move around the body <u>on its own</u>, of course. It needs a <u>pump</u>.

Learn This **Diagram** of the **Heart** with All Its **Labels**

1) The <u>right atrium</u> of the heart receives <u>deoxygenated</u> blood from the <u>body</u> (through the <u>vena cava</u>).
   (The plural of atrium is atria.)

2) The deoxygenated blood moves through to the <u>right ventricle</u>, which pumps it to the <u>lungs</u> (via the <u>pulmonary artery</u>).

3) The <u>left atrium</u> receives <u>oxygenated</u> blood from the <u>lungs</u> (through the <u>pulmonary vein</u>).

4) The oxygenated blood then moves through to the <u>left ventricle</u>, which pumps it out round the <u>whole body</u> (via the <u>aorta</u>).

5) The <u>left</u> ventricle has a much <u>thicker wall</u> than the <u>right</u> ventricle. It needs more <u>muscle</u> because it has to pump blood around the <u>whole body</u>, whereas the right ventricle only has to pump it to the <u>lungs</u>. This also means that the blood in the left ventricle is under <u>higher pressure</u> than the blood in the right ventricle.

6) The <u>valves</u> prevent the <u>backflow</u> of blood.

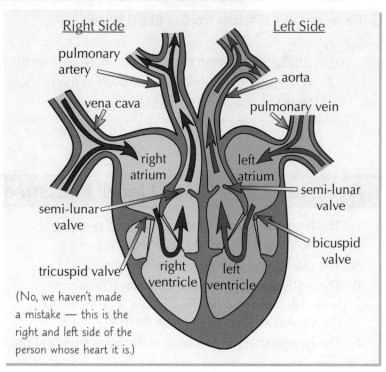

Right Side   Left Side

pulmonary artery

aorta

vena cava

pulmonary vein

right atrium

left atrium

semi-lunar valve

semi-lunar valve

bicuspid valve

tricuspid valve

right ventricle

left ventricle

(No, we haven't made a mistake — this is the right and left side of the person whose heart it is.)

Exercise Increases **Heart Rate**

There's more on respiration on p.49-50.

1) When you <u>exercise</u>, your muscles need <u>more energy</u>, so you <u>respire more</u>.

2) You need to get <u>more oxygen</u> into the cells and <u>remove</u> more <u>carbon dioxide</u>. For this to happen the blood has to flow faster, so your <u>heart rate increases</u>. Here's how:

- Exercise <u>increases</u> the amount of <u>carbon dioxide</u> in the <u>blood</u>.
- High levels of blood CO_2 are detected by <u>receptors</u> in the <u>aorta</u> and <u>carotid artery</u> (an artery in the neck).
- These receptors <u>send signals</u> to the <u>brain</u>.
- The brain sends signals to the <u>heart</u>, causing it to contract <u>more frequently</u> and with <u>more force</u>.

The **Hormonal System** Also Helps to **Control Heart Rate**

1) When an organism is <u>threatened</u> (e.g. by a predator) the <u>adrenal glands</u> release <u>adrenaline</u>.

2) Adrenaline <u>binds</u> to <u>specific receptors</u> in the <u>heart</u>. This causes the cardiac muscle to <u>contract more frequently</u> and with <u>more force</u>, so <u>heart rate increases</u> and the heart <u>pumps more blood</u>.

3) This <u>increases oxygen supply</u> to the <u>tissues</u>, getting the body <u>ready for action</u>.

You need to know the heart in a fair bit of detail
Sketch out the <u>heart diagram</u> and see if you can put all the <u>labels</u> on. Keep trying till you can.

Circulation and Coronary Heart Disease

The <u>circulation system</u> is made up of the <u>heart</u> and the <u>blood vessels</u>. It gets the <u>blood</u> to where it needs to be, so that useful substances (e.g. <u>glucose</u> and <u>oxygen</u>) can be delivered and wastes removed.

You Need to Know the **Structure** of the **Circulation System**

The diagram below shows the <u>human circulation system</u>.

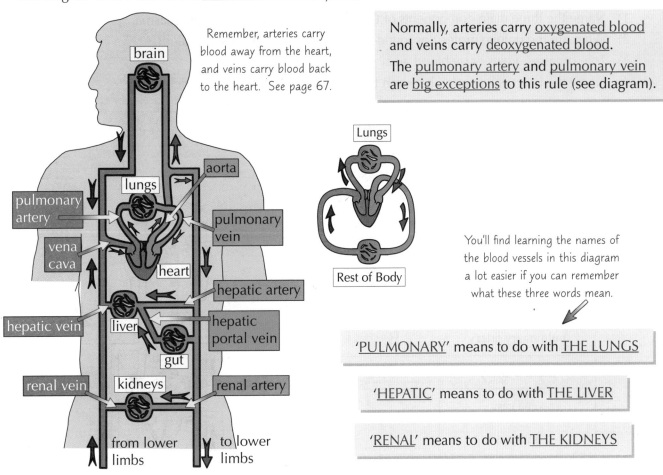

Remember, arteries carry blood away from the heart, and veins carry blood back to the heart. See page 67.

Normally, arteries carry <u>oxygenated blood</u> and veins carry <u>deoxygenated blood</u>.
The <u>pulmonary artery</u> and <u>pulmonary vein</u> are <u>big exceptions</u> to this rule (see diagram).

You'll find learning the names of the blood vessels in this diagram a lot easier if you can remember what these three words mean.

'PULMONARY' means to do with THE LUNGS

'HEPATIC' means to do with THE LIVER

'RENAL' means to do with THE KIDNEYS

Several Factors can Lead to **Coronary Heart Disease**

1) <u>Coronary heart disease</u> is when the <u>coronary arteries</u> that supply the <u>blood</u> to the muscle of the heart get <u>blocked</u> by <u>layers of fatty material building up</u>.

2) This causes the arteries to become <u>narrow</u>, so blood flow is <u>restricted</u> and there's a <u>lack of oxygen</u> to the heart muscle — this can lead to a <u>heart attack</u>.

3) There are many <u>risk factors</u> for coronary heart disease. Risk factors are things that are linked to an <u>increase</u> in the <u>likelihood</u> that a person will develop a certain disease during their lifetime.

4) One risk factor for coronary heart disease is having a <u>diet</u> high in <u>saturated fat</u>. This can lead to <u>fatty deposits</u> forming inside <u>arteries</u>, which can lead to <u>coronary heart disease</u>.

5) <u>Smoking</u> is another risk factor for coronary heart disease. Smoking <u>increases blood pressure</u>, which can cause <u>damage</u> to the inside of the coronary arteries. Chemicals in cigarette smoke can also cause <u>damage</u>. The damage makes it more likely that <u>fatty deposits</u> will form, <u>narrowing</u> the coronary arteries.

6) Another risk factor for coronary heart disease is being <u>inactive</u>. It can lead to <u>high blood pressure</u>, which can damage the lining of arteries. This damage makes it more likely that <u>fatty deposits</u> will form.

Warm-Up & Exam Questions

There are some nice diagrams to learn on the previous few pages. If you don't bother, you'll feel pretty silly if you turn over the exam paper and the first question asks you to label a diagram of the heart. Just saying... Anyway, let's see if these questions get your blood pumping...

Warm-Up Questions

1) Name the three main components of the blood that are carried by the plasma.
2) What are the unique molecules found on the surface of pathogens called?
3) True or false? Veins carry blood away from the heart.
4) Name the heart valve found between the left atrium and the left ventricle.

Exam Questions

1 The diagram shows the circulation system with some structures labelled A to H. Complete the table by writing in the letter that represents each structure. The first one has been done for you.

Grade 4-6

Structure	Letter
pulmonary artery	B
hepatic artery	....
vena cava	....
kidneys	....
aorta	....
hepatic portal vein	....

[5 marks]

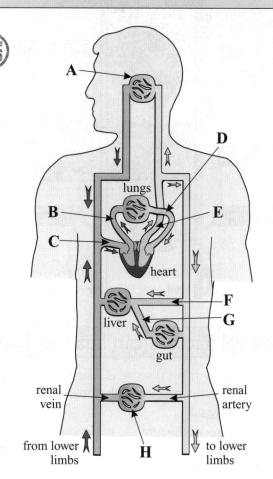

2 The cell shown transports oxygen around the body. *Grade 4-6*

(a) Explain how this cell's shape is adapted for transporting oxygen.

[2 marks]

(b) Describe and explain **one** other way in which this cell is adapted for carrying oxygen.

[2 marks]

View from above   Cut through view

Exam Questions

3 The human immune system fights pathogens using a number of different mechanisms.

   (a) Describe the mechanism for destroying pathogens which is shown in the diagram below.

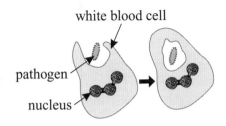

                            [2 marks]

   (b) Explain the role of antibodies in the immune response.

                            [3 marks]

4 A diagram of a capillary is shown to the right.

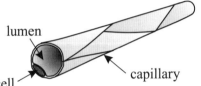

   (a) Name **two** substances that diffuse through capillary walls.

                  [2 marks]

   (b) Explain how the structure of a capillary is adapted for its function.

                            [6 marks]

5 Doctors were assessing the heart of a patient who had recently suffered from a heart attack. They noticed that one of the main arteries supplying the heart muscle was narrowed.

   (a) The patient is a smoker. Explain **one** way that smoking may have contributed to the narrowing of the artery.

                            [2 marks]

   (b) The patient is advised to stop smoking. Give **two** other pieces of lifestyle advice the doctors are likely to give to the patient.

                            [2 marks]

6 A dog barks at a cat, causing the cat's heart rate to increase from 145 beats per minute to 170 beats per minute.

   (a) Explain the process which caused the cat's heart rate to increase.

                            [3 marks]

   (b) Suggest how an increased heart rate prepares the cat for action.

                            [1 mark]

> **PAPER 2**

7 Child A and child B are born to different women on the same day. Child A is vaccinated with the rubella vaccine, but child B is not. Three years later the two children are exposed to the rubella virus. Explain why child B becomes ill but child A does not.

                            [5 marks]

Excretion — The Kidneys

Excretion is the removal of waste products. Carbon dioxide is a waste product from the lungs, and sweat is a waste product from the skin. Excretion is also carried out by the kidneys.

The Kidneys are Excretion Organs

The kidneys are part of the urinary system. They perform three main roles:

1) Removal of urea from the blood. Urea is produced in the liver from excess amino acids.

2) Adjustment of ion (salt) levels in the blood.

3) Adjustment of water content of the blood.

They do this by filtering stuff out of the blood under high pressure, and then reabsorbing the useful things. The end product is urine.

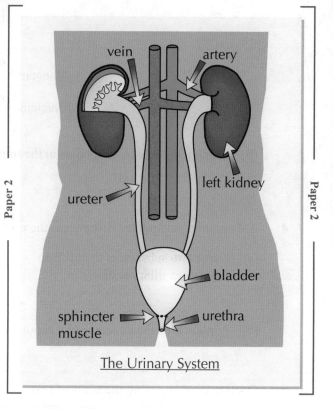

The Urinary System

Nephrons are the Filtration Units in the Kidneys

Each kidney contains thousands of nephrons.

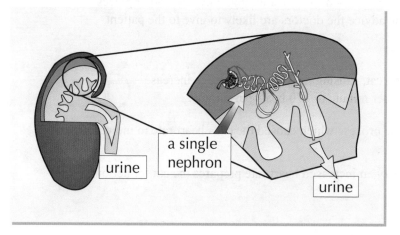

You can find out what happens at the nephron on the next page.

The kidneys remove urea and control salt and water levels

Scientists have made a machine which can do the kidneys' job for us — a kidney dialysis machine. People with kidney failure have to use it for 3-4 hours, 3 times a week. Unfortunately it's not something you can carry around with you, which makes life difficult for people with kidney failure.

Excretion — The Kidneys

Here's what happens as <u>blood</u> passes through the <u>nephron</u>...

1) Ultrafiltration:

1) Blood from the <u>renal artery</u> flows through the <u>glomerulus</u> — a bundle of capillaries at the start of the nephron (see diagram below).

2) A <u>high pressure</u> is built up which squeezes <u>water</u>, <u>urea</u>, <u>ions</u> and <u>glucose</u> out of the blood and into the <u>Bowman's capsule</u>.

3) The membranes between the blood vessels in the glomerulus and the Bowman's capsule act like <u>filters</u>, so <u>big</u> molecules like <u>proteins</u> and <u>blood cells</u> are <u>not</u> squeezed out. They stay in the blood. The <u>filtered liquid</u> in the Bowman's capsule is known as the <u>glomerular filtrate</u>.

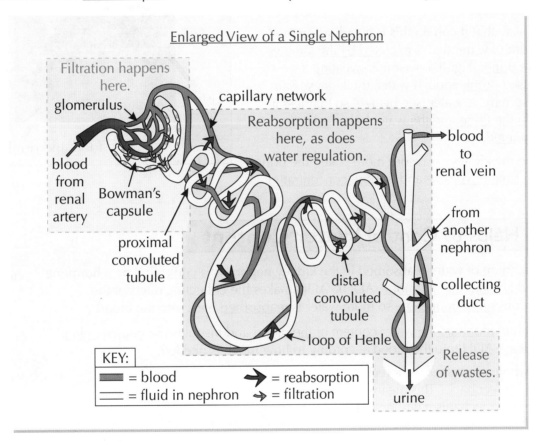

Enlarged View of a Single Nephron

2) Reabsorption:

It's called selective reabsorption because only some substances are reabsorbed.

As the filtrate flows along the nephron, <u>useful</u> substances are <u>selectively reabsorbed</u> back into the blood:

1) <u>All</u> the <u>glucose</u> is reabsorbed from the <u>proximal convoluted tubule</u> so that it can be used in <u>respiration</u>. The reabsorption of glucose involves the process of <u>active transport</u> (see p.18) against the concentration gradient.

2) <u>Sufficient ions</u> are reabsorbed. Excess ions aren't.

3) <u>Sufficient water</u> is reabsorbed from the <u>collecting duct</u> into the bloodstream by <u>osmosis</u> (see p.15).

3) Release of Wastes:

The remaining substances (including <u>water</u>, <u>ions</u> and <u>urea</u>) form <u>urine</u>. This continues out of the <u>nephron</u>, through the ureter and down to the <u>bladder</u>, where it is stored before being released via the <u>urethra</u>.

Paper 2

Paper 2

Osmoregulation — The Kidneys

The kidneys are <u>really important</u> organs. Not only do they filter the blood (see previous page), they also play a key role in controlling the amount of water inside your body. Whether you're interested in it or not, I'm afraid <u>you need to know this page</u> for your exam — so <u>pay attention</u>.

The Kidneys Also Adjust the Body's Water Content

1) Water is taken into the body as <u>food and drink</u> and is <u>lost</u> from the body in <u>three main ways</u>: sweating, breathing and weeing (see page 85).

2) The body has to <u>constantly balance</u> the water coming <u>in</u> against the water going <u>out</u> — this is <u>osmoregulation</u>.

3) One way that it can do this is by adjusting the amount of water that is <u>excreted by the kidneys</u> in the <u>urine</u>. E.g. If a person is <u>sweating</u> a lot or hasn't <u>drunk</u> enough water, the kidneys can reabsorb more water (see below), so that less is <u>lost in the urine</u> and the water balance is <u>maintained</u>.

4) When the kidneys reabsorb more water, the urine has a <u>smaller volume</u> and is <u>more concentrated</u>.

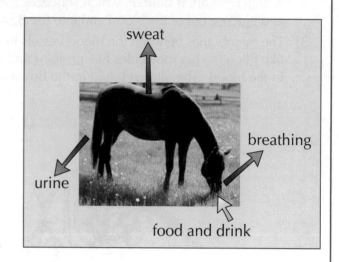

ADH Helps to Control Water Content

1) The amount of water reabsorbed in the kidney nephrons is <u>controlled</u> by a hormone called <u>anti-diuretic hormone</u> (ADH). ADH makes the collecting ducts of the nephrons <u>more permeable</u> so more water is <u>reabsorbed</u> back into the blood.

2) The brain <u>monitors the water content of the blood</u> and instructs the <u>pituitary gland</u> to release <u>ADH</u> into the blood according to how much is needed.

3) The whole process of osmoregulation is controlled by a mechanism called <u>negative feedback</u>. This means that if the water content gets <u>too high</u> or <u>too low</u> a mechanism will be triggered that brings it back to <u>normal</u>.

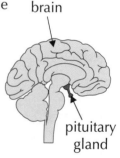

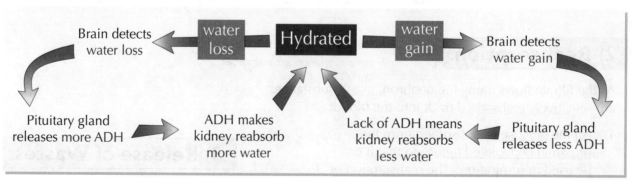

Don't try to kid me that you know it all — learn it properly

So the kidneys make sure you don't end up like a dry sponge or a massive water balloon — thank goodness. Make sure you remember which way round <u>ADH</u> works. Basically, <u>low</u> blood water content means <u>increased</u> ADH production and <u>more water</u> reabsorbed in the kidneys. <u>High</u> blood water content means <u>decreased</u> ADH production and <u>less water</u> reabsorbed. What could be simpler...

Warm-Up & Exam Questions

It's question time again. Don't skip this page — use it to check how well you know your stuff.

Warm-Up Questions

1) Where is urea produced?
2) Is blood entering the glomerulus under high pressure or low pressure?
3) Where is urine stored before being released from the body?

Exam Questions

PAPER 2

1 The kidneys play a key role in osmoregulation. *Grade 4-6*

(a) What is meant by the term **osmoregulation**?

[1 mark]

(b) Name the fluid in which excess water is removed from the body.

[1 mark]

(c) (i) Which of the following hormones controls the reabsorption of water in the kidneys?

☐ **A** oestrogen ☐ **B** ADH

☐ **C** adrenaline ☐ **D** insulin

[1 mark]

(ii) Name the part of the brain where this hormone is released.

[1 mark]

PAPER 2

2 Ultrafiltration in the kidneys results in the production of glomerular filtrate. *Grade 6-7*

(a) Name the part of the nephron where ultrafiltration occurs.

[1 mark]

(b) (i) Describe how glomerular filtrate is produced in the body.

[3 marks]

(ii) The substances below are all involved in the process of ultrafiltration.
1. glucose
2. urea
3. proteins
Which of these substances are present in the glomerular filtrate?

☐ **A** 1 only ☐ **B** 2 only ☐ **C** 1 and 2 only ☐ **D** 2 and 3 only

[1 mark]

PAPER 2

3 A runner went for a 10 mile run on a warm day. When she got home she noticed that her urine was darker in colour than normal. Explain why the runner produced darker coloured urine. In your answer, refer to the functioning of the kidneys. *Grade 7-9*

[6 marks]

Revision Summary for Section 5

That wraps up Section 5. You know what it's time for now...
- Try these questions and tick off each one when you get it right.
- When you've done all the questions under a heading and are completely happy with it, tick it off.

Functions of the Blood, White Blood Cells and Immunity (p.64-66) ☑

1) Name six things that blood plasma transports around the body. ☑
2) What are platelets? What role do they play in the body? ☑
3) Describe the shape of a red blood cell. ☑
4) How do lymphocytes defend the body from pathogens? ☑
5) Explain the role of memory cells in the immune system's response against pathogens. ☑
6) Explain how vaccination prevents you from getting a particular infection. ☑

Blood Vessels and The Heart (p.67-68) ☑

7) Why do arteries need very muscular, elastic walls? ☑
8) What is the purpose of valves in blood vessels? ☑
9) Which blood vessels have valves? ☑
10) Draw and label a simple diagram of the heart. ☑
11) Name the blood vessel that joins to the right ventricle of the heart.
    Where does it take the blood? ☑
12) Why does the left ventricle have a thicker wall than the right ventricle? ☑
13) How does heart rate change during exercise? Why? ☑
14) What hormone causes heart rate to rise? ☑

Circulation and Coronary Heart Disease (p.69) ☐

15) What is the name of the blood vessel that carries blood away from the liver? ☑
16) What is the function of the renal artery? ☑
17) What are the names of the two main blood vessels associated with the lungs? ☑
18) What is coronary heart disease? ☑
19) Give a risk factor for coronary heart disease. ☑

The Kidneys — Excretion and Osmoregulation (p.72-74) ☑

20) Draw and label a diagram of the urinary system. ☑
21) Describe the process of ultrafiltration. ☑
22) What happens in the collecting duct of a nephron? ☑
23) Describe the path taken by urine once it leaves the nephron. ☑

The Nervous System and Responding to Stimuli

The <u>nervous system</u> means that humans can <u>react to their surroundings</u> and <u>coordinate their behaviour</u>.

Responding to Their Environment Helps Organisms Survive

1) <u>Animals increase</u> their <u>chances of survival</u> by <u>responding</u> to <u>changes</u> in their <u>external environment</u>, e.g. by avoiding places that are too hot or too cold.

2) They also respond to changes in their <u>internal environment</u> to make sure that the <u>conditions</u> are always <u>right</u> for their <u>metabolism</u> (all the chemical reactions that go on inside them).

3) <u>Plants</u> also <u>increase</u> their <u>chances of survival</u> by responding to changes in their environment (see page 87).

4) Any <u>change</u> in the internal or external <u>environment</u> is called a <u>stimulus</u>.   *The plural of 'stimulus' is 'stimuli'.*

Receptors Detect Stimuli and Effectors Produce a Response

1) <u>Receptors detect stimuli</u>. Receptors in the <u>sense organs</u> (the eyes, ears, nose, tongue and skin) are groups of cells that <u>detect external stimuli</u>. E.g. <u>rod</u> and <u>cone cells</u> in the <u>eye</u> detect changes in <u>light</u> (see page 79).

2) <u>Effectors</u> are cells that bring about a <u>response</u> to <u>stimuli</u>. They include <u>muscle cells</u> and cells found in <u>glands</u>, e.g. the pancreas. Effectors respond in different ways — muscle cells <u>contract</u>, whereas glands <u>secrete hormones</u>.

3) Receptors <u>communicate</u> with effectors via the <u>nervous system</u> (see below), the <u>hormonal system</u> (see page 83) or sometimes <u>both</u>.

The Central Nervous System (CNS) Coordinates Information

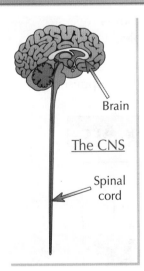

Brain

The CNS

Spinal cord

1) The <u>nervous system</u> is made up of all the <u>neurones</u> (nerve cells) in your body. There are three main types of neurone — <u>sensory</u> neurones, <u>relay</u> neurones and <u>motor</u> neurones.

2) The <u>central nervous system</u> (CNS) consists of the <u>brain</u> and <u>spinal cord</u> only.

3) When <u>receptors</u> in a sense organ <u>detect a stimulus</u>, they send <u>electrical impulses</u> along <u>sensory neurones</u> to the <u>CNS</u>.

4) The CNS then sends electrical impulses to an <u>effector</u> along a <u>motor neurone</u>. The effector then <u>responds</u> accordingly.

5) The job of the CNS is to <u>coordinate</u> the response. Coordinated responses always need a <u>stimulus</u>, a <u>receptor</u> and an <u>effector</u>.

6) Because neurones transmit information using <u>high speed electrical impulses</u>, the nervous system is able to bring about <u>very rapid responses</u>.

Synapses Connect Neurones

1) The <u>connection</u> between <u>two neurones</u> is called a <u>synapse</u>.

2) The nerve signal is transferred by <u>chemicals</u> called <u>neurotransmitters</u> which <u>diffuse</u> (move) across the gap.

3) These chemicals then set off a <u>new electrical signal</u> in the <u>next</u> neurone.

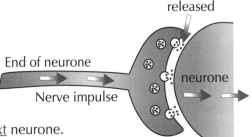

neurotransmitters released

End of neurone

neurone

Nerve impulse

Reflexes

Your brain can <u>decide</u> how to respond to a stimulus <u>pretty quickly</u>. But sometimes waiting for your brain to make a decision is just <u>too slow</u>. That's why you have <u>reflexes</u>.

Reflexes Help Prevent Injury

1) <u>Reflexes</u> are <u>automatic</u> responses to certain stimuli — they can reduce the chances of being injured.

2) For example, if someone shines a <u>bright light</u> in your eyes, your <u>pupils</u> automatically get smaller so that less light gets into the eyes — this stops them getting <u>damaged</u> (see next page).

3) Or if you get a shock, your body releases the <u>hormone</u> adrenaline automatically — it doesn't wait for you to <u>decide</u> that you're shocked.

4) The route taken by the information in a reflex (from receptor to effector) is called a <u>reflex arc</u>.

The Reflex Arc Goes Through the Central Nervous System

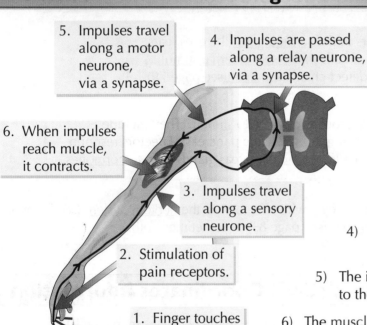

5. Impulses travel along a motor neurone, via a synapse.

4. Impulses are passed along a relay neurone, via a synapse.

6. When impulses reach muscle, it contracts.

3. Impulses travel along a sensory neurone.

2. Stimulation of pain receptors.

1. Finger touches hot object.

1) The neurones in reflex arcs go through the <u>spinal cord</u> or through an <u>unconscious part of the brain</u>.

2) When a <u>stimulus</u> (e.g. touching a hot object) is detected by receptors, an impulse is sent along a <u>sensory neurone</u> to the CNS.

3) In the CNS the sensory neurone passes on the message to another type of neurone — a <u>relay neurone</u>.

4) Relay neurones <u>relay</u> the impulse to a <u>motor neurone</u>.

5) The impulse then travels along the <u>motor neurone</u> to the <u>effector</u> (in this example it's a muscle).

6) The <u>muscle</u> then <u>contracts</u> and moves your hand away from the hot object.

7) Because you don't have to think about the response (which takes time) it's <u>quicker</u> than normal responses.

You Can Draw a Block Diagram to Represent a Reflex Arc

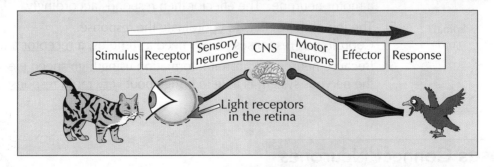

Stimulus | Receptor | Sensory neurone | CNS | Motor neurone | Effector | Response

Light receptors in the retina

Don't let the thought of exams play on your nerves...

Reflexes <u>bypass</u> your conscious brain completely — when a <u>quick response</u> is essential, your body just gets on with things. If you had to stop and think first, you'd end up a lot more sore (or worse).

The Eye

The eye is a good example of a sense organ, and there are several parts you need to learn about.

Learn the Eye with All Its Labels

1) The CONJUNCTIVA lubricates and protects the surface of the eye.

2) The SCLERA is the tough outer layer that protects the eye.

3) The CORNEA refracts (bends) light into the eye. The cornea is transparent and has no blood vessels to supply it with oxygen, so oxygen diffuses in from the outer surface.

4) The IRIS controls the diameter of the PUPIL (the hole in the middle) and therefore how much light enters the eye.

5) The LENS focuses the light onto the RETINA (the light-sensitive part — it's covered in light receptors called rods and cones).

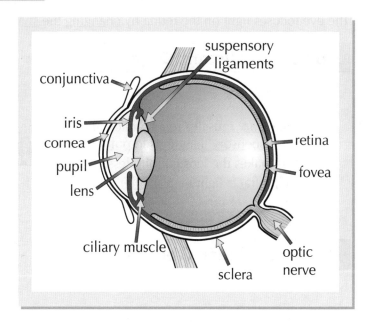

Rods are more sensitive in dim light but can't sense colour. Cones are sensitive to colours but aren't so good in dim light. Cones are found all over the retina, but there are loads of them at the FOVEA.

6) The OPTIC NERVE carries impulses from the receptors to the brain.

The Iris Reflex — Adjusting for Bright Light

Very bright light can damage the retina — so you have a reflex to protect it.

1) Very bright light triggers a reflex that makes the pupil smaller, allowing less light in.

(See the previous page for more about reflexes... but basically, in this case, light receptors detect the bright light and send a message along a sensory neurone to the brain. The message then travels along a relay neurone to a motor neurone, which tells circular muscles in the iris to contract, making the pupil smaller.)

2) The opposite process happens in dim light. This time, the brain tells the radial muscles to contract, which makes the pupil bigger.

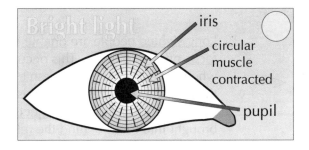

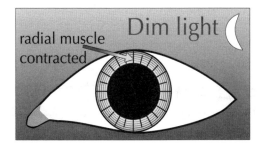

The iris reflex prevents damage to the eye

REVISION TIP

There's no getting round the fact that you need to learn the structure of the eye. Sketch it out and see if you can add the labels to all of the parts. If you can't, you need to study it again.

The Eye

Another page, another reflex. This one's known as accommodation.

Focusing on Near and Distant Objects — Another Reflex

The eye focuses light on the retina by changing the shape of the lens — this is known as accommodation.

To Look at **Distant Objects**:

1) The ciliary muscles relax, which allows the suspensory ligaments to pull tight.
2) This makes the lens go thin (less curved).
3) So it refracts light by a smaller amount.

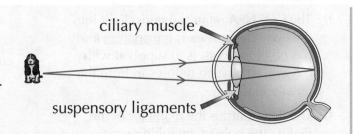

To Look at **Near Objects**:

1) The ciliary muscles contract, which slackens the suspensory ligaments.
2) The lens becomes fat (more curved).
3) This increases the amount by which it refracts light.

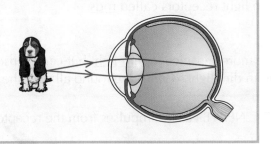

As you get older, your eye's lens loses flexibility, so it can't easily spring back to a round shape.
This means light can't be focused well for near viewing, so older people often have to use reading glasses.

Long- and **Short-Sightedness** Can Be **Corrected**

1) Short-sighted people are unable to focus on distant objects. This occurs when the cornea or lens bends the light too much or the eyeball is too long. The images of distant objects are brought into focus in front of the retina.

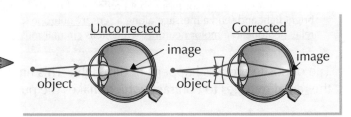

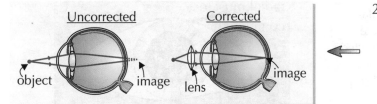

2) Long-sighted people are unable to focus on near objects. This occurs when the cornea or lens doesn't bend the light enough or the eyeball is too short. The images of near objects are brought into focus behind the retina.

A thinner (less curved) lens is used to look at distant objects...

... while a fatter (more curved) lens is needed to focus on nearby objects. The ciliary muscles and suspensory ligaments contract and relax to change the shape of the lens. And remember: it's a reflex.

Warm-Up & Exam Questions

Welcome to the first set of questions in this section. I can't guarantee you a laugh per minute, but it's one of the best ways of figuring out just what you know. So it's a case of grin and bear it, I'm afraid...

Warm-Up Questions

1) What are the five sense organs in the human body?
2) Name the two parts of the body which make up the central nervous system.
3) In what form is information transmitted along nerve cells?
4) Why are reflexes useful?
5) Give an example of a reflex.

Exam Questions

1   Animals are able to detect changes in their environment. These changes are known as stimuli.

   (a)   Suggest why it's important for animals to be able to detect changes in their external environment.

                                                                           [1 mark]

   (b)   Cells in the sense organs detect stimuli. What name is given to these cells?

                                                                           [1 mark]

   (c)   Suggest what the **stimulus**, **sense organ** and **effectors** are in this scenario:
       When a hungry animal sees a source of food, it moves towards it.

                                                                      [3 marks]

   (d)   The nervous system coordinates responses to stimuli.
       Name the other communication system in the body that coordinates responses to stimuli.

                                                                      [1 mark]

2   A man picked up a plate without realising it was hot, then immediately dropped it.
   The diagram below shows the reflex arc for this incident.

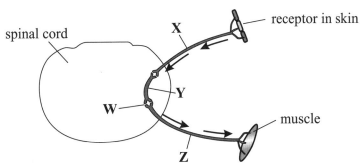

   (a)   Name the **three** types of neurone labelled **X**, **Y** and **Z**.

                                                                            [3 marks]

   (b)   What name is given to the small gap between neurones, marked **W** on the diagram?

                                                                            [1 mark]

   (c)   State what the effectors are in this reflex arc and describe their response.

                                                                             [2 marks]

Exam Questions

3   The diagram below shows a cross section through the eye.

   (a)   Name the parts labelled **A** and **B**.

                                                          [2 marks]

   (b)   Describe the function of the iris.

                                                           [1 mark]

   (c)   (i)   Name the **two** types of light receptor
            found on the retina.

                                                    [2 marks]

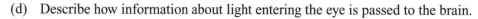

      (ii) Name the part of the retina that has the greatest
             number of colour-sensitive light receptors.

                                                 [1 mark]

   (d)   Describe how information about light entering the eye is passed to the brain.

                                                                       [2 marks]

4   The eye adjusts its shape slightly to focus light.

   (a)   Describe how the eye adjusts to focus on distant objects.

                                                                      [3 marks]

   (b)   Presbyopia is a condition in which the lens of the eye becomes
        less elastic and isn't easily able to form a rounded shape.
        Suggest how having presbyopia will affect a person's vision.

                                                                      [2 marks]

5   The eye adjusts to different light levels. The diagrams
   below show the eye in two different light conditions.

                   A   **B**

   (a)   Which diagram, **A** or **B**, shows the eye in bright light? Explain your answer.

                                                                      [2 marks]

   (b)   (i)   The response of the eye to bright light is a reflex. Suggest why it is an advantage
            to have this type of response controlling the action of the eye.

                                                                      [2 marks]

      (ii) Describe the reflex arc which is triggered by bright light entering the eye.

                                                                      [5 marks]

Hormones

The other way to send information around the body (apart from along nerves) is by using hormones.

Hormones Are **Chemical Messengers** Sent in the **Blood**

1) Hormones are chemicals released directly into the blood. They're carried in the blood plasma to other parts of the body, but only affect particular cells (called target cells) in particular places. Hormones control things in organs and cells that need constant adjustment.

2) Hormones are produced in glands. They travel quite slowly and tend to have relatively long-lasting effects.

Each **Different Hormone** in the Body has its **Own Job**

You need to know where each of these hormones is made and what they do.

Hormone	Source	Role	Effects
Adrenaline	Adrenal glands (on top of the kidneys)	Readies the body for a 'fight or flight' response (see page 84).	Increases heart rate, blood flow to muscles and blood sugar level.
Insulin	Pancreas	Helps control the blood sugar level.	Stimulates the liver to turn glucose into glycogen for storage.
Testosterone	Testes	Main male sex hormone.	Promotes male secondary sexual characteristics, e.g. facial hair (see p.109).
Progesterone	Ovaries	Supports pregnancy.	Maintains the lining of the uterus (see p.110).
Oestrogen	Ovaries	Main female sex hormone.	Controls the menstrual cycle and promotes female secondary sexual characteristics, e.g. widening of the hips (see p.109 and 110).
ADH (anti-diuretic hormone)	Pituitary gland (in the brain)	Controls water content.	Increases the permeability of the kidney tubules to water (see p.74).
FSH	Pituitary gland	Female sex hormone.	Causes an egg to mature in an ovary. Stimulates the ovaries to produce oestrogen.
LH	Pituitary gland	Female sex hormone.	Stimulates the release of an egg from an ovary.

Nerves, hormones — no wonder revision makes me tense...

Hormones control various organs and cells in the body, though they tend to control things that aren't immediately life-threatening (so things like sexual development, blood sugar level, water content, etc.).

Hormones and Nerves

Now you know that there are <u>two ways</u> information can be sent round the body
— via the <u>nervous</u> or <u>hormonal</u> systems — here's a recap of the <u>differences</u> between them...

There Are **Differences** in How **Hormones** and **Nerves** Work

<u>Hormones</u> and <u>nerves</u> do similar jobs — they both <u>carry information</u> and <u>instructions</u> about the body.
But there are some important <u>differences</u> between them that you need to know too:

Nerves

1) Very <u>FAST</u> message.

2) Act for a very <u>SHORT TIME</u>.

3) Act on a very <u>PRECISE AREA</u>.

Hormones

1) <u>SLOWER</u> message.

2) Act for a <u>LONG TIME</u>.

3) Act in a more <u>GENERAL</u> way.

If you're not sure whether a response is nervous or hormonal, have a think about the <u>speed</u>
of the reaction and <u>how long it lasts</u>:

1) If the Response is **Really Quick**, It's Probably **Nervous**

1) Some information needs to be passed to effectors really quickly (e.g. <u>pain signals</u>,
or information from your <u>eyes</u> telling you about the <u>lion</u> heading your way).

2) It's no good using <u>hormones</u> to carry the message — they're <u>too slow</u>.

2) But if a Response **Lasts For a Long Time**, It's Probably **Hormonal**

For example, when you get a shock, a hormone called <u>adrenaline</u>
is released into the bloodstream (causing the <u>fight-or-flight</u>
response, where your body is <u>hyped up</u> ready for action).

Nervous and hormonal responses are pretty different

You could be asked to work out if a response in the body is controlled by nerves or hormones.
Just remember — <u>nervous</u> responses are really <u>fast</u> whereas <u>hormonal</u> responses are <u>slower</u>.

Homeostasis

Homeostasis involves balancing body functions to maintain a "constant internal environment". Hormones are sometimes (but not always) involved.

Homeostasis — it's all about Balance

Conditions in your body need to be kept steady so that cells can function properly. This involves balancing inputs (stuff going into your body) with outputs (stuff leaving). For example...

> Water content — you need to keep a balance between the water you gain and the water you lose (see below).

> Body temperature — you need to get rid of excess body heat when you're hot, but retain heat when the environment is cold.

Homeostasis is what keeps these conditions balanced. Don't forget:

> **Homeostasis is the maintenance of a constant internal environment.**

Water is Lost from the Body in Various Ways

Water is taken into the body as food and drink and is lost from the body in the following ways:

1) through the skin as sweat...
2) via the lungs in breath...
3) via the kidneys as urine.

Some water is also lost in faeces.

The balance between sweat and urine can depend on what you're doing, or what the weather's like...

- On a hot day, or when you're exercising, you sweat a lot.
- You will produce less urine, but this will be more concentrated (and hence a deeper colour).
- You will also lose more water through your breath when you exercise because you breathe faster.

- On a cold day, or when you're not exercising, you don't sweat much.
- You'll produce more urine, which will be pale (since the waste carried in the urine is more diluted).

Body Temperature is Kept at About 37 °C

1) All enzymes work best at a certain optimum temperature (see page 10). The enzymes in the human body work best at about 37 °C — and so this is the temperature your body tries to maintain.

2) A part of the brain acts as your own personal thermostat. It's sensitive to the blood temperature in the brain, and it receives messages from temperature receptors in the skin that provide information about skin temperature.

3) Based on the signals from these receptors, your central nervous system can activate the necessary effectors to make sure your body temperature stays just right.

More On Homeostasis

Homeostasis is so <u>important</u> for organisms (and for science students) that I just couldn't <u>resist</u> writing a second page on it for you.

The **Skin** Helps to **Maintain Body Temperature**

To <u>stay</u> at a <u>cosy-but-not-too-warm</u> 37 °C your body has a few <u>tricks</u> up its sleeve:

When You're **Too Hot**:

1) <u>Lots of sweat</u> is produced — when it <u>evaporates</u> it <u>transfers energy</u> from your skin to the environment, cooling you down.

2) <u>Blood vessels</u> close to the surface of the skin <u>widen</u> — this is called <u>vasodilation</u>. It allows more blood to flow near the surface, so it can <u>transfer more energy</u> into the <u>surroundings</u>, which cools you down.

3) <u>Hairs</u> lie flat.

When You're **Too Cold**:

1) <u>Very little sweat</u> is produced.

2) <u>Blood vessels</u> near the surface of the skin <u>constrict</u> (<u>vasoconstriction</u>). This means <u>less blood</u> flows near the surface, so <u>less energy</u> is transferred to the surroundings.

3) You <u>shiver</u>, which increases your rate of <u>respiration</u>, which transfers more <u>energy</u> to <u>warm</u> the body. <u>Exercise</u> does the same.

4) <u>Hairs</u> stand on end to trap an insulating layer of air, which helps keep you warm.

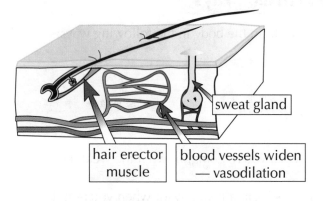

sweat gland

hair erector muscle

blood vessels widen — vasodilation

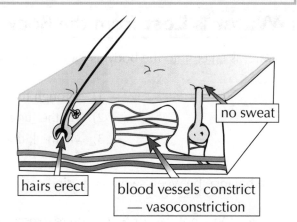

no sweat

hairs erect

blood vessels constrict — vasoconstriction

Smaller Organisms Can **Cool Down Quicker**

1) <u>Smaller organisms</u> have <u>bigger surface area to volume ratios</u> (see page 19).

2) Organisms with bigger surface area to volume ratios can <u>gain</u> (or <u>lose</u>) <u>heat faster</u> because there is <u>more area</u> for the heat to transfer across.

3) This allows <u>small organisms</u> to lose body heat more easily in <u>hot climates</u> and reduces the chance of them <u>overheating</u>. It also means that they're very <u>vulnerable</u> in <u>cold environments</u>.

4) Organisms with <u>smaller</u> surface area to volume ratios <u>gain</u> (or <u>lose</u>) <u>heat more slowly</u> because there is <u>less area</u> for the heat to transfer across.

5) This is why animals living in <u>cold</u> conditions have a <u>compact</u> (rounded) shape to keep their <u>surface area</u> to a minimum, <u>reducing heat loss</u>.

EXAM TIP

The skin plays a key role in adjusting the body's temperature

If you're asked to describe the role of the <u>skin</u> in <u>temperature regulation</u>, there are a few things to remember — the <u>blood vessels</u> change their width, the amount of <u>sweat</u> changes, and the <u>hairs</u> stand up or lie down. Remember those things, and you'll be able to write the perfect answer.

Responses in Plants

You're <u>nearly</u> done for this section. Just this <u>little bit</u> about plants still to go — they're just as important...

Plants Need to Respond to Stimuli Too

1) Plants, like animals, <u>increase</u> their chances of <u>survival</u> by responding to changes in their environment. For example:

- They sense the direction of <u>light</u> and <u>grow</u> towards it to <u>maximise</u> light absorption for <u>photosynthesis</u>.
- They can sense <u>gravity</u>, so their roots and shoots <u>grow</u> in the <u>right direction</u>.
- <u>Climbing</u> plants have a sense of <u>touch</u>, so they can find things to climb and <u>reach</u> the <u>sunlight</u>.

2) Plants are more likely to survive if they respond to the presence of <u>predators</u> to avoid being eaten. For example:

> <u>White clover</u> is a plant that can produce substances that are <u>toxic</u> to <u>cattle</u>. Cattle start to <u>eat</u> lots of white clover when fields are <u>overgrazed</u> — the white clover <u>responds</u> by <u>producing toxins</u>, to <u>avoid</u> being <u>eaten</u>.

3) Plants are more likely to survive if they respond to <u>abiotic stress</u> — anything harmful that's natural but non-living, like a drought. For example:

> <u>Carrots</u> produce <u>antifreeze proteins</u> at low temperatures — the proteins <u>bind</u> to <u>ice crystals</u> and <u>lower</u> the <u>temperature</u> that water <u>freezes</u> at, <u>stopping</u> more ice crystals from <u>growing</u>.

Auxins are Plant Growth Hormones

1) <u>Auxins</u> are <u>plant hormones</u> which control <u>growth</u> at the <u>tips</u> of <u>shoots</u> and <u>roots</u>.
2) They move through the plant in <u>solution</u> (dissolved in water).
3) Auxin is produced in the <u>tips</u> and <u>diffuses backwards</u> to stimulate the <u>cell elongation process</u> which occurs in the cells <u>just behind</u> the tips.
4) Auxin <u>promotes</u> growth in the <u>shoot</u>, but actually <u>inhibits</u> growth in the <u>root</u>.
5) Auxins are involved in the <u>growth</u> responses of plants to <u>light</u> (phototropism) and <u>gravity</u> (geotropism).

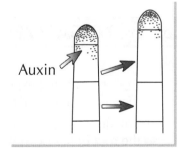

Auxin

I bet I can guess your response to learning about plants...

Everyone seems to think that plants are boring, but they're actually pretty amazing. They can <u>sense</u> their <u>environment</u> and <u>respond</u> to it accordingly — and they don't even have a nervous system.

Responses in Plants

Remember: auxins are plant hormones that control the growth responses
of plants to light (phototropism) and gravity (geotropism).

Auxins Change the Direction of Root and Shoot Growth

Shoots are POSITIVELY PHOTOTROPIC (grow towards light)

1) When a shoot tip is exposed to light, it accumulates more auxin
   on the side that's in the shade than the side that's in the light.
2) This makes the cells grow (elongate) faster on the shaded side,
   so the shoot bends towards the light.

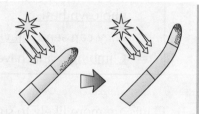

Shoots are NEGATIVELY GEOTROPIC (grow away from gravity)

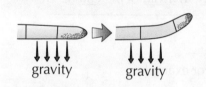

gravity   gravity

1) When a shoot is growing sideways, gravity produces an
   unequal distribution of auxin in the tip, with more auxin
   on the lower side.
2) This causes the lower side to grow faster, bending the
   shoot upwards.

Roots are POSITIVELY GEOTROPIC (grow towards gravity)

1) A root growing sideways will also have
   more auxin on its lower side.
2) But in a root the extra auxin inhibits growth.
   This means the cells on top elongate faster,
   and the root bends downwards.

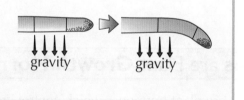

gravity   gravity

Roots are NEGATIVELY PHOTOTROPIC (grow away from light)

1) If a root starts being exposed to some light, more auxin
   accumulates on the more shaded side.
2) The auxin inhibits cell elongation on the shaded side,
   so the root bends downwards, back into the ground.

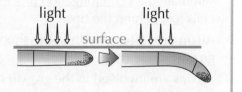

light   light

surface

Roots that are underground aren't exposed to light. They grow downwards due to positive gravitropism.

'Photo' comes from the Greek word for light

...and PHOTOtropism is growing in response to light, so use that to help you remember the
difference between phototropism and geotropism. If a shoot is growing towards the light,
then you could say it must be positive about it — so that's positive phototropism.

Warm-Up & Exam Questions

Have a go at these questions to see if you've taken all of the last six pages on board.

Warm-Up Questions

1) State the sources of the following hormones: (a) oestrogen (b) progesterone (c) adrenaline.
2) Name the hormone that prepares the body for the 'fight or flight' response.
3) What effect does the hormone ADH have on the body?
4) Why is human body temperature maintained at around 37 °C?
5) What are auxins?

Exam Questions

1 A cyclist goes for a bike ride. It is a hot day and he has to work hard on some steep hills. Homeostasis helps to regulate the water content in his body.

   (a) What is meant by the term **homeostasis**?

   [1 mark]

   (b) (i) Describe **two** ways in which the cyclist's body loses water while he is cycling.

   [2 marks]

   (ii) When the cyclist returns home, he notices that his urine is dark in colour. Suggest why.

   [2 marks]

   (c) The cyclist does exactly the same bike ride the following day, but notices afterwards that his urine is not as dark in colour this time. Suggest **one** possible reason for this.

   [1 mark]

2 A student placed some germinating beans on the surface of some damp soil and left them for five days. The appearance of the beans before and after the five day period is shown.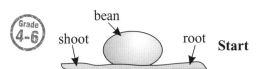

   (a) (i) What is meant by the term **negative geotropism**?
   [1 mark]

   (ii) Which part of the seedling is demonstrating negative geotropism after five days?
   [1 mark]

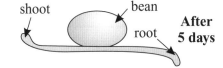

   (b) (i) After the five day period, the student turned the seeds upside down.

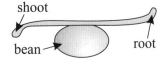

   State the direction in which the root will grow after the seed is turned upside down.

   [1 mark]

   (ii) Which of the following explains this direction of root growth?

   ☐ **A** Auxin builds up on the upper side of the root, inhibiting growth of upper cells.

   ☐ **B** Auxin builds up on the upper side of the root, inhibiting growth of lower cells.

   ☐ **C** Auxin builds up on the lower side of the root, inhibiting growth of upper cells.

   ☐ **D** Auxin builds up on the lower side of the root, inhibiting growth of lower cells.

   [1 mark]

Exam Questions

3 Changes in the skin are an important part of temperature regulation. The diagram shows a cross-section through the skin of a person who is cold.

(a) In the diagram, blood vessels close to the surface of the skin have narrowed.

(i) Give the scientific name for this process.

[1 mark]

(ii) Explain why the blood vessels have narrowed.

[2 marks]

(b) Explain the response of a sweat gland when a person is cold.

[2 marks]

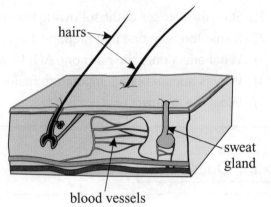

4 Responses to stimuli can be either nervous or hormonal.

Describe the differences between responses brought about by hormones and those brought about by the nervous system.

[4 marks]

5 An investigation was done to find out how plant shoots respond to light. Three plant shoots (**A**, **B** and **C**) were exposed to a light stimulus. The diagram below shows the shape of each shoot before and after the experiment.

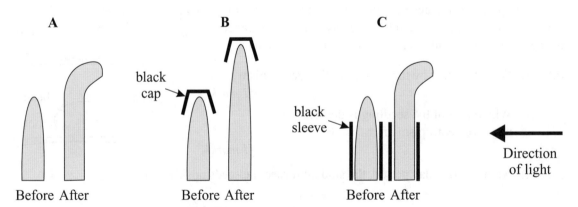

(a) Using the results of the experiment, suggest which part of the plant shoot is most sensitive to light.

[1 mark]

(b) Explain the growth of shoot **B** during the experiment.

[3 marks]

(c) Give **two** variables that should have been controlled in this experiment.

[2 marks]

(d) Suggest how the results of the experiment may have been different if the tips of the shoots were removed at the start of the experiment. Explain your answer.

[2 marks]

Revision Summary for Section 6

That's <u>Section 6</u> done and dusted. Stick around for a few more minutes to put yourself to the test.
- Try these questions and <u>tick off each one</u> when you <u>get it right</u>.
- When you've done <u>all the questions</u> under a heading and are <u>completely happy</u> with it, tick it off.

The Nervous System, Responding to Stimuli and Reflexes (p.77-78) ☐

1) What is a stimulus? How are stimuli detected?
2) Give two types of effector.
3) What does the central nervous system do?
4) What is the purpose of a reflex action?
5) Describe the pathway of a reflex arc from stimulus to response.

The Eye (p.79-80) ☑

6) Draw a labelled diagram of a human eye.
7) Explain the roles of the following parts of the eye:
   a) cornea   b) pupil   c) lens
8) Describe the iris reflex. Why is this needed?
9) How does accommodation of the eye work?
   Is the lens fat or thin when looking at distant objects?

Hormones and Homeostasis (p.83-86) ☑

10) Define the term 'hormone'.
11) What is the role of the hormone adrenaline? What effects does it have on the body?
12) Where is insulin made? Describe insulin's role in the body.
13) Where is FSH made?
14) Describe the role of LH in the body.
15) List three differences between nervous and hormonal responses.
16) Write down two conditions that the body needs to keep fairly constant.
17) Give three ways in which water is lost from the body.
18) Describe how the amount and concentration of urine you produce varies depending on
   how much exercise you do and how hot it is.
19) At what temperature do most of the enzymes in the human body work best?
20) Describe how body temperature is reduced when you're too hot.

Responses in Plants (p.87-88) ☐

21) Give two ways in which plants respond to stimuli.
22) Name the hormones in plants that control the growth responses of plants to light and gravity.
23) What is: a) positive phototropism?   b) positive geotropism?
24) Shoots are negatively geotropic. What does this mean?

DNA, Genes and Chromosomes

It's <u>dead important</u> you get to grips with this stuff — you'll need it to understand the <u>rest of the section</u>.

Chromosomes are Found in the Nucleus

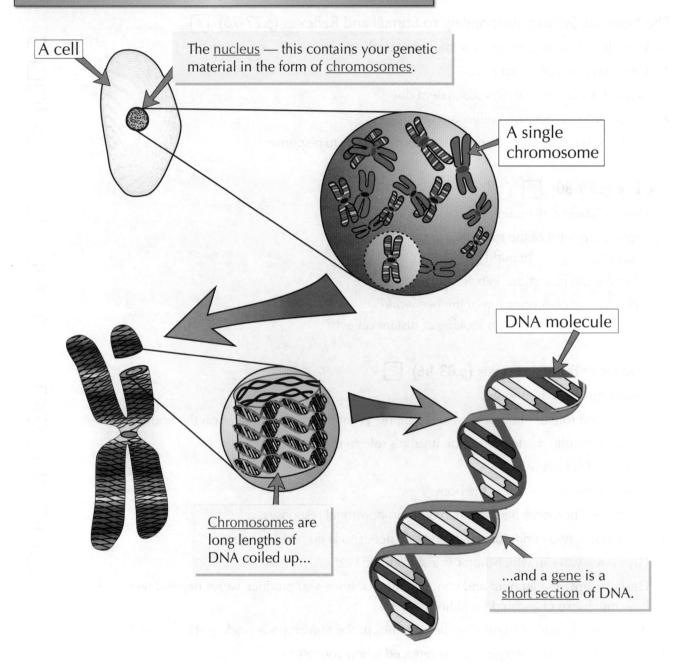

A cell

The <u>nucleus</u> — this contains your genetic material in the form of <u>chromosomes</u>.

A single chromosome

DNA molecule

<u>Chromosomes</u> are long lengths of DNA coiled up...

...and a <u>gene</u> is a <u>short section</u> of DNA.

Human Body Cells are Diploid

1) Human body cells are <u>diploid</u> — this means they have <u>two copies</u> of each chromosome, arranged in <u>pairs</u>.

2) A human cell nucleus contains <u>46 chromosomes</u> in total — so the <u>diploid number</u> for a human is <u>46</u>.

DNA, Genes and Chromosomes

Genes are Chemical Instructions

1) DNA is a long list of instructions on how to put an organism together and make it work.

2) All of an organism's DNA makes up the organism's genome.

3) Each separate gene in a DNA molecule is a chemical instruction that codes for (says how to make) a particular protein.

4) Proteins are important because they control most processes in the body. They also determine inherited characteristics, e.g. eye colour, blood type.

5) By controlling the production of proteins, genes also control our inherited characteristics.

6) There can be different versions of the same gene, which give different versions of a characteristic — like blue or brown eyes. The different versions of the same gene are called alleles.

DNA is a Double Helix

1) A DNA molecule has two strands coiled together in the shape of a double helix (two spirals).

2) The two strands are held together by chemicals called bases. There are four different bases (shown in the diagram as different colours) — adenine (A), cytosine (C), guanine (G) and thymine (T).

3) The bases are paired, and they always pair up in the same way — it's always A-T and C-G. This is called complementary base-pairing.

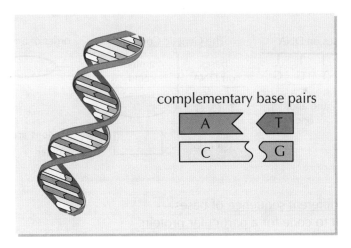

complementary base pairs

A — T

C — G

Every living organism has DNA

Remember, DNA contains all the instructions to 'build' an organism. The instructions are different for each type of organism on Earth (otherwise all living things would be the same). There's a lot more about DNA and chromosomes coming up in this topic so make sure you understand these pages before you move on.

Protein Synthesis

So here's how <u>life</u> works — <u>DNA molecules</u> contain a <u>genetic code</u> that determines which <u>proteins</u> are built. The proteins determine how all the <u>cells</u> in the body <u>function</u>.

Proteins are Made by **Reading the Code** in **DNA**

1) DNA controls the <u>production of proteins</u> (protein synthesis) in a cell.

2) Proteins are made up of chains of molecules called <u>amino acids</u>.
   Each different protein has its own particular <u>number</u> and <u>order</u> of amino acids.

3) The amino acid chains <u>fold up</u> to give each protein a <u>different</u>, <u>specific shape</u> — which means each protein can have a <u>different function</u>. This is why <u>enzymes</u> have active sites with a specific shape, and so only catalyse a specific reaction (see page 9).

4) Remember, a section of DNA that codes for a <u>particular protein</u> is called a <u>gene</u> (see previous page). It's the <u>order</u> of the <u>bases</u> in a gene that decides the <u>order</u> of <u>amino acids</u> in a protein.

5) Each amino acid is coded for by a sequence of <u>three bases</u> in the gene — this is called a <u>codon</u>.

6) DNA contains <u>four</u> different bases and each codon in a gene contains <u>three</u> bases.
   So there are 4 × 4 × 4 = <u>64 possible codons</u>. Since there are only 20 amino acids, some codons code for the <u>same amino acid</u>.

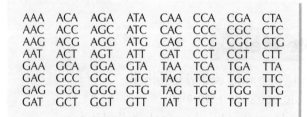

AAA	ACA	AGA	ATA	CAA	CCA	CGA	CTA
AAC	ACC	AGC	ATC	CAC	CCC	CGC	CTC
AAG	ACG	AGG	ATG	CAG	CCG	CGG	CTG
AAT	ACT	AGT	ATT	CAT	CCT	CGT	CTT
GAA	GCA	GGA	GTA	TAA	TCA	TGA	TTA
GAC	GCC	GGC	GTC	TAC	TCC	TGC	TTC
GAG	GCG	GGG	GTG	TAG	TCG	TGG	TTG
GAT	GCT	GGT	GTT	TAT	TCT	TGT	TTT

Codons are also known as base triplets.

7) The amino acids are <u>joined together</u> to make proteins, following the order of the bases in the gene.

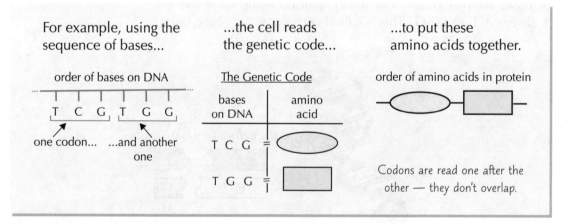

For example, using the sequence of bases...

...the cell reads the genetic code...

...to put these amino acids together.

order of bases on DNA

one codon... ...and another one

The Genetic Code

bases on DNA	amino acid
T C G	⬭
T G G	▭

order of amino acids in protein

Codons are read one after the other — they don't overlap.

8) Each gene contains a <u>different sequence</u> of bases — which is what allows it to code for a <u>particular protein</u>.

DNA Also Contains **Non-Coding Regions**

1) Many regions of DNA are <u>non-coding</u> — that means that they <u>don't code</u> for any <u>amino acids</u>.

2) Despite this, some of these regions are still involved in <u>protein synthesis</u> (see next page).

Protein Synthesis

This page is all about how you actually <u>use</u> the DNA code to <u>make</u> the proteins that you need.

Proteins are Made in Two Stages

1) Transcription

1) Proteins are made in the <u>cell cytoplasm</u> by subcellular structures called <u>ribosomes</u> (see p.2). DNA is found in the cell <u>nucleus</u> and can't move out of it because it's <u>really big</u>. The cell needs to get the information from the DNA to the ribosome in the cytoplasm.

2) This is done using a molecule called <u>messenger RNA</u> (<u>mRNA</u>). Like DNA, mRNA is made up of a sequence of bases, but it's <u>shorter</u> and only a <u>single strand</u>. It also uses <u>uracil</u> (U) instead of <u>thymine</u> (T) as a <u>base</u>.

Uracil still pairs with adenine, A-U.

3) <u>RNA polymerase</u> is the <u>enzyme</u> involved in <u>joining together</u> the base sequence to make mRNA. This stage of protein synthesis is called <u>transcription</u>. Here's how it works:

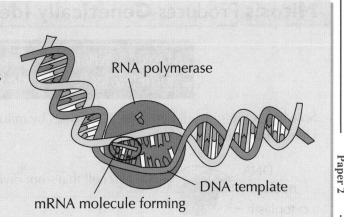

1) <u>RNA polymerase</u> binds to a region of <u>non-coding DNA</u> in front of a gene.

2) The two DNA strands <u>unzip</u> and the RNA polymerase <u>moves along</u> one of the strands of the DNA.

3) It uses the <u>coding DNA</u> in the <u>gene</u> as a <u>template</u> to make the <u>mRNA</u>. <u>Base pairing</u> between the DNA and RNA ensures that the mRNA is <u>complementary</u> to the gene.

4) Once made, the mRNA molecule moves <u>out</u> of the nucleus and joins with a <u>ribosome</u> in the cytoplasm.

RNA polymerase

mRNA molecule forming

DNA template

2) Translation

Once the <u>mRNA</u> is bound to a ribosome, the <u>protein</u> can be assembled. This stage is called <u>translation</u>.

1) <u>Amino acids</u> are brought to the <u>ribosome</u> by another RNA molecule called <u>transfer RNA</u> (<u>tRNA</u>).

2) The <u>order</u> in which the amino acids are brought to the ribosome <u>matches</u> the order of the <u>codons</u> in mRNA.

3) Part of the tRNA's structure is called an <u>anticodon</u> — it is <u>complementary</u> to the <u>codon</u> for the amino acid. The pairing of the codon and anticodon makes sure that the amino acids are brought to the ribosome in the <u>correct order</u>.

4) The amino acids are <u>joined together</u> by the ribosome. This makes a <u>protein</u>.

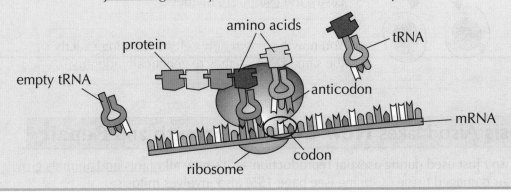

empty tRNA

protein

amino acids

tRNA

anticodon

mRNA

codon

ribosome

Asexual Reproduction and Mitosis

There are two ways an organism can reproduce (asexually and sexually) and two ways a cell can divide (mitosis and meiosis). This page, as you might have guessed, is about asexual reproduction and mitosis.

Asexual Reproduction Involves Mitosis

1) An ordinary cell can make a new cell by simply dividing in two. Both new cells are genetically identical to the original cell — they both contain exactly the same genetic information.

2) This type of cell division is known as mitosis (see below).

3) Some organisms produce offspring (children) using mitosis. This is known as asexual reproduction. Organisms which reproduce asexually include bacteria and some plants (see page 105).

Asexual reproduction involves only one parent. The offspring have identical genes to the parent — so there's no variation between parent and offspring.

Mitosis Produces Genetically Identical Cells

Mitosis is when a cell reproduces itself by splitting to form two cells with identical sets of chromosomes.

So when a diploid cell (see page 92) divides by mitosis, you get two cells that are both diploid. Here's how mitosis works:

DNA
nucleus
cytoplasm
cell membrane

In a cell that's not dividing, the DNA is all spread out in long strings.

If the cell gets a signal to divide, it needs to duplicate its DNA — so there's one copy for each new cell. The DNA forms X-shaped chromosomes. Each 'arm' of the chromosome is an exact duplicate of the other.

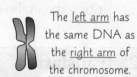

The left arm has the same DNA as the right arm of the chromosome.

The chromosomes then line up at the centre of the cell and cell fibres pull them apart. The two arms of each chromosome go to opposite ends of the cell.

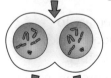

Membranes form around each of the sets of chromosomes. These become the nuclei of the two new cells.

Lastly, the cytoplasm divides.

You now have two new cells containing exactly the same DNA — they're genetically identical.

Mitosis Also Makes New Cells for Growth and Repair

Mitosis isn't just used during asexual reproduction — it's how all plants and animals grow and repair damaged tissue. Cloning (see page 155) also involves mitosis.

Sexual Reproduction

Another page, another form of reproduction...

Sexual Reproduction Produces Genetically Different Cells

Sexual reproduction is where genetic information from two organisms (a father and a mother) is combined to produce offspring which are genetically different to either parent.

Sexual Reproduction Involves Gametes...

1) In sexual reproduction, the mother and father produce gametes. Gametes are sperm cells and egg cells.

2) Gametes are haploid — this means they have half the number of chromosomes in a normal cell. In humans, each gamete contains 23 chromosomes — so the haploid number is 23.

...and Fertilisation

1) At fertilisation, a male gamete fuses with a female gamete to form a zygote (fertilised egg). The zygote ends up with the full set of chromosomes.

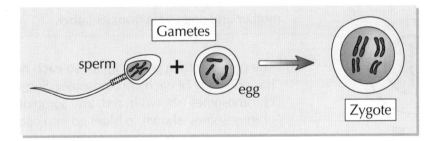

2) The zygote then undergoes cell division (by mitosis — see previous page) and develops into an embryo.

3) The embryo inherits features from both parents — it's received a mixture of chromosomes from its mum and its dad (and it's the chromosomes that decide how you turn out).

4) The fertilisation of gametes is random — this produces genetic variation in the offspring.

Sexual reproduction involves the fusion of male and female gametes. Because there are two parents, the offspring contain a mixture of their parents' genes.

You might need to reproduce these facts in the exam...

Here's a summary of reproduction... 1) sexual reproduction needs two parents and forms cells that are genetically different to the parents, so there's lots of genetic variation. And 2) asexual reproduction needs just one parent to make genetically identical cells, so there's no genetic variation in the offspring.

Meiosis

This page is a little bit tricky, so take your time.

Gametes are Produced by Meiosis

1) Meiosis is another type of <u>cell division</u>.
2) It's different to mitosis (on the page 96) because it <u>doesn't produce identical cells</u>.
3) In humans, meiosis <u>only</u> happens in the <u>reproductive organs</u> (ovaries and testes).

> <u>Meiosis</u> produces <u>four haploid cells</u> whose chromosomes are <u>not identical</u>.

Meiosis Involves Two Divisions

Here's how meiosis works:

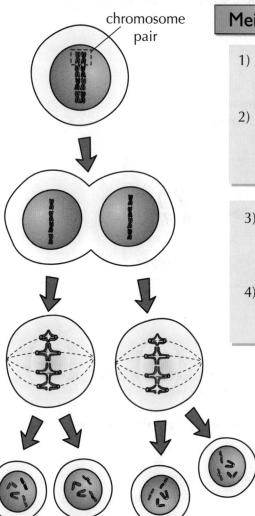

chromosome pair

Meiosis — Division 1

Step 1 is like the start of mitosis. Step 2 is different though.

1) Before the cell starts to divide, it <u>duplicates</u> its <u>DNA</u> (so there's enough for each new cell). One arm of each X-shaped chromosome is an <u>exact copy</u> of the other arm.
2) In the <u>first division</u> in meiosis (there are two divisions) the chromosomes <u>line up</u> in pairs in the centre of the cell. One chromosome in each pair came from the organism's mother and one came from its father.

3) The <u>pairs</u> are then <u>pulled apart</u>, so each new cell only has one copy of each chromosome. <u>Some</u> of the father's chromosomes (shown in red) and <u>some</u> of the mother's chromosomes (shown in blue) go into each new cell.
4) Each new cell will have a <u>mixture</u> of the mother's and father's chromosomes. Mixing up the genes like this is <u>really important</u> — it creates <u>genetic variation</u> in the offspring.

Meiosis — Division 2

5) In the <u>second division</u> the chromosomes <u>line up</u> again in the centre of the cell. It's a lot like mitosis. The <u>arms</u> of the chromosomes are <u>pulled apart</u>.
6) You get <u>four haploid gametes</u>. Each <u>gamete</u> only has a <u>single set</u> of chromosomes. The gametes are all <u>genetically different</u>.

REVISION TIP

Meiosis produces gametes for sexual reproduction

With <u>meiosis</u> you end up with <u>four haploid cells</u> that are all <u>genetically different</u>. With <u>mitosis</u> (page 96), you only get <u>two cells</u> and they're <u>genetically identical</u>. Learn all the details on this page and then come up with a rhyme to help you remember the key differences between the two.

Warm-Up & Exam Questions

Take a deep breath and go through these warm-up questions one by one.
If you sort out the basic facts, you'll stand a much better chance with the exam questions.

Warm-Up Questions

1) What is a chromosome?
2) Which base does adenine pair with?
3) Does asexual reproduction use mitosis or meiosis?
4) An organism is produced through asexual reproduction. How many parents does it have?
5) How many divisions are there in meiosis?

Exam Questions

1   DNA in plants and animals is found in the form of chromosomes.   *(Grade 4-6)*

(a)   Name the part of the cell where chromosomes are found.

[1 mark]

(b)   (i) The body cells of most mammals are **diploid**. Explain what this means.

[1 mark]

(ii) State the diploid number for humans.

[1 mark]

PAPER 2

2   To make a protein, the base sequence in the coding DNA of a gene is copied into mRNA.   *(Grade 4-6)*

(a)   Which of the following sets of bases are found in mRNA?

☐ **A** A, T, C, G   ☐ **C** A, U, C, G

☐ **B** A, T, C, U   ☐ **D** A, E, C, G

[1 mark]

(b)   Which of the following is the name for a set of three bases in mRNA?

☐ **A** an amino acid   ☐ **C** a gene

☐ **B** a codon   ☐ **D** a variant

[1 mark]

(c)   Name the part of the cell in which mRNA is made.

[1 mark]

(d)   Name the process that ensures the mRNA produced is a complementary copy of the gene.

[1 mark]

(e)   Describe the role of tRNA in protein synthesis.

[1 mark]

(f)   Explain the purpose of mRNA.

[2 marks]

Exam Questions

3 Genes are short sections of DNA. Grade 6-7

(a) Explain the relationship between genes and the characteristics of an organism.

[2 marks]

(b) Fur length in cats is controlled by a single gene.
A female cat gave birth to a litter of two kittens, shown below.

One kitten is long-haired and the other is short-haired.
Explain why the kittens show different characteristics.

[3 marks]

4 The graph below shows how the amount of DNA per cell changes as a cell undergoes two cell divisions by mitosis. Point **C** is the time when the chromosomes first become visible in the new cells. Grade 7-9

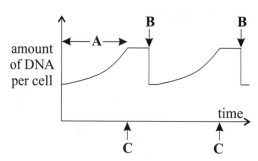

(a) Describe what is happening to the DNA during stage **A**.
Suggest why this needs to happen.

[2 marks]

(b) Suggest what happens at time **B**.

[1 mark]

(c) How many cells are there after the first cell division?

[1 mark]

PAPER 2

5 The diagram below shows a section of DNA containing coding and non-coding regions. Grade 7-9

Non-coding DNA   Gene (coding DNA)   Non-coding DNA

Explain how a protein would be produced from this section of DNA in a cell.

[6 marks]

Sexual Reproduction in Plants

Some types of plants reproduce asexually (see page 105), whilst others reproduce sexually (see below).

The **Flower** Contains both **Male** and **Female Gametes**

Flowering plants have both male and female structures — they're contained in the flower:

The **Stamen** is the **Male** Reproductive Part

The stamen consists of the anther and filament:

The anther contains pollen grains — these produce the male gametes (sperm).

The filament is the stalk that supports the anther.

The **Carpel** is the **Female** Reproductive Part

The carpel consists of the ovary, style and stigma.

The stigma is the end bit that the pollen grains attach to.

The style is the rod-like section that supports the stigma.

The ovary contains the female gametes (eggs) inside ovules.

Sexual Reproduction in Plants Involves Pollination

1) Pollination is the transfer of pollen from an anther to a stigma, so that the male gametes can fertilise the female gametes in sexual reproduction.

2) Cross-pollination is a type of sexual reproduction where pollen is transferred from the anther of one plant to the stigma of another.

3) Plants that cross-pollinate rely on things like insects or the wind to help them pollinate.

Plants can reproduce using gametes

If you're struggling to get it right, remember: the staMEN is the MALE part of the flower.

Plant Pollination

As you saw on the previous page, <u>sexual reproduction</u> in plants involves the transfer of pollen from an <u>anther</u> to a <u>stigma</u>. This is called <u>pollination</u> and plants sometimes need a bit of outside help, e.g. from <u>bees</u> and <u>butterflies</u> or a <u>gust of wind</u>, to get it done.

Some Plants are **Adapted** for **Insect Pollination**

Here's how plants can be <u>adapted</u> for <u>pollination by insects</u>...

1) They have <u>brightly coloured petals</u> to <u>attract insects</u>.

2) They also have <u>scented flowers</u> and <u>nectaries</u> (glands that secrete <u>nectar</u>) to <u>attract insects</u>.

3) They make <u>big, sticky pollen grains</u> — the grains <u>stick to insects</u> as they go from plant to plant.

4) The <u>stigma</u> is also <u>sticky</u> so that any <u>pollen</u> picked up by insects on other plants will <u>stick to the stigma</u>.

Other Plants are **Adapted** for **Wind Pollination**

Features of plants that are <u>adapted</u> for <u>pollination by wind</u> include...

1) <u>Small</u>, <u>dull petals</u> on the flower (they don't need to attract insects).

2) <u>No nectaries</u> or strong <u>scents</u> (for the same reason).

3) A <u>lot</u> of <u>pollen</u> grains — they're <u>small</u> and <u>light</u> so that they can easily be <u>carried</u> by the wind.

4) <u>Long filaments</u> that <u>hang</u> the anthers <u>outside</u> the flower, so that a lot of the <u>pollen</u> gets <u>blown away</u> by the wind.

5) A <u>large</u> and <u>feathery stigma</u> to <u>catch pollen</u> as it's carried past by the wind. The stigma often <u>hangs outside</u> the flower too.

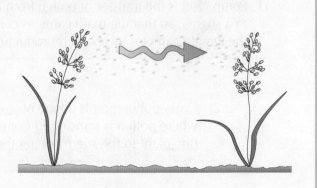

 EXAM TIP

Pollination is the transfer of pollen from an anther to a stigma

Flowers like roses (big, bright petals, a strong scent) are pollinated by <u>insects</u>. The feathery looking flowers you sometimes see in long grass, and fluffy willow catkins, are pollinated by the <u>wind</u>. If you're given a picture of a flower in the exam, you should be able to say whether it's most likely to be insect- or wind-pollinated and explain your answer. So get learning this page.

Fertilisation and Germination in Plants

Once the pollen has found its way to a lovely stigma, it's time for <u>fertilisation</u> to take place...

Fertilisation is the Fusion of Gametes

1) A <u>pollen</u> grain lands on the <u>stigma</u> of a flower, usually with help from insects or the wind (see previous page).

2) A <u>pollen tube</u> grows out of the pollen grain and down through the <u>style</u> to the <u>ovary</u> and into the <u>ovule</u>.

3) A <u>nucleus</u> from the male gamete <u>moves down the tube</u> to join with a female gamete in the <u>ovule</u>. <u>Fertilisation</u> is when the two nuclei <u>fuse</u> together to make a zygote. This divides by mitosis to form an <u>embryo</u>.

4) Each <u>fertilised</u> female gamete forms a <u>seed</u>. The <u>ovary</u> develops into a <u>fruit</u> around the seed.

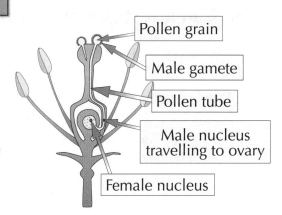

Pollen grain

Male gamete

Pollen tube

Male nucleus travelling to ovary

Female nucleus

Flowering plants can only be fertilised by pollen grains from the same species (or a closely related species).

Germination is when Seeds Start to Grow

A seed will often lie <u>dormant</u> until the <u>conditions</u> around it are right for <u>germination</u>. Seeds need the right <u>conditions</u> to start germinating:

1) <u>Water</u> — to <u>activate</u> the enzymes that <u>break down</u> the <u>food</u> reserves in the seed.

2) <u>Oxygen</u> — for respiration (see page 49), which transfers the <u>energy</u> from food for growth.

3) A suitable <u>temperature</u> — for the enzymes inside the seed to work. This depends on what <u>type</u> of seed it is.

Germination only starts when all these conditions are suitable.

first green leaves

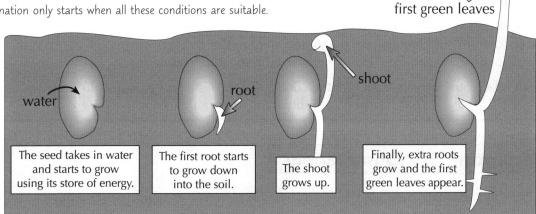

water

root

shoot

The seed takes in water and starts to grow using its store of energy.

The first root starts to grow down into the soil.

The shoot grows up.

Finally, extra roots grow and the first green leaves appear.

Germinating Seeds get Energy from Food Stores

1) A developed seed contains an <u>embryo</u> and a store of <u>food reserves</u>, wrapped in a <u>hard seed coat</u>.

2) When a seed starts to <u>germinate</u>, it gets <u>glucose</u> for respiration from its own <u>food store</u>. This transfers the <u>energy</u> it needs to grow.

3) Once the plant has grown enough to produce <u>green leaves</u> (see above), it can get its own food for energy from <u>photosynthesis</u> (see page 33).

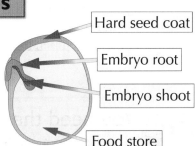

Hard seed coat

Embryo root

Embryo shoot

Food store

 **Investigating Seed Germination**

If you've always wanted to <u>investigate</u> the different <u>conditions</u> needed for <u>germination</u> to take place, then today is your lucky day...

You Can Investigate the **Conditions** Needed for **Germination**

You saw on the last page that seeds need <u>water</u>, <u>oxygen</u> and a <u>suitable temperature</u> for <u>germination</u> to happen. Here's an experiment you can do to investigate these <u>conditions</u>.

1) Take <u>four boiling tubes</u> and put some <u>cotton wool</u> at the bottom of each one.

2) Put <u>10 seeds</u> on top of the <u>cotton wool</u> in each boiling tube.

3) <u>Set up</u> each boiling tube as follows:

Tube 1	water, oxygen, room temperature (the <u>control</u>).
Tube 2	<u>no water</u>, oxygen, room temperature.
Tube 3	water, oxygen, <u>low temperature</u>.
Tube 4	water, <u>no oxygen</u>, room temperature.

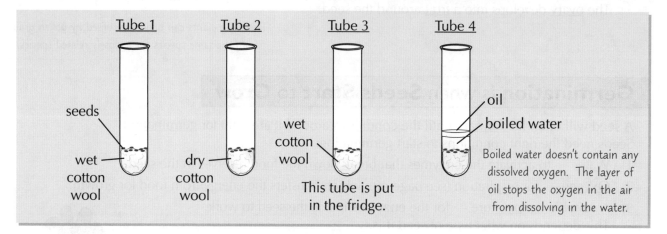

Tube 1 — seeds, wet cotton wool
Tube 2 — dry cotton wool
Tube 3 — wet cotton wool — This tube is put in the fridge.
Tube 4 — oil, boiled water — Boiled water doesn't contain any dissolved oxygen. The layer of oil stops the oxygen in the air from dissolving in the water.

4) <u>Leave</u> the tubes for a few days and then <u>observe</u> what has happened.

5) It's important to <u>control</u> all of the <u>variables</u> during the experiment. You should only be changing <u>one condition</u> at a time so you know that any effect on germination is due to the change in that one condition.

6) So, in Tube 2, the only change from the control (Tube 1) is a <u>lack of water</u>. In Tube 3, only the <u>temperature</u> has changed. In Tube 4, the only change is the <u>lack of oxygen</u>.

Interpreting Your Observations

1) You should only see germination happening in <u>Tube 1</u>.

2) This is because <u>all</u> of the conditions needed for germination are present.

3) The seeds in the other boiling tubes <u>won't</u> germinate — this shows that the seeds need <u>water</u>, <u>oxygen</u> and a <u>suitable temperature</u> to germinate.

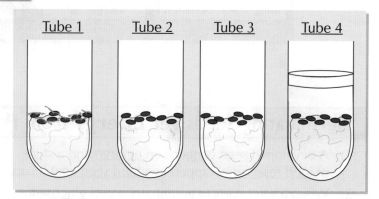

Tube 1   Tube 2   Tube 3   Tube 4

 You need the right conditions for germination to happen

It's really important that you <u>label</u> your four boiling tubes — if you don't, you'll end up with no idea about what conditions are set up in each tube, and your results won't mean anything.

Asexual Reproduction in Plants

Some plants reproduce <u>asexually</u>. They do this in the wild (<u>naturally</u>) and when we force them to (<u>artificially</u>). Artificial asexual reproduction is also called <u>cloning</u>.

Plants Can **Reproduce Asexually** Using **Natural Methods...**

Plants have several different ways of reproducing asexually.
Some plants do so by growing <u>new plants</u> from their stems — for example, <u>strawberry plants</u>...

1) The parent strawberry plant sends out <u>runners</u> — <u>fast-growing stems</u> that grow out <u>sideways</u>, just above the ground.

2) The runners <u>take root</u> at various points (a short distance away) and <u>new plants</u> start to grow.

3) The new plants are <u>clones</u> of the <u>parent</u> strawberry plant, so there's <u>no</u> genetic variation between them.

Some plants reproduce asexually <u>and</u> sexually, e.g. strawberry plants send out runners and produce fruit (seeds).

runner

parent plant

new plant

...or We Can **Clone** Them Using **Artificial Methods**

Asexual reproduction can be used to <u>clone plants</u>. And it's not all high-tech crazy science stuff either — gardeners have been using <u>cuttings</u> for a long time.

1) Gardeners can take <u>cuttings</u> from good parent plants, and then plant them to produce <u>genetically identical copies</u> (clones) of the parent plant.

2) These plants can be produced <u>quickly and cheaply</u>.

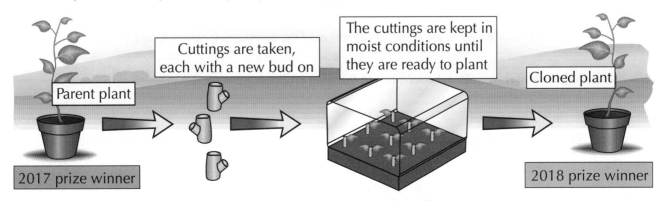

Cuttings are taken, each with a new bud on

The cuttings are kept in moist conditions until they are ready to plant

Parent plant

Cloned plant

2017 prize winner

2018 prize winner

Warm-Up & Exam Questions

It's that time again. Don't turn the page just yet — give these questions a go before you move on. They're the only way of finding out if you really know your stuff.

Warm-Up Questions

1) Name the two structures that make up a flower's stamen.
2) What is: a) the stigma? b) the style?
3) What is germination?
4) Give three conditions that are needed for germination to happen.

Exam Questions

1 Flowering plants contain both male and female organs. They are able to reproduce sexually via pollination. Grade 4-6

(a) Describe what happens during pollination.

[3 marks]

(b) Cross-pollination is the term used to describe sexual reproduction involving two different plants. Suggest what is meant by the term **self-pollination**.

[1 mark]

2 The diagram below shows cross-sections through two flowers. Grade 6-7

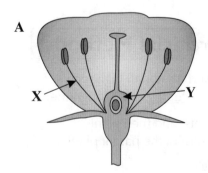
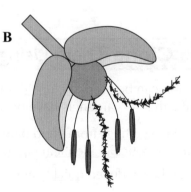

(a) Look at flower **A**. State the name and function of the structures labelled **X** and **Y**.

[4 marks]

(b) Which flower, **A** or **B**, is better adapted for wind pollination? Explain your answer.

[2 marks]

(c) Describe and explain **two** ways in which flowers can be adapted for pollination by insects.

[2 marks]

Exam Questions

3 Some plants, such as daffodils and strawberry plants, can reproduce asexually.

(a) Strawberry plants reproduce asexually using **runners**.
Explain what is meant by the term **runners** and describe how they allow plants to reproduce.

[2 marks]

(b) A strawberry plant is genetically susceptible to a particular virus.
Explain why any offspring the plant produces through
asexual reproduction will also be susceptible to the virus.

[1 mark]

4 A scientist has bred a high yield grapevine that seems to be
resistant to the grapevine chrome mosaic virus. She wants to
clone the vine to produce new plants to continue her research.

(a) Suggest **one** reason why the scientist wants to clone the plants
rather than allow them to reproduce sexually.

[2 marks]

(b) Give **one** artificial method that the scientist could use to clone
the grapevine.

[1 mark]

PRACTICAL

5 A student set up a controlled experiment to investigate the conditions needed for germination.

She placed moist cotton wool and soaked alfalfa seeds in two large sealed flasks.
Flask **A** contained sodium pyrogallate solution, which absorbs oxygen from the air.
Flask **B** contained sodium hydroxide solution, which absorbs carbon dioxide from the air.

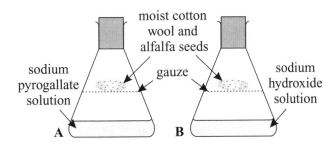

After 24 hours, the student found that the seeds had germinated in flask **B** only.

(a) Explain why germination did not occur in flask **A**.

[2 marks]

(b) How did the germinating alfalfa seeds obtain energy for growth during the experiment?

[1 mark]

(c) The student left flask B for a further 6 days.
She observed that the seedlings produced green leaves after 4 days,
but then showed no further growth despite still being alive.
Suggest why the seedlings in flask **B** stopped growing after they had produced green leaves.

[3 marks]

Human Reproductive Systems

If you skipped to this page in the book first, shame on you...
But now you're here, it's time to learn all about the <u>male</u> and <u>female reproductive systems</u>.

The **Male Reproductive System** Makes **Sperm**

1) Sperm are <u>male gametes</u>. They're made in the <u>testes</u>, <u>all the time</u> after puberty.

2) Sperm mix with a <u>liquid</u> to make <u>semen</u>, which is <u>ejaculated</u> from the penis into the <u>vagina</u> of the female during <u>sexual intercourse</u>.

See page 98 for more on gametes.

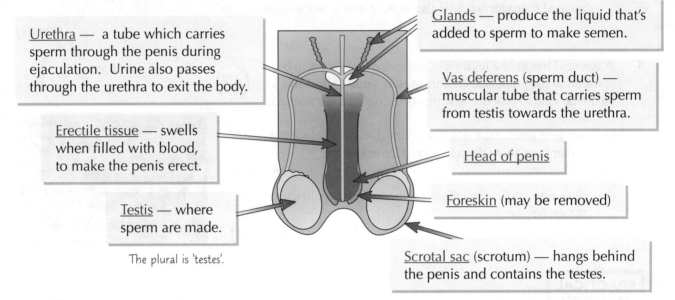

<u>Urethra</u> — a tube which carries sperm through the penis during ejaculation. Urine also passes through the urethra to exit the body.

<u>Erectile tissue</u> — swells when filled with blood, to make the penis erect.

<u>Testis</u> — where sperm are made.

The plural is 'testes'.

<u>Glands</u> — produce the liquid that's added to sperm to make semen.

<u>Vas deferens</u> (sperm duct) — muscular tube that carries sperm from testis towards the urethra.

<u>Head of penis</u>

<u>Foreskin</u> (may be removed)

<u>Scrotal sac</u> (scrotum) — hangs behind the penis and contains the testes.

The **Female Reproductive System** Makes **Ova (Eggs)**

1) Ova are <u>female gametes</u>. An <u>ovum</u> (egg) is produced <u>every 28 days</u> from one of the two <u>ovaries</u>.

2) It then passes into the <u>Fallopian tube</u> — this is where it might <u>meet sperm</u> that have entered the vagina during <u>sexual intercourse</u>.

3) If it <u>isn't fertilised</u> by sperm, the ovum will <u>break up</u> and pass out of the <u>vagina</u>.

4) If it <u>is fertilised</u>, the ovum starts to divide.

5) The new cells will travel down the Fallopian tube to the <u>uterus</u> (womb) and attach to the <u>endometrium</u> (uterus lining). A fertilised ovum develops into an <u>embryo</u>.

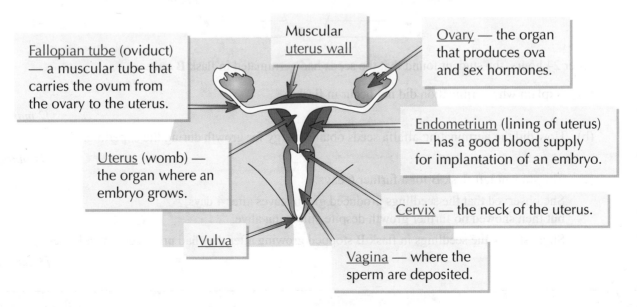

<u>Fallopian tube</u> (oviduct) — a muscular tube that carries the ovum from the ovary to the uterus.

Muscular <u>uterus wall</u>

<u>Ovary</u> — the organ that produces ova and sex hormones.

<u>Endometrium</u> (lining of uterus) — has a good blood supply for implantation of an embryo.

<u>Uterus</u> (womb) — the organ where an embryo grows.

<u>Cervix</u> — the neck of the uterus.

<u>Vulva</u>

<u>Vagina</u> — where the sperm are deposited.

Puberty and the Menstrual Cycle

You need to learn the science behind what happens at puberty. Read on, my friend...

Hormones Promote Sexual Characteristics at Puberty

At puberty, your body starts releasing <u>sex hormones</u> — <u>testosterone</u> in men and <u>oestrogen</u> in women. These trigger off the <u>secondary sexual characteristics</u>:

Oestrogen in women causes...

1) <u>Extra hair</u> on underarms and pubic area.
2) <u>Hips</u> to <u>widen</u>.
3) Development of <u>breasts</u>.
4) <u>Ovum</u> release and <u>start of periods</u>.

See page 83 for more on hormones.

Testosterone in men causes...

1) <u>Extra hair</u> on face and body.
2) <u>Muscles</u> to <u>develop</u>.
3) <u>Penis and testicles</u> to enlarge.
4) <u>Sperm</u> production.
5) <u>Deepening</u> of <u>voice</u>.

The Menstrual Cycle Has Four Stages

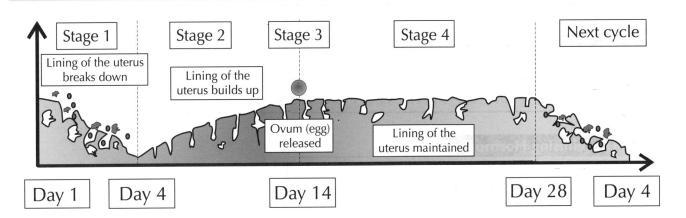

Stage 1 | Stage 2 | Stage 3 | Stage 4 | Next cycle

Lining of the uterus breaks down

Lining of the uterus builds up

Ovum (egg) released

Lining of the uterus maintained

Day 1 | Day 4 | Day 14 | Day 28 | Day 4

<u>Stage 1:</u> <u>Day 1 — menstruation starts</u>. The uterus lining breaks down for about four days.

<u>Stage 2:</u> <u>The uterus lining builds up again</u>, from day 4 to day 14, into a thick spongy layer full of blood vessels, ready to receive a fertilised egg.

<u>Stage 3:</u> <u>An egg develops and is released</u> from the ovary at day 14 — this is called <u>ovulation</u>.

<u>Stage 4:</u> <u>The wall is then maintained</u> for about 14 days until day 28. If no fertilised egg has landed on the uterus wall by day 28, the spongy lining starts to break down and the whole cycle starts again.

The Menstrual Cycle and Pregnancy

There's <u>more than one</u> hormone involved in the menstrual cycle...

The **Menstrual Cycle** is **Controlled** by **Four Hormones**

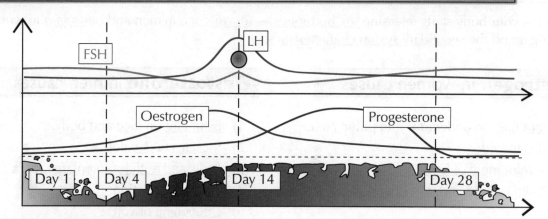

FSH (Follicle-Stimulating Hormone)

1) Produced in the <u>pituitary gland</u>.
2) Causes an <u>egg to mature</u> in one of the ovaries, in a structure called a <u>follicle</u>.
3) <u>Stimulates</u> the <u>ovaries</u> to produce <u>oestrogen</u>.
4) <u>Oestrogen</u> then <u>inhibits</u> the release of FSH.

Oestrogen

1) Produced in the <u>ovaries</u>.
2) Causes the lining of the uterus to <u>grow</u>.
3) <u>Stimulates</u> the release of <u>LH</u> (which causes the release of an egg).

LH (Luteinising Hormone)

1) Produced by the <u>pituitary gland</u>.
2) Stimulates the <u>release of an egg</u> at day 14 (<u>ovulation</u>).

Progesterone

1) Produced in the <u>ovaries</u> by the remains of the <u>follicle</u> after ovulation.
2) <u>Maintains</u> the lining of the uterus during the <u>second half</u> of the cycle. When the level of progesterone <u>falls</u>, the lining <u>breaks down</u>.
3) <u>Inhibits</u> the release of <u>LH</u> and <u>FSH</u>.

The **Embryo Develops** During **Pregnancy**

Once an ovum has been fertilised, it develops into an <u>embryo</u> and implants in the uterus. In <u>later stages</u> of pregnancy (when it starts to look human) the embryo is called a <u>fetus</u>.

Once the embryo has implanted, the <u>placenta</u> develops — this lets the blood of the embryo and mother get very close to allow the exchange of <u>food</u>, <u>oxygen</u> and <u>waste</u>.

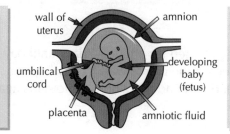

The <u>amnion membrane forms</u> — this surrounds the embryo and is full of <u>amniotic fluid</u>. Amniotic fluid <u>protects</u> the embryo against knocks and bumps.

Warm-Up & Exam Questions

There's only one way to do well in the exam — learn the facts and then practise lots of exam questions to see what it'll be like on the big day. We couldn't have made it easier for you — so do it.

Warm-Up Questions

1) What is the function of the testes?
2) What is the function of the vas deferens?
3) What is the name of the male sex hormone?
4) What secondary sexual characteristics does oestrogen produce in women?

Exam Questions

PAPER 2

1 Which of the following hormones is responsible for stimulating egg maturation?

☐ **A** oestrogen ☐ **B** progesterone ☐ **C** LH ☐ **D** FSH

[1 mark]

2 The diagram shows the uterus during pregnancy.

Describe the role of the following features shown in the diagram:

placenta   amniotic fluid

(a) the placenta

[1 mark]

(b) the amniotic fluid

[1 mark]

3 The diagram shows the levels of oestrogen and progesterone over a 28 day menstrual cycle.

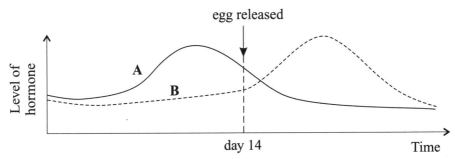

(a) State which curve, **A** or **B**, represents oestrogen. Explain your answer.

[1 mark]

(b) During which part of the cycle is the lining of the uterus thickest? Explain your answer.

[2 marks]

Alleles and Inheritance

This page is all about how <u>characteristics</u> (like eye colour) are <u>inherited</u>. Before you start, you might want to refresh your memory of <u>genes</u>, <u>chromosomes</u> and <u>DNA</u> on page 92. It'll make life a lot easier.

Alleles are Different Versions of the Same Gene

1) What <u>genes</u> you <u>inherit</u> control what <u>characteristics</u> you <u>develop</u>. <u>Some</u> characteristics are controlled by a <u>single gene</u>. However <u>most</u> characteristics are controlled by <u>several genes interacting</u>.

2) Most of the time you have <u>two copies</u> of each gene (i.e. <u>two alleles</u>, see p.92) — one from each parent.

3) If the alleles are different, you have <u>instructions</u> for <u>two different versions</u> of a characteristic (e.g. blue eyes or brown eyes) but you only <u>show one version</u> of the two (e.g. brown eyes).

4) The version of the characteristic that appears is caused by the <u>dominant allele</u>. The other allele is said to be <u>recessive</u>.

5) The characteristic caused by the recessive allele only appears if <u>both alleles</u> are recessive.

Codominant Alleles

Some characteristics are caused by <u>codominant alleles</u>. Neither allele is recessive, so you <u>show characteristics</u> from <u>both alleles</u> (e.g. not blood group A or B, but blood group <u>AB</u>).

In Genetic Diagrams, Letters are Used to Represent Genes

The inheritance of a <u>single</u> characteristic is called <u>monohybrid inheritance</u>. You can use a <u>monohybrid cross</u> to show how <u>recessive</u> and <u>dominant</u> traits for a <u>single characteristic</u> are inherited. They're covered in more detail over the next few pages.

1) In genetic diagrams, <u>letters</u> are used to represent <u>genes</u>. <u>Dominant alleles</u> are always shown with a <u>capital letter</u> (e.g. 'C') and <u>recessive alleles</u> with a <u>small letter</u> (e.g. 'c').

2) If you're <u>homozygous</u> for a trait you have <u>two alleles the same</u> for that particular gene, e.g. <u>CC</u> or <u>cc</u>.

3) If you're <u>heterozygous</u> for a trait you have <u>two different alleles</u> for that particular gene, e.g. <u>Cc</u>.

4) Your <u>genotype</u> is the <u>alleles</u> that you have. Your <u>phenotype</u> is the <u>characteristics</u> the alleles produce.

Genetic diagrams show how alleles can be inherited

Lots of tricky, <u>technical words</u> to learn on this page. It's really important that you do learn them all though, so you can use them correctly and explain what they mean. Try covering up the page and scribbling down everything you can remember. Keep going till you've got it all.

Genetic Diagrams

If you haven't read the previous page, do it now. Trust me — you won't be able to make head nor tails of this lot if you haven't learnt what all the words mean first.

Genetic Diagrams show the Possible Alleles in the Offspring

Imagine you're cross-breeding hamsters, and that some have superpowers.
And suppose you know that the behaviour is due to one gene...

Let's say that the allele which causes the superpowers is recessive — so use a 'b'.
And normal behaviour is due to a dominant allele — call it 'B'.

1) A superpowered hamster must have the genotype bb (i.e. it must be homozygous for this trait).

2) However, a normal hamster could have two possible genotypes — BB (homozygous) or
   Bb (heterozygous), because the dominant allele (B) overrules the recessive one (b).

3) Here's what happens if you breed from two heterozygous hamsters:

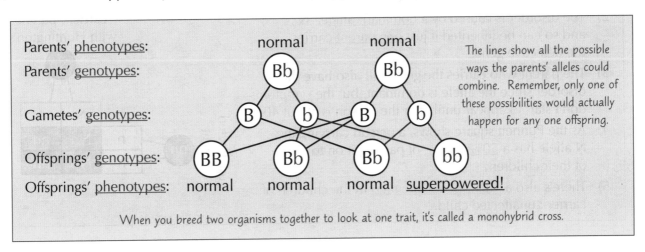

Parents' phenotypes: normal   normal
Parents' genotypes: Bb   Bb

The lines show all the possible ways the parents' alleles could combine. Remember, only one of these possibilities would actually happen for any one offspring.

Gametes' genotypes: B   b   B   b

Offsprings' genotypes: BB   Bb   Bb   bb
Offsprings' phenotypes: normal   normal   normal   superpowered!

When you breed two organisms together to look at one trait, it's called a monohybrid cross.

Results of the Heterozygous Cross

There's a 75% chance of having a normal hamster, and a 25% chance of a superpowered one.
To put that another way... you'd expect a 3 : 1 ratio of normal : superpowered hamsters.
This ratio is called a phenotypic ratio (because it's a ratio of different phenotypes).

Breeding Two Homozygous Hamsters

If you breed two homozygous hamsters there's only one possible offspring you can end up with.

For example, breeding BB and bb hamsters can only give offspring
with a Bb genotype — and they'd all have a normal phenotype.

Genetic diagrams aren't that scary — you just need to practise them

There's one type of genetic diagram on this page, and you're about to meet another type on the next page.
Make sure you know how to produce and interpret genetic diagrams before exam day.

More Genetic Diagrams

Here are some more lovely examples of genetic diagrams to help you out.

There's Another Way to Draw Genetic Diagrams

You can also draw a type of genetic diagram called a Punnett square.
They're dead easy to do. You start by drawing a grid like this.
Then you fill it in like this:

1) Put the possible gametes from one parent down the side,
and those from the other parent along the top.

2) In each middle square, fill in the letters from the top and side that line up with that square.
The pairs of letters in the middle show the possible combinations of the gametes.

For example:

1) Huntington's is a genetic disorder of the nervous system.

2) The disorder is caused by a dominant allele, 'N',
and so can be inherited if just one parent carries
the defective gene.

3) The parent who carries the gene will also have the
disorder since the allele is dominant, but the symptoms
don't start to appear until after the person is about 40.

4) As the Punnett square shows, a person carrying the
N allele has a 50% chance of passing it on to each
of their children.

5) There's also a 1 : 1 phenotypic ratio in the children of
carrier : unaffected child.

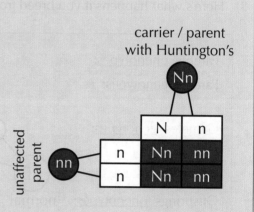

You Can Draw Genetic Diagrams for Codominant Inheritance

You might need to work out the outcome of a monohybrid cross
involving codominant alleles (see p 112).

Don't worry, it's pretty straightforward — you can use a genetic diagram like the one above to help you.

Here's an example:

1) Your blood type is determined by two codominant
alleles (A and B) and one recessive one (O).

2) Blood can be type A (AA or AO genotype),
type B (BB or BO genotype), type AB
(AB genotype) or type O (OO genotype).

3) As the Punnett square shows, for two people with
type AB blood there's a 50% chance their children
will be type AB, a 25% chance they'll be type A
and a 25% chance they'll be type B.

'O' is a recessive allele,
but it's usually written as
a capital letter. There's an
exception to every rule...

Parent 1

		A	B
Parent 2 — AB	A	AA	AB
	B	AB	BB

Family Pedigrees

Once you've got your head around genetic diagrams (see pages 113-114), family pedigrees are really quite straightforward. Which is probably something of a relief.

You Need to Understand **Family Pedigrees**

Knowing how inheritance works helps you to interpret a family pedigree (a family tree of genetic disorders).

Here's a worked example using cystic fibrosis — a genetic disorder of the cell membranes.

Example: Inheritance of **Cystic Fibrosis**

1) The allele which causes cystic fibrosis is a recessive allele, 'f', carried by about 1 person in 30.

2) Because it's recessive, people with only one copy of the allele won't have the disorder — they're known as carriers.

3) For a child to have a chance of inheriting the disorder, both parents must either have the disorder themselves or be carriers.

4) As the diagram shows, there's a 1 in 4 chance of a child having the disorder if both parents are carriers.

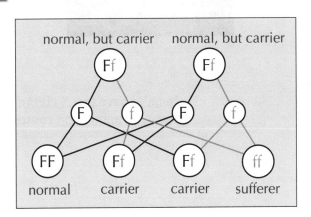

Example: **Family Pedigree** Showing Inheritance of **Cystic Fibrosis**

Below is a family pedigree for a family that includes carriers of cystic fibrosis.

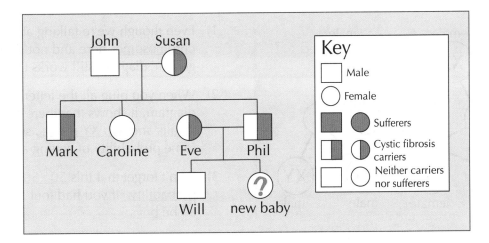

1) The allele for cystic fibrosis isn't dominant because plenty of the family carry the allele but don't have the disorder.

2) There is a 25% chance that the new baby will have cystic fibrosis and a 50% chance that it will be a carrier because both of its parents are carriers but do not have the disorder.

3) The case of the new baby is just the same as in the genetic diagram above — so the baby could be unaffected (FF), a carrier (Ff) or have cystic fibrosis (ff).

Sex Determination

Now for a couple of <u>very important</u> little chromosomes...

Your **Chromosomes** Control Whether You're **Male** or **Female**

There are <u>23 matched pairs</u> of <u>chromosomes</u> in every human body cell. The <u>23rd pair</u> is labelled <u>XX</u> or <u>XY</u>. They're the two chromosomes that decide whether you turn out <u>male</u> or <u>female</u>.

Males have an <u>X</u> and a <u>Y</u> chromosome: XY
The <u>Y chromosome</u> causes <u>male characteristics</u>.

<u>Females</u> have <u>two X chromosomes</u>:   XX
The <u>XX combination</u> causes <u>female characteristics</u>.

This is true for all mammals, but not for some other organisms, e.g. plants.

There's an **Equal Chance** of Having a **Boy** or a **Girl**...

Here's a genetic diagram to prove it.

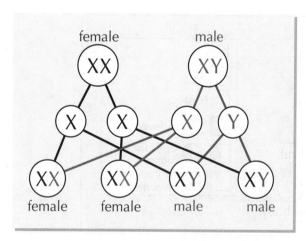

1) Even though we're talking about inheriting <u>chromosomes</u> here and not single genes, the genetic diagram still works the same way.

2) When you plug all the letters into the diagram, it shows that there are <u>two XX results</u> and <u>two XY results</u>, so there's the same probability of getting a boy or a girl.

3) Don't forget that this <u>50 : 50 ratio</u> is only a <u>probability</u>. If you had four kids they <u>could</u> all be <u>boys</u>.

All <u>eggs</u> have one <u>X chromosome</u>, but a <u>sperm</u> can have either an <u>X chromosome</u> or a <u>Y chromosome</u>. So <u>sex determination</u> in humans depends on whether the <u>sperm</u> that <u>fertilises</u> an egg carries an <u>X</u> or a <u>Y</u>.

The X and Y chromosomes determine the sex of all mammals

The genetic diagrams you've seen so far have concentrated on a <u>gene</u>, instead of a <u>chromosome</u>, but the principle's the same. Sex determination is a nice easy topic to end all this genetics business on — which is double the reason to make sure you know it all inside out.

Warm-Up & Exam Questions

By doing these questions, you'll soon find out what you know and what you don't.
Once you've finished, take the time to go back over the bits you've struggled with.

Warm-Up Questions

1) What are alleles?
2) What does genotype mean?
3) In a genetic diagram, what are capital letters used to represent?
4) Which chromosome causes male characteristics?

Exam Questions

1 An individual carries a recessive allele, **b**, for red hair and a dominant allele, **B**, for brown hair.

   (a) What is the individual's phenotype?

[1 mark]

   (b) The individual's genotype is **Bb**.
What is the term used to describe this genotype?

[1 mark]

2 Fruit flies usually have red eyes. However, there are a small number of white-eyed fruit flies. Having white eyes is a recessive characteristic.

Two fruit flies with red eyes have the heterozygous genotype for this characteristic.
They are crossed to produce offspring.

   (a) Complete the genetic diagram below to show the genotypes of the parent flies, the genotypes of the parents' gametes and the genotypes and phenotypes of the possible offspring.

      Use **R** to represent the dominant allele and **r** to represent the recessive allele.

Genotypes of parents:

Genotypes of gametes:

Genotypes of offspring:

Phenotypes of offspring:

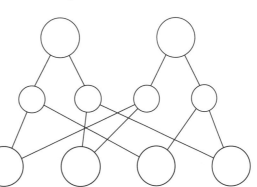

[3 marks]

   (b) (i) State the probability that one of the fruit flies' offspring will have white eyes.

[1 mark]

      (ii) The fruit flies have 60 offspring. Calculate how many of the offspring are likely to have red eyes. Show your working.

[2 marks]

Exam Questions

3 Polydactyly is a genetic disorder transmitted by the dominant allele **D**. The corresponding recessive allele is **d**. The family pedigree of a family with a history of polydactyly is shown.

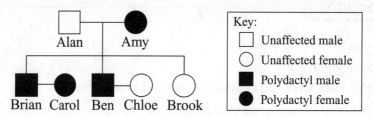

Key:
☐ Unaffected male
○ Unaffected female
■ Polydactyl male
● Polydactyl female

Using the information given above, state what Amy's genotype must be.
Explain your answer.

[2 marks]

4 Albinism is a condition characterised by the lack of pigment in the hair and skin.
It is caused by the recessive allele **a**. The dominant allele **A** results in normal pigmentation.
A rabbit with albinism mated with a rabbit that showed no symptoms of the condition.
They produced 12 offspring, 7 of which had albinism.

   (a) Deduce the genotypes of the parent rabbits. Use a genetic diagram to show the parents' genotypes, the genotypes of their gametes, and the possible genotypes and phenotypes of the offspring.

[4 marks]

   (b) From your genetic diagram, what percentage of offspring are likely to have albinism?

[1 mark]

   (c) Explain why the percentage of offspring with albinism you calculated in part (b) is not the same as that suggested by the genetic diagram.

[1 mark]

5 Colour blindness in humans is caused by a recessive allele located on the X chromosome.
It is more common in men because men carry only one X chromosome.

A man who is colour blind has a child with a woman who does not have the recessive allele.

   (a) Draw a genetic diagram to show the chromosomes of the parents and the gametes they produce, the possible combinations of sex chromosomes in the offspring and the sex of the offspring.

[4 marks]

   (b) The child is a boy. Explain why the boy will not be colour blind.

[1 mark]

   (c) State the probability that a daughter of this couple would be colour blind.

[1 mark]

PAPER 2

6 A gardener is cultivating a species of camellia flower. He crosses two plants that both have red and white spotted flowers. When the offspring plants flower, some have pure red flowers, some have pure white flowers, and some have red and white spotted flowers.

   (a) Are the alleles that control camellia flower colour recessive, dominant or codominant?
Explain your answer.

[2 marks]

   (b) Use a Punnett square to show the genotypes of the parent plants and their gametes, and the genotypes of the offspring. Use **R** and **W** for the alleles that produce red and white flowers.

[3 marks]

   (c) State the phenotypic ratio of the offspring produced by this cross.

[1 mark]

Variation

All variation means is how animals or plants of the same species look or behave slightly differently from each other. There are two kinds of variation — genetic and environmental.

Genetic Variation is Caused by... Genes (Surprise)

1) All animals (including humans) are bound to be slightly different from each other because their genes are slightly different.

2) You might remember from p.93 that genes determine how your body turns out — they control your inherited traits, e.g. eye colour. We all end up with a different set of genes. The exceptions to this rule are identical twins, because their genes are exactly the same.

Sexual reproduction produces genetic variation in other species too, e.g. plants.

Most Variation in Animals is Due to Genes AND Environment

1) Most variation in animals is caused by a mixture of genetic and environmental factors.

2) Almost every single aspect of a human (or other animal) is affected by our environment in some way, however small. In fact it's a lot easier to list the factors which aren't affected in any way by environment:

> - Eye colour,
> - Hair colour in most animals (in humans, vanity plays a big part),
> - Inherited disorders like haemophilia, cystic fibrosis, etc.,
> - Blood group.

3) Environment can have a large effect on human growth even before someone's born. For example, a baby's weight at birth can be affected by the mother's diet.

4) And having a poor diet whilst you're growing up can stunt your growth — another environmental variation.

5) For some characteristics, it's hard to say which factor is more important — genes or environment...

> - Health — Some people are more likely to get certain diseases (e.g. cancer and heart disease) because of their genes. But lifestyle also affects the risk, e.g. if you smoke or only eat junk food.
> - Intelligence — One theory is that although your maximum possible IQ might be determined by your genes, whether you get to it depends on your environment, e.g. your upbringing and school life.
> - Sporting ability — Again, genes probably determine your potential, but training is important too.

Environmental Variation in Plants is Much Greater

Plants are strongly affected by:

1) sunlight, 2) moisture level, 3) temperature, 4) the mineral content of the soil.

For example, plants may grow twice as big or twice as fast due to fairly modest changes in environment such as the amount of sunlight or rainfall they're getting, or how warm it is or what the soil is like.

Evolution and Natural Selection

The <u>theory of evolution</u> states that one of your (probably very distant) ancestors was a <u>blob</u> in a swamp somewhere. Something like that, anyway. It's probably best to read on for more details...

Make Sure You Know the **Theory of Evolution**

> Theory of Evolution:
> Life began as simple organisms from which more complex organisms evolved (rather than just popping into existence).

1) The whole <u>process</u> of evolution usually takes place gradually over <u>millions of years</u>.

2) It's still going on today, e.g. some <u>bacteria</u> are evolving to become <u>resistant to antibiotics</u> (see page 122).

Natural Selection Means the "Survival of the Fittest"

<u>Charles Darwin</u> came up with the theory of <u>evolution by natural selection</u>.

At the time, he didn't know how <u>characteristics</u> were passed on to <u>offspring</u> — but we now know that they're passed on in the <u>genes</u> that parents contribute to their offspring.

Scientists have developed Darwin's theory over time, using what we now know about genetics.

1) Darwin knew that organisms in a species show <u>variation</u> in their characteristics.

Charles Darwin

2) Darwin also knew that the <u>resources</u> that organisms need to survive are <u>limited</u> and individuals have to <u>compete</u> for these resources to <u>survive</u>.

3) Darwin concluded that the organisms with the <u>most suitable characteristics</u> for the environment would be <u>more successful competitors</u> and so would have a <u>better chance</u> of survival — this is known as the "<u>survival of the fittest</u>".

4) The successful organisms will then have an increased chance of <u>breeding</u> and passing on their <u>genes</u>.

5) This means that a <u>greater</u> proportion of individuals in the next generation will have the better <u>alleles</u>, and so the <u>characteristics</u>, that help <u>survival</u>.

6) Over many generations, the <u>characteristic</u> that <u>increases survival</u> becomes <u>more common</u> in the population, making the species become better and better able to <u>survive</u>. The 'best' features are <u>naturally selected</u> and the species becomes more and more <u>adapted</u> to its environment. There's an example of this on the next page.

I wonder what exams evolved from...

Natural selection's all about the organisms with the <u>best characteristics</u> surviving to pass on their <u>genes</u> so that the whole species ends up adapted to its environment. It doesn't happen overnight though.

Evolution and Natural Selection

Here's an Example of **Natural Selection**

1) Once upon a time maybe all rabbits had <u>short ears</u> and managed OK.

2) Then one day out popped a rabbit with <u>big ears</u> who could hear better and was always the first to dive for cover at the sound of a predator.

FOX!

3) Pretty soon he's fathered a whole family of rabbits with <u>big ears</u>, all diving for cover before the other rabbits, and before you know it there are only <u>big-eared</u> rabbits left — because the rest just didn't hear trouble coming quick enough.

This is how populations <u>adapt</u> to survive better in their environment (an organism doesn't actually change when it's alive — changes only occur from generation to generation).

The **Best Genes** for a **Particular Environment** Tend to Survive

1) The individuals who are <u>less suited</u> to an environment are <u>less likely</u> to survive than those that are better suited, and so have <u>less chance</u> to pass their <u>alleles</u> on.

2) Gradually, over time, this results in a population which is extremely <u>well suited</u> to the environment in which it lives.

3) Remember — <u>variations</u> that are caused by the <u>environment</u> itself (e.g. accidentally losing a finger) <u>aren't</u> involved in natural selection. Variations in a species can have either <u>environmental</u> or <u>genetic causes</u>, but only the <u>genetic</u> ones are passed on to the next generation and influence the <u>evolution</u> of the species.

Natural selection — the fittest pass on their characteristics

It's no good being really great at surviving if for some reason you don't breed and <u>pass on your genes</u>. Also remember that it's only <u>genetic traits</u> that get passed on. So if you change your hair colour, or get any scars, your kids will still inherit your genetic traits and not your new characteristics.

Mutations and Antibiotic Resistance

Everyone is <u>slightly different</u>. One reason for this is that we have different sets of <u>alleles</u>. This is partly because of how <u>sexual reproduction</u> works (see page 97) and partly due to <u>mutation</u>.

Mutations are Changes to the Genetic Code

1) <u>Occasionally</u> a gene may <u>mutate</u>. A mutation is a <u>rare</u>, <u>random change</u> in an organism's <u>DNA</u> that can be <u>inherited</u>.

2) Mutations <u>change the sequence</u> of the <u>DNA bases</u> in a gene, which produces a <u>genetic variant</u> (different form of the gene). As the <u>sequence</u> of DNA bases <u>codes</u> for the sequence of <u>amino acids</u> that make up a <u>protein</u> (p.94), mutations to a gene <u>sometimes</u> lead to <u>changes</u> in the protein that it codes for.

> <u>Enzymes</u> are proteins which need an active site with a <u>very specific shape</u> to be able to work properly. A mutation in the gene that codes for an enzyme could lead to a <u>change in the shape</u> of an enzyme's active site — altering its function. A mutation could also <u>stop the production</u> of the enzyme altogether.

3) Mutations can lead to a different <u>phenotype</u>, <u>increasing variation</u>.

- <u>Most</u> mutations have <u>no effect</u> on the phenotype — they're neutral. For example, if the mutation occurs in an unimportant region of the DNA, or if a mutated codon still codes for the same amino acid, the protein's <u>structure</u> and <u>function</u> will be <u>unaffected</u>. A mutation will also usually have no effect if it occurs in a <u>recessive</u> allele.

  See page 94 for more on codons.

- <u>Some</u> mutations have a <u>small effect</u> on the phenotype. This happens when the change in amino acid only has a <u>slight effect</u> on the protein's structure and function — so the individual's characteristics are only altered <u>very slightly</u>.

- Very <u>rarely</u>, a mutation will have a <u>significant effect</u> on phenotype. For example, it might result in a <u>very different</u> protein which can <u>no longer</u> carry out its function. These mutations can be <u>harmful</u> (such as those which lead to cancer) or <u>beneficial</u> (giving a survival advantage, e.g. antibiotic resistance in bacteria — see below).

4) Mutations can happen <u>spontaneously</u> — when a chromosome doesn't quite copy itself properly. However, the chance of mutation is <u>increased</u> by exposing yourself to:

- <u>ionising radiation</u>, e.g. X-rays, gamma rays or ultraviolet rays,
- <u>chemicals</u> called <u>mutagens</u>, e.g. chemicals in tobacco.

If the mutations can lead to cancer then the chemicals causing them are called carcinogens.

Paper 2

Bacteria can Evolve and Become Antibiotic-Resistant

1) Like all organisms, bacteria sometimes develop <u>random mutations</u> in their DNA. These can lead to <u>changes</u> in a bacterium's characteristics. Sometimes, they mean that a bacterium is <u>less affected</u> by a particular <u>antibiotic</u>.

2) For the bacterium, this ability to resist antibiotics is a big <u>advantage</u>. It's better able to survive, even in a host who's being treated to get rid of the infection, so it lives for longer and <u>reproduces</u> many more times.

3) This leads to the <u>allele</u> for resistance being <u>passed on</u> to lots of offspring — it's just <u>natural selection</u>. This is how it spreads and becomes <u>more common</u> in a population of bacteria over time.

4) This is a problem for people who become <u>infected</u> with these bacteria, because you <u>can't</u> easily get rid of them with antibiotics. Sometimes drug companies can come up with a <u>new</u> antibiotic that's effective, but '<u>superbugs</u>' that are resistant to most known antibiotics (e.g. MRSA) are becoming more common.

Making sure you finish the whole course of any prescribed antibiotics helps to prevent the spread of antibiotic resistance. Doctors only prescribing antibiotics when they're really needed helps too.

Warm-Up & Exam Questions

You need to test your knowledge with a few warm-up questions, followed by some exam questions...

Warm-Up Questions

1) Give four environmental conditions that strongly affect plant characteristics.
2) Outline the theory of evolution.
3) What is meant by the term 'mutation'?
4) Name three types of ionising radiation. What effect can ionising radiation have on DNA?
5) Give an example of where chemical mutagens can be found.

Exam Questions

PAPER 2

1   Genetic variation in a population arises partly due to mutations.

Explain how mutations can increase variation in a species.

[3 marks]

2   *Staphylococcus aureus* (SA) is a common bacterium that is found on the skin and mucous membranes. It can cause a range of infections. Some strains of SA have developed resistance to the antibiotic methicillin, and are known as methicillin-resistant *Staphylococcus aureus* (MRSA).

(a)   Name the process that leads to the spread of antibiotic resistance in bacteria.

[1 mark]

(b)   The statements below describe the different stages that led to *Staphylococcus aureus* becoming resistant to methicillin.

Put them in the correct order by writing the numbers
1 to 4 in the boxes, where 1 represents the first stage.

Stage	Order
The gene for methicillin resistance became more common in the population over time.	....
Individual bacteria with the mutated genes were more likely to survive and reproduce in a host being treated with methicillin.	....
Random mutations in the DNA of *Staphylococcus aureus* led to it being less affected by methicillin.	....
The gene for methicillin resistance was passed on to lots of offspring, who also survived and reproduced.	....

[2 marks]

Exam Questions

3 Helen and Stephanie are identical twins.

   (a) Helen has brown hair and Stephanie has blonde hair.
Are these likely to be the natural hair colours of both girls? Explain your answer.

[2 marks]

   (b) Helen weighs 7 kg more than Stephanie.
Explain whether this is due to genes, environmental factors or both.

[2 marks]

   (c) Stephanie has a birthmark on her shoulder. Helen doesn't.
State whether birthmarks are caused by genes and explain your answer.

[1 mark]

4 A racehorse owner wants to produce a successful
foal from one of his thoroughbred mares. He takes
the mare to breed with a prize-winning stallion.

Suggest whether or not the racehorse owner can
confidently expect the foal to be a successful racehorse.
Explain your answer.

[4 marks]

5 The photograph shows an adult buff tip moth.

The buff tip moth's appearance mimics a broken twig, making it well camouflaged.

Explain how the moth might have evolved to look like this.

[5 marks]

6 A population of finches on an island mainly eat seeds. The finches vary in
the size of their beaks. Larger beaks are better for breaking apart larger seeds,
whereas smaller beaks are better for picking up and eating smaller seeds.
A storm kills off many of the plants that produce larger seeds.

Describe how evolution by natural selection may lead to a change
in the beak size in the population of finches, following the storm.

[6 marks]

Revision Summary for Section 7

Section 7 was a long one, but don't go just yet — try out these final questions to find out what you know.
- Try these questions and tick off each one when you get it right.
- When you've done all the questions under a heading and are completely happy with it, tick it off.

DNA and Protein Synthesis (p.92-95) ☐

1) What is a gene?
2) Describe the shape of a DNA molecule.
3) Give one difference between a molecule of DNA and a molecule of RNA.
4) Name the two main stages of protein synthesis.

Reproduction and Cell Division (p.96-98) ☐

5) a) Name the type of cell division used in asexual reproduction.
   b) Apart from asexual reproduction, what else is this type of cell division used for?
6) Name the type of cell division that creates gametes. Where does it take place in humans?

Reproduction, Fertilisation and Germination in Plants (p.101-105) ☐

7) Name the male and female reproductive parts of a flower.
8) What is pollination?
9) What is fertilisation? How does the pollen get from the stigma to the ovary?
10) What conditions are needed for seed germination?
    Outline an experiment you could do to investigate these conditions.
11) Give an example of a plant that reproduces asexually and briefly describe how it happens.
12) Describe how to make plant clones from cuttings.

Male and Female Reproductive Systems and Hormones (p.108-110) ☐

13) Where are sperm made? Where are ova made?
14) What secondary sexual characteristics does testosterone trigger in males?
15) Sketch a timeline of the 28-day menstrual cycle. Label the four stages of the cycle.
16) Name the hormone that is produced in the pituitary gland and stimulates the release of an egg.

Inheritance and Genetic Diagrams (p.112-116) ☐

17) What does it mean if you are homozygous for a particular trait?
18) What are codominant alleles?
19) How are carriers shown on a family pedigree?
20) Draw a genetic diagram showing that there's an equal chance of a baby being a boy or a girl.

Variation, Evolution, Mutations and Antibiotic Resistance (p.119-122) ☐

21) List four features of animals which aren't affected at all by their environment, and three which are.
22) Who proposed the theory of evolution by natural selection?
23) Explain what is meant by natural selection.
24) What is a 'superbug'?

Ecosystems and Biodiversity

This is where the <u>fun</u> starts. Studying <u>ecology</u> gives you the chance to <u>rummage around</u> in bushes, get your hands <u>dirty</u> and look at some <u>real organisms</u>, living in the <u>wild</u>.

You Need to Learn Some **Definitions** to Get You Started

Habitat — The <u>place</u> where an organism <u>lives</u>, e.g. a rocky shore or a field.

Population — <u>All</u> the organisms of <u>one species</u> in a <u>habitat</u>.

Community — All the <u>different species</u> in a habitat.

Ecosystem — All the <u>organisms</u> living in a <u>particular area</u> and all the <u>non-living</u> (abiotic) <u>conditions</u>, e.g. temperature, climate, soil-type.

Biodiversity is all About the **Variety of Life** in an Area

<u>Biodiversity</u> is the variety of different species of organisms on Earth, or within an ecosystem.

1) <u>High</u> biodiversity is important. It makes sure that <u>ecosystems</u> are <u>stable</u> because different species depend on each other for things like <u>shelter</u> and <u>food</u>. Different species can also help to maintain the right <u>physical environment</u> for each other (e.g. the acidity of the soil).

2) Lots of human actions, including <u>deforestation</u> (see p.140), <u>pollution</u> (p.136 and 139), as well as <u>global warming</u> (p.137) are reducing biodiversity.

Environmental Changes **Affect Communities** in **Different Ways**

The <u>environment</u> in which plants and animals live <u>changes all the time</u>. These changes are caused by <u>abiotic</u> (non-living) and <u>biotic</u> (living) factors and affect communities in different ways — for some species <u>population size</u> may <u>increase</u>, for others it may <u>decrease</u>, or the <u>distribution</u> of populations (where they live) may change.

Here are some <u>examples</u> of the effects of changes in <u>abiotic</u> and <u>biotic</u> factors:

Abiotic Factors Affect Communities...

1) <u>Environmental conditions</u> — e.g. the distribution of <u>bird species</u> in Germany appears to be changing because of a <u>rise</u> in average <u>temperature</u>. Other environmental conditions that affect the abundance and distribution of organisms include <u>light intensity</u> (plants only), <u>moisture level</u> and <u>soil pH</u>.

2) <u>Toxic chemicals</u> — e.g. chemical pesticides or fertilisers. Pesticides can <u>build up</u> in food chains through <u>bioaccumulation</u> — this is where, at each stage of the food chain, concentration of the pesticide increases, so <u>organisms</u> at the <u>top</u> of the chain receive a <u>toxic dose</u>. <u>Excess fertilisers</u> released into <u>lakes</u> and <u>ponds</u> cause <u>eutrophication</u> (see p.139) which leads to the <u>death</u> of organisms (e.g. fish).

... and so do **Biotic** Factors

1) <u>Availability of food</u> — e.g. in a <u>bumper year</u> for <u>berries</u>, the population of <u>blackbirds</u> might <u>increase</u> because there'll be <u>enough food</u> for all of them, so they're more likely to <u>survive</u> and <u>reproduce</u>.

2) <u>Number of predators</u> — e.g. if the <u>number of lions</u> (predator) <u>decreases</u> then the number of <u>gazelles</u> (prey) might <u>increase</u> because <u>fewer</u> of them will be <u>eaten</u> by the lions.

3) <u>Competition</u> — organisms <u>compete with other species</u> (and members of their own species) for the <u>same resources</u>. E.g. <u>plants</u> need things like <u>light</u>, <u>space</u>, <u>water</u> and <u>minerals</u> from the soil. Animals compete for things like <u>space</u> (territory), <u>shelter</u>, <u>food</u>, <u>water</u> and <u>mates</u>.

Paper 2

Using Quadrats

Time to put some ecology investigations into action now...

Use a Quadrat to Study The Population Size of Small Organisms

A quadrat is a square frame enclosing a known area, e.g. 1 m². To compare the population size of an organism in two sample areas just follow these simple steps:

1) Place a 1 m² quadrat on the ground at a random point within the first sample area. You could do this by dividing the sample area into a grid and using a random number generator to pick coordinates to place your quadrats at. This will help to make sure the results you get are representative of the whole sample area.

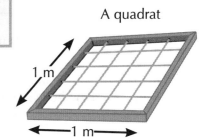
A quadrat

1 m

1 m

2) Count all the organisms you're interested in within the quadrat.

3) Repeat steps 1 and 2 lots of times.

4) Work out the mean number of organisms per quadrat within the first sample area.

5) Repeat steps 1 to 4 in the second sample area.

$$\text{Mean} = \frac{\text{total number of organisms}}{\text{number of quadrats}}$$

6) Finally compare the two means. E.g. you might find a mean of 2 daisies per m² in one area, and 22 daisies per m² (lots more) in another area.

Estimate Population Size from a Small Sample Area

To work out the population size of an organism in one sample area you need to work out the mean number of organisms per m² (if your quadrat has an area of 1 m², this is the same as the mean number of organisms per quadrat, worked out above). Then just multiply the mean by the total area of the habitat:

Students used 0.5 m² quadrats to randomly sample daisies in a field.
They found a mean of 10 daisies per quadrat. The field's area was 800 m².
Estimate the population of daisies in the field.
1) Work out the mean number of organisms per m².   1 ÷ 0.5 = 2   2 × 10 = 20 daisies per m²
2) Multiply the mean per m² by the total area (in m²) of the habitat.   20 × 800 = 16 000 daisies in the field

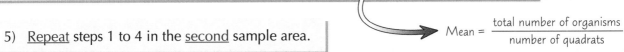

You should put your quadrat down in a random place...

...rather than choosing where to put it, which could mean your results are biased. That's if you're just looking at the population size though — the next page explains how placing your quadrats along a transect can help you investigate the distribution of a species...

 **Using Quadrats**

So, now you think you've learnt all about <u>quadrats</u>. Well hold on — there's more fun to be had.

Use **Belt Transects** to Study **Distribution Across** a **Habitat**

Sometimes <u>abiotic factors</u> will <u>change across a habitat</u>. You can use quadrats to help find out how organisms (like plants) are <u>distributed</u> across a habitat.

> For example, how a species becomes <u>more or less common</u> as you move from an area of <u>shade</u> (near a hedge at the edge of a field) to an area of full sun (the middle of the field).

The quadrats are laid out along a <u>line</u>, forming a <u>belt transect</u>:

1) <u>Mark out a line</u> in the area you want to study, e.g. from the hedge to the middle of the field.

2) Then <u>collect data</u> along the line using <u>quadrats</u> placed <u>next to</u> each other. If your transect is <u>quite long</u>, you could place the quadrats at <u>regular intervals</u> (e.g. every 2 metres) instead. <u>Count</u> all the organisms of the species you're interested in, or <u>estimate percentage cover</u> (estimating the <u>percentage area</u> of a quadrat covered by a particular type of organism).

3) You could also <u>record</u> other data, such as the <u>mean height</u> of the plants you're counting or the <u>abiotic factors</u> in each quadrat (e.g. you could use a <u>light meter</u> to measure the light intensity).

4) <u>Repeat</u> steps 1-3 several times, then find the <u>mean</u> number of organisms or mean percentage cover for <u>each quadrat</u>.

You can measure biodiversity in an area by recording the number of different species that are present, and using quadrats to work out how many organisms of each species there are.

5) Plot graphs to see if the <u>changing abiotic factor</u> is <u>correlated</u> with a change in the <u>distribution</u> of the species you're studying.

tape measure

quadrat 1

 ## You don't need fancy kit to study the distribution of organisms

You might investigate the relationship between the <u>distribution</u> of organisms and any of the <u>biotic</u> or <u>abiotic</u> factors listed on p.126. But when you're analysing your results, remember that just because two things are <u>correlated</u>, it doesn't always mean a change in one is <u>causing</u> the change in the other. There might be <u>other factors</u> involved.

Paper 2

Food Chains and Food Webs

A <u>trophic level</u> is a <u>feeding</u> level. It comes from the Greek word <u>trophe</u> meaning 'nourishment'.

Food Chains Show What's Eaten by What in an Ecosystem

1) <u>Food chains</u> always start with a <u>producer</u>, e.g. a plant.
Producers <u>make</u> (produce) <u>their own food</u> using energy from the Sun.

Consumers are organisms that eat other organisms. 'Primary' means 'first', so primary consumers are the first consumers in a food chain. Secondary consumers are second and tertiary consumers are third.

2) Producers are eaten by <u>primary consumers</u>.
Primary consumers are then eaten by <u>secondary consumers</u> and secondary consumers are eaten by <u>tertiary consumers</u>.

3) All these organisms eventually die and get eaten by <u>decomposers</u>, e.g. bacteria. Decomposers <u>break down</u> (decompose) <u>dead material</u> and <u>waste</u>.

4) Each <u>stage</u> (e.g. producers, primary consumers) is called a <u>trophic level</u>.

Here's an <u>example</u> of a food chain:

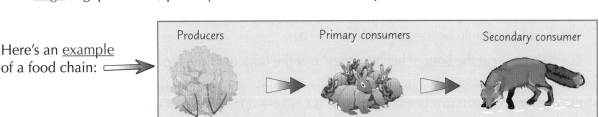

Producers Primary consumers Secondary consumer

<u>5000</u> dandelions... feed... <u>100</u> rabbits... which feed... <u>1</u> fox.

Food Webs Show How Food Chains are Linked

1) There are many different species within an environment — which means <u>lots of different</u> possible <u>food chains</u>. You can draw a <u>food web</u> to show them.

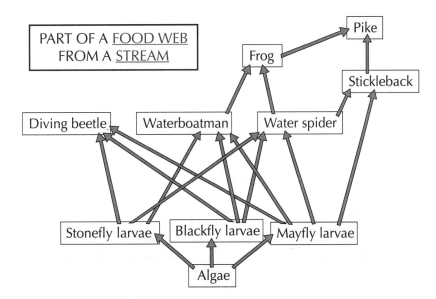

PART OF A <u>FOOD WEB</u>
FROM A <u>STREAM</u>

Pike

Frog

Stickleback

Diving beetle Waterboatman Water spider

Stonefly larvae Blackfly larvae Mayfly larvae

Algae

2) All the species in a food web are <u>interdependent</u>, which means if one species changes, it <u>affects all the others</u>. For example, in the food web above, if lots of water spiders died, then:

• There would be <u>less food</u> for the <u>frogs</u>, so their numbers might <u>decrease</u>.
• The number of <u>mayfly larvae</u> might <u>increase</u> since the water spiders wouldn't be eating them.
• The <u>diving beetles</u> wouldn't be <u>competing</u> with the water spiders for food, so their numbers might <u>increase</u>.

Pyramids of Number, Biomass and Energy

Lots of pyramids to learn here. They're <u>not always pyramid-shaped</u> mind you, but that's biology for you.

You Need to Understand **Pyramids of Numbers**

Here's a <u>pyramid of numbers</u> for the dandelions, rabbits and fox food chain on the previous page.

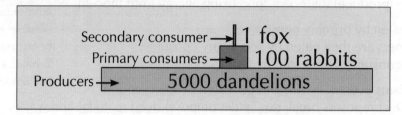

Secondary consumer → 1 fox
Primary consumers → 100 rabbits
Producers → 5000 dandelions

1) Each bar on a pyramid of numbers shows the <u>number of organisms</u> at that stage of the food chain.

2) So the '<u>dandelions</u>' bar on this pyramid would need to be <u>longer</u> than the '<u>rabbits</u>' bar, which in turn should be <u>longer</u> than the '<u>fox</u>' bar.

3) <u>Dandelions</u> go at the <u>bottom</u> because they're at the bottom of the food chain.

4) This is a <u>typical pyramid of numbers</u>, where every time you go up a <u>trophic level</u>, the number of organisms goes <u>down</u>. This is because it takes a <u>lot</u> of food from the level below to keep one animal alive.

5) There are cases where a number pyramid is <u>not a pyramid at all</u>. For example 1 fox may feed 500 fleas.

You Have to Understand **Pyramids of Biomass** Too

1) Each bar on a <u>pyramid of biomass</u> shows the <u>mass of living material</u> at that stage of the food chain — basically how much all the organisms at each level would '<u>weigh</u>' if you put them <u>all together</u>.

2) So the one fox would have a <u>big biomass</u> and the <u>hundreds of fleas</u> would have a <u>very small biomass</u>. Biomass pyramids are <u>practically always the right shape</u>.

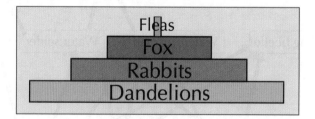

Fleas
Fox
Rabbits
Dandelions

Pyramids of Energy Transfer Are **Always** Pyramid-Shaped

1) <u>Pyramids of energy</u> show the <u>energy</u> transferred to each trophic level in a food chain. E.g. when a rabbit eats dandelions it gets energy, which the dandelions got from the Sun.

2) Pyramids of energy transfer are <u>always the right shape</u> — a nice, regular pyramid.

MATHS TIP — **If you have to construct a pyramid, check it's to scale.**
For example, if one square = 10 units, 5 units of fox biomass would be half a square, but 500 units of dandelion biomass would need a 50 square block (e.g. 5 × 10 squares).

Energy Transfer

Some organisms get their <u>energy</u> from the Sun and some get it from other organisms.

Energy is Transferred Along a Food Chain

1) Energy from the <u>Sun</u> is the source of energy for nearly <u>all</u> life on Earth.

2) <u>Plants</u> use energy from the Sun to make <u>food</u> during photosynthesis. This energy then works its way through the food chain as animals eat the plants and each other.

3) Not all the energy that's available to the organisms in a trophic level is passed on to the next trophic level — around <u>90%</u> of the energy is <u>lost</u> in various ways.

4) Some parts of food, e.g. roots or bones, <u>aren't eaten</u> by organisms so the energy isn't <u>taken in</u>. Some parts of food are <u>indigestible</u> (e.g. fibre) so pass through organisms and come out as <u>waste</u>, e.g. faeces.

Material and energy are both lost at each stage of the food chain — which explains why you get pyramids of biomass and energy.

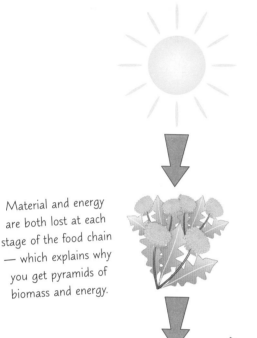

5) A lot of the energy that does get taken in is used for <u>staying alive</u>, i.e. in <u>respiration</u> (see page 49), which powers all life processes.

6) Most of this energy is eventually transferred to the surroundings by <u>heat</u>.

ENERGY TRANSFERRED BY HEAT

MATERIALS LOST IN ANIMALS' WASTE

7) Only around <u>10%</u> of the total energy available becomes <u>biomass</u>, i.e. it's <u>stored</u> or used for <u>growth</u>.

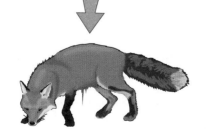

8) This is the <u>energy</u> that's <u>transferred</u> from one trophic level to the next.

Energy is lost at each trophic level

That's why pyramids of <u>energy transfer</u> (p.130) are always pyramid-shaped — most of the energy from the <u>producers</u> doesn't make it to the <u>top</u> of the food chain. Make sure you know the different reasons why.

Warm-Up & Exam Questions

Right, now you've got to grips with how energy and material move through a food chain, have a go at these practice questions. If there's anything you're struggling with, go back and read that bit again.

Warm-Up Questions

1) What is the correct scientific term for:
   a) all the different species in a habitat?
   b) all the organisms in a particular area and all the non-living (abiotic) conditions?
2) What is meant by the term producer? What is a consumer?
3) What is a trophic level?

Exam Questions

1   A student is studying the following food chain on the beach.   Grade 4-6

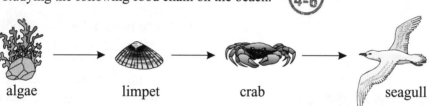

algae   limpet   crab   seagull

(a)   State the number of trophic levels in this food chain.

[1 mark]

(b)   Name the organism in this food chain which is the secondary consumer.

[1 mark]

(c)   When the organisms in the food chain above die, they are broken down by microorganisms.
      What name is given to the microorganisms that break down dead material?

[1 mark]

PAPER 2   **PRACTICAL**

2   A student investigated the distribution of dandelions across a field   Grade 6-7
     next to a wood. A sketch the student drew of the area is shown below.

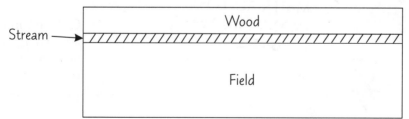

The following table shows the results of the student's investigation.

Number of dandelions per m²	5	9	14	19	26
Distance from wood (m)	2	4	6	8	10

(a)   Describe how the student could have used quadrats to obtain these results.

[3 marks]

(b)   Describe the trend in the student's results.

[1 mark]

Exam Questions

3   A diagram of energy transfer is shown on the right.

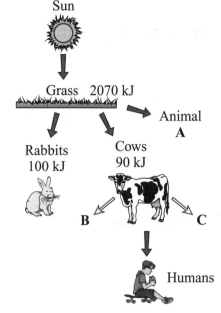

   (a) The efficiency of energy transfer from the
        grass to the next trophic level is 10%.
        Calculate how much energy is available
        to animal **A**. Show your working.

        [2 marks]

   (b) **B** and **C** are processes that represent energy loss.
        Suggest what these processes could be.

        [2 marks]

   (c) Suggest why this food chain cannot support any more
        trophic levels.

        [2 marks]

4   The diagram shows part of a food web
    from Nebraska, USA. The flowerhead
    weevil is not native to this area.
    It was introduced by farmers to eat
    the musk thistle, which is a weed.

    Explain how the introduction of the
    flowerhead weevil could affect the amount
    of wild honey produced in the area.

        [2 marks]

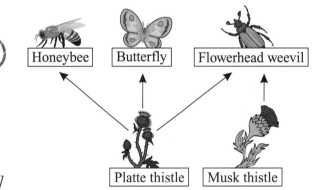

5   In the 1950s a chemical called DDT was used to control insect pests. DDT was later discovered
    to be toxic to other animals and was detected at very high levels in the tissues of organisms across
    food chains. The pyramid of biomass below shows the concentration of DDT in the tissues of
    organisms at each trophic level in parts per million (ppm).

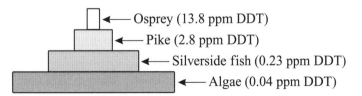

   (a) Describe what happens to the concentration of DDT in organisms as you go up the trophic levels.

        [1 mark]

   (b) Calculate how many times the concentration of DDT has risen by between the producer and the
        tertiary consumer. Show your working.

        [2 marks]

   (c) Suggest why a pyramid of biomass is a suitable diagram for displaying the problem with DDT.

        [1 mark]

The Carbon Cycle

All the <u>nutrients</u> in our environment are constantly being <u>recycled</u> — there's a nice balance between what <u>goes in</u> and what <u>goes out</u> again. This page is all about the recycling of <u>carbon</u>.

Materials are Constantly **Recycled** in an **Ecosystem**

1) Remember, an <u>ecosystem</u> is a <u>community</u> of <u>organisms</u> living in an area, as well as all the <u>non-living</u> (abiotic) conditions, e.g. soil quality, availability of water, temperature. There's more on these on p.126.

2) Materials that organisms need to survive, such as <u>carbon</u> and <u>nitrogen</u> (see next page) are <u>recycled</u> through <u>both</u> the <u>biotic</u> and <u>abiotic</u> components of ecosystems.

3) This means they pass through both <u>living organisms</u> (the biotic components of an ecosystem) and things like the <u>air</u>, <u>rocks</u> and <u>soil</u> (abiotic components of an ecosystem) in a <u>continuous cycle</u>.

The **Carbon Cycle** Shows How **Carbon** is **Recycled**

<u>Carbon</u> is an important element in the materials that living things are made from. But there's only a <u>fixed amount</u> of carbon in the world. This means it's constantly <u>recycled</u>:

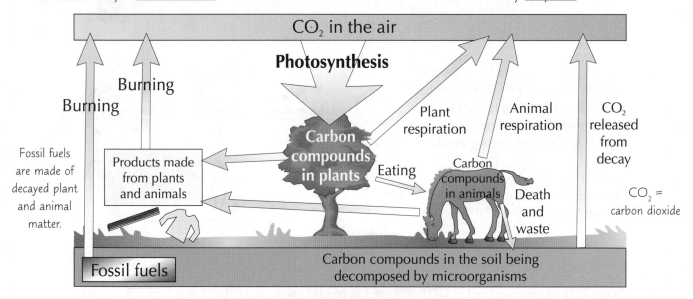

This diagram isn't half as bad as it looks. <u>Learn</u> these important points:

1) There's only <u>one arrow</u> going <u>down</u> from <u>CO_2</u> in the air. The whole thing is 'powered' by <u>photosynthesis</u> (see page 33). Green <u>plants</u> use the carbon from <u>CO_2</u> to make <u>carbohydrates</u>, <u>lipids</u> and <u>proteins</u>.

2) <u>Eating</u> passes the carbon compounds in the plant along to <u>animals</u> in a food chain or web (p.129-131).

3) <u>Respiration</u> (see page 49) by living plants and animals <u>releases CO_2</u> back into the <u>air</u>.

4) Plants and animals eventually <u>die</u> and <u>decompose</u>, or are killed and turned into <u>useful products</u>.

5) When plants and animals decompose they're broken down by microorganisms, such as <u>bacteria</u> and <u>fungi</u>. These microorganisms are known as <u>decomposers</u> and they release <u>enzymes</u>, which <u>catalyse</u> the breakdown of dead material into <u>smaller molecules</u>. Decomposers <u>release CO_2</u> back into the air by <u>respiration</u> as they break down the material.

6) Some useful plant and animal <u>products</u>, e.g. wood and fossil fuels, are <u>burned</u> (<u>combustion</u>). This also releases <u>CO_2</u> back into the air.

7) <u>Decomposition</u> of materials means that <u>habitats</u> can be <u>maintained</u> for the organisms that live there, e.g. <u>nutrients</u> are <u>returned</u> to the soil and <u>waste material</u> (such as dead leaves) doesn't just <u>pile up</u>.

The Nitrogen Cycle

Nitrogen, just like carbon, is constantly being <u>recycled</u>. So the nitrogen in your proteins might once have been in the <u>air</u>. And before that it might have been in a <u>plant</u>. Or even in some <u>horse wee</u>. Nice.

Nitrogen is Recycled in the Nitrogen Cycle

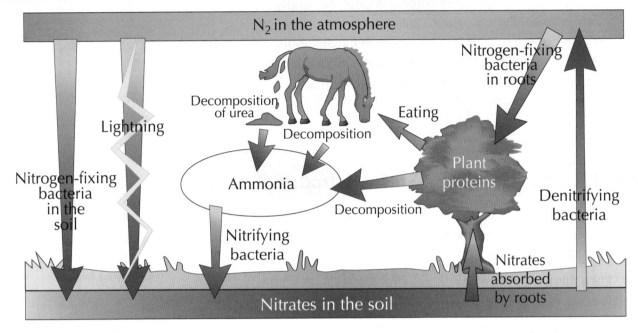

1) The <u>atmosphere</u> contains about <u>78% nitrogen gas</u>, N_2. This is <u>very unreactive</u> and so it can't be used <u>directly</u> by plants or animals.

2) <u>Nitrogen</u> is <u>needed</u> for making <u>proteins</u> for growth, so living organisms have to get it somehow.

3) Plants get their nitrogen from the <u>soil</u>, so nitrogen in the air has to be turned into <u>nitrogen compounds</u> (such as nitrates) before plants can use it. <u>Animals</u> can only get <u>proteins</u> by eating plants (or each other).

4) <u>Nitrogen fixation</u> isn't an obsession with nitrogen — it's the process of turning <u>N_2 from the air</u> into <u>nitrogen compounds</u> in the soil which <u>plants can use</u>. There are <u>two main ways</u> that this happens:

    a) <u>LIGHTNING</u> — there's so much <u>energy</u> in a bolt of lightning that it's enough to make nitrogen <u>react with oxygen</u> in the air to give nitrates.

    b) <u>NITROGEN-FIXING BACTERIA</u> in soil and the roots of some plants (see below).

5) There are <u>four</u> different types of <u>bacteria</u> involved in the nitrogen cycle:

    a) <u>DECOMPOSERS</u> — break down <u>proteins</u> (in rotting plants and animals) and <u>urea</u> (in animal waste) and turn them into <u>ammonia</u> (a nitrogen compound). This forms <u>ammonium ions</u> in the soil.

    b) <u>NITRIFYING BACTERIA</u> — turn <u>ammonium ions</u> in decaying matter into <u>nitrates</u> (nitrification).

    c) <u>NITROGEN-FIXING BACTERIA</u> — turn <u>atmospheric N_2</u> into <u>nitrogen compounds</u> that plants can use.

    d) <u>DENITRIFYING BACTERIA</u> — turn <u>nitrates</u> back into <u>N_2 gas</u>. This is of no benefit to living organisms.

When ammonia is dissolved in water, ammonium ions are formed.

Some of these bacteria live in the <u>soil</u> and some of them live in <u>nodules</u> on plant roots.

Air Pollution

Air pollutants can cause lots of problems when they're released into the atmosphere.

Carbon Monoxide is Poisonous

1) When fossil fuels are burnt without enough air supply they produce the gas carbon monoxide (CO).

2) It's a poisonous gas. If it combines with haemoglobin in red blood cells, it prevents them from carrying oxygen.

3) Carbon monoxide's mostly released in car emissions. Most modern cars are fitted with catalytic converters that turn the carbon monoxide into carbon dioxide, decreasing the amount of CO that's released into the atmosphere.

Acid Rain is Caused by Sulfur Dioxide

1) Burning fossil fuels releases harmful gases like CO_2 (a greenhouse gas, see next page) and sulfur dioxide (SO_2).

2) The sulfur dioxide comes from sulfur impurities in the fossil fuels.

3) When this gas mixes with rain clouds it forms dilute sulfuric acid.

4) This then falls as acid rain.

5) Internal combustion engines in cars and power stations are the main causes of acid rain.

Acid rain is also caused by nitrogen oxides that are produced by burning fossil fuels.

Acid Rain Kills Fish and Trees

1) Acid rain can cause a lake to become more acidic. This has a severe effect on the lake's ecosystem. Many organisms are sensitive to changes in pH and can't survive in more acidic conditions. Many plants and animals die.

2) Acid rain can kill trees. The acid damages leaves and releases toxic substances from the soil, making it hard for the trees to take up nutrients.

Learn all the facts on this page

Exam questions on this topic might ask you to describe the effects of air pollution, mini-essay style. Or they may give you a graph or table to interpret — you'll have to apply your knowledge.

The Greenhouse Effect

The greenhouse effect is always in the news. We need it, since it makes Earth a suitable temperature for living on. But unfortunately it's starting to trap more heat than is necessary.

Greenhouse Gases Trap Energy from the Sun

1) The temperature of the Earth is a balance between the energy it gets from the Sun and the energy it radiates back out into space.

2) Gases in the atmosphere absorb most of the heat that would normally be radiated out into space, and re-radiate it in all directions (including back towards the Earth). This is the greenhouse effect.

This is what happens in a greenhouse. The Sun shines in, and the glass helps keeps some of the energy in.

3) If this didn't happen, then at night there'd be nothing to keep any energy in, and we'd quickly get very cold indeed.

4) There are several different gases in the atmosphere that help keep the energy in. They're called "greenhouse gases" (oddly enough) and they include water vapour, carbon dioxide and methane.

Global Warming — the Earth is Heating Up

1) Human beings are increasing the amount of carbon dioxide in the atmosphere (see next page). We're also increasing levels of other gases that can act as greenhouse gases, e.g. CFCs and nitrous oxide (again, see next page). This has enhanced the greenhouse effect.

2) As a result of all this, the Earth is heating up — this is global warming.

3) Global warming is a type of climate change and causes other types of climate change, e.g. changing rainfall patterns.

4) Climate change could lead to things like extreme weather, and rising sea levels and flooding due to the polar ice caps melting. This could cause habitat loss, and could affect food webs and crop growth.

We need the greenhouse effect, but it's starting to go too far

There's a consensus among scientists that global warming is happening and that human activity has caused most of the recent warming. But, they don't know exactly what the effects will be.

The Greenhouse Effect

Humans are increasing the levels of greenhouse gases in the atmosphere. Here's how...

Human Activity Produces Lots of Greenhouse Gases

Carbon Dioxide

1) Humans release carbon dioxide into the atmosphere all the time as part of our everyday lives — in car exhausts, industrial processes, as we burn fossil fuels etc.

2) People around the world are also cutting down large areas of forest (deforestation) for timber and to clear land for farming — and this activity affects the level of carbon dioxide in the atmosphere (see page 140).

Methane

1) Methane gas is produced naturally from various sources, e.g. rotting plants in marshland.

2) However, two 'man-made' sources of methane are on the increase: rice growing and cattle rearing — it's the cows' "pumping" that's the problem, believe it or not.

Nitrous Oxide

1) Nitrous oxide is released naturally by bacteria in soils and the ocean.

2) A lot more is released from soils after fertiliser is used.

3) It's also released from vehicle engines and industry.

CFCs

1) CFCs are man-made chemicals that were once used in aerosol sprays (e.g. deodorant) and fridges. They're really powerful greenhouse gases.

2) Most countries have agreed not to produce them any more because they also damage the ozone layer that prevents UV radiation from reaching the Earth.

3) But some CFCs still remain and get released, e.g. by leaks from old fridges.

Water Pollution

I'm sorry to bring so much <u>gloom</u> in such a short space, but here's another environmental problem for you to learn about — <u>river pollution</u> by fertiliser or sewage.

Fertilisers Can Leach into Water and Cause Eutrophication

You might think <u>fertiliser</u> would be a good thing for the environment because it makes plants grow faster. Unfortunately it causes <u>big problems</u> when it ends up in <u>lakes</u> and <u>rivers</u> — here's how...

1) <u>Nitrates</u> and <u>phosphates</u> are put onto fields as <u>mineral fertilisers</u>.
2) If <u>too much fertiliser</u> is applied and it <u>rains</u> afterwards, nitrates are easily <u>leached</u> (washed through the soil) into rivers and lakes.
3) The result is <u>eutrophication</u>, which can cause serious damage to river and lake ecosystems:

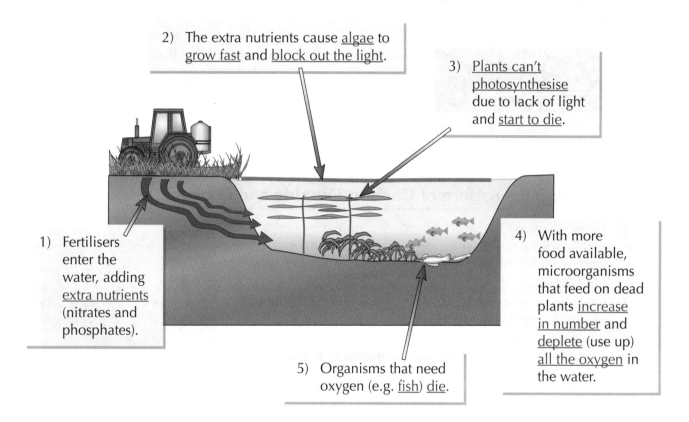

2) The extra nutrients cause <u>algae</u> to <u>grow fast</u> and <u>block out the light</u>.

3) <u>Plants can't photosynthesise</u> due to lack of light and <u>start to die</u>.

1) Fertilisers enter the water, adding <u>extra nutrients</u> (nitrates and phosphates).

4) With more food available, microorganisms that feed on dead plants <u>increase in number</u> and <u>deplete</u> (use up) <u>all the oxygen</u> in the water.

5) Organisms that need oxygen (e.g. <u>fish</u>) <u>die</u>.

Sewage can Also Cause Eutrophication

1) Another cause of <u>eutrophication</u> is pollution by <u>sewage</u>.
2) Sewage contains lots of <u>phosphates</u> from <u>detergents</u>, e.g. washing powder. It also contains <u>nitrates</u> from urine and faeces.
3) These extra nutrients cause eutrophication in the <u>same way that fertilisers do</u>.

Lots of tricky words on this page...

...like 'nitrates', 'phosphates', 'eutrophication' and 'leached'. If you're writing an answer on this stuff in the exam, using <u>technical words</u> like these will really <u>impress</u> the <u>examiners</u>.

Deforestation

Deforestation Has Lots of **Negative Effects**

Deforestation is bad. Chop down all the trees, and the animals and insects that lived there will disappear too. But there are some other <u>nasty effects</u> that you need to know about...

Soil Erosion

1) Tree roots <u>hold the soil together</u>.
2) When trees are <u>removed</u>, soil can be <u>washed away</u> by the rain (<u>eroded</u>) leaving <u>infertile</u> ground.

Leaching

1) Trees <u>take up nutrients</u> from the soil <u>before</u> they can be <u>washed away</u> (<u>leached</u>) by rain, but return them to the soil when leaves die.
2) When trees are removed nutrients get <u>leached away</u>, but <u>don't</u> get <u>replaced</u>, leaving <u>infertile soil</u>.

Disturbing the Balance of **Carbon Dioxide** and **Oxygen**

1) Forests take up CO_2 by <u>photosynthesis</u>, <u>store</u> it in <u>wood</u>, and slowly release it when they <u>decompose</u> (microorganisms feeding on bits of <u>dead wood</u> release CO_2 as a waste product of <u>respiration</u>).
2) When trees are cut down and <u>burnt</u>, the stored carbon is <u>released</u> at once as CO_2. This disturbs the <u>carbon cycle</u> and contributes to <u>global warming</u> (see page 137).
3) Fewer trees in the forest also means that <u>less photosynthesis</u> takes place, releasing <u>less oxygen</u>. This causes the oxygen level in the atmosphere to <u>drop</u>.

Disturbing Evapotranspiration

1) <u>Evapotranspiration</u> includes both the processes of water <u>evaporating</u> from the <u>Earth's surface</u> and from <u>plant transpiration</u> (page 42).
2) This water falls back to the Earth as <u>rain</u> (or hail or snow).
3) So, when <u>trees</u> are <u>cut down</u>, evapotranspiration is <u>reduced</u>, which can make the <u>local climate drier</u>.

Removing trees affects soil, evapotranspiration and the carbon cycle

Trees <u>remove CO_2</u> from the atmosphere as they grow — but once they <u>die</u> and <u>decompose</u>, the CO_2 is <u>released</u>. But if the carbon gets <u>stored</u> in wood products, it is <u>permanently</u> removed from the atmosphere.

Warm-Up & Exam Questions

It's finally the end of the section, but before you go on to the next one a few questions need answering.

Warm-Up Questions

1) Describe one problem caused by the release of carbon monoxide.
2) Methane is a greenhouse gas.
   Explain why the level of methane in the atmosphere is increasing.
3) CFCs are also greenhouse gases. Give two man-made products that used to contain CFCs.

Exam Questions

1 Carbon is constantly being recycled. The diagram below shows some of the processes occurring in the carbon cycle.

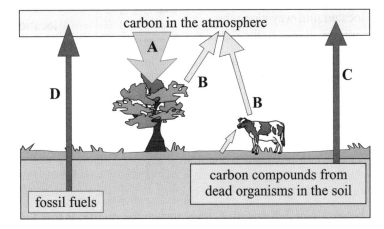

   (a) (i) Name the process, labelled **A**, that removes carbon from the atmosphere.

[1 mark]

        (ii) Name the gas in which carbon is removed from the atmosphere by process **A**.

[1 mark]

   (b) Name the process, labelled **B**, by which all living organisms return carbon to the atmosphere.

[1 mark]

   (c) Explain how carbon is released from dead organisms in the soil (process **C**).

[2 marks]

   (d) (i) Explain why fossil fuels contain carbon.

[1 mark]

        (ii) Describe how the carbon from fossil fuels is released back into the atmosphere (process **D**).

[1 mark]

PAPER 2

2 Several different types of bacteria are involved in the nitrogen cycle. Which bacteria convert nitrogen in the atmosphere into nitrogen compounds that plants can use?

    ☐ **A** nitrifying   ☐ **B** denitrifying   ☐ **C** nitrogen-fixing   ☐ **D** decomposers

[1 mark]

Exam Questions

3 The Earth is kept warm by greenhouse gases.

(a) Explain the role of greenhouse gases in keeping the Earth warm.

[2 marks]

(b) Give **one** way in which conditions on Earth would be different if there were no greenhouse gases.

[1 mark]

(c) Explain the relationship between greenhouses gases and global warming.

[3 marks]

(d) Give **one** possible consequence of global warming and explain how it could affect humans.

[2 marks]

4 An investigation was carried out into the number of microorganisms along a stream. A sewage outflow pipe was located mid-way along the study site. The results are shown to the right.

Describe and explain the change in number of microorganisms downstream from the outflow pipe.

[4 marks]

| PAPER 2 |

5 Read the passage below about deforestation, then answer the questions that follow.

Forests cover around 30% of the Earth's land surface, but the destruction of tropical forests is taking place at rapid rate. Tropical forests are home to more than half of animal and plant species, so this deforestation has a devastating effect on biodiversity. It is also thought to contribute to global warming by disturbing the balance of carbon dioxide in the atmosphere, as well as
5 contributing to a drier local climate.

Studying areas that have been cleared of trees in the past provides insight into other effects of deforestation. The Huangtu Plateau is a large area in north central China characterised by a fine, loose soil called loess. In the past, the plateau was forested and highly fertile, but human activity over the past two thousand years has greatly decreased the tree cover. The removal of trees has
10 been linked to increased soil erosion and increasingly infertile land. Deforestation in this area also appears to be linked to an increasing number of natural disasters, including floods.

(a) Explain how deforestation contributes to global warming (line 4).

[4 marks]

(b) Suggest how deforestation could lead to a drier local climate (line 5)

[2 marks]

(c) Explain how the removal of trees could cause increased soil erosion (line 10).

[2 marks]

(d) Describe **one** way, other than soil erosion, in which deforestation results in infertile land (line 10).

[2 marks]

Revision Summary for Section 8

You've battled to the end of Section 8, but don't stop now — pit yourself against these questions to claim glory.

* Try these questions and tick off each one when you get it right.
* When you've done all the questions for a topic and are completely happy with it, tick off the topic.

Ecosystems, Biodiversity and Using Quadrats (p.126-128) ☑

1) Define the following:
   a) a habitat
   b) a population
   c) an ecosystem
   d) biodiversity ☑
2) How could you estimate a population size in a habitat using a quadrat? ☑
3) How could you investigate the distribution of organisms across a habitat using quadrats? ☑

Pyramids, Energy Transfer and Food Webs (p.129-131) ☑

4) What's a secondary consumer? ☑
5) Give an example of a decomposer. ☑
6) Explain why pyramids of number are not always pyramid-shaped. ☑
7) What is the source of all the energy in a typical food chain? ☑
8) Give two reasons why energy is lost between trophic levels. ☑
9) Approximately how much energy is passed on to the next trophic level? ☑
10) What does a food web show? ☑

The Carbon Cycle and the Nitrogen Cycle (p.134-135) ☑

11) How does carbon enter the carbon cycle from the air? ☑
12) Give two ways that carbon can enter the air from dead plants and animals. ☑
13) What role do decomposers play in the nitrogen cycle? ☑
14) What role do nitrogen-fixing bacteria play in the nitrogen cycle? ☑

Pollution, The Greenhouse Effect and Deforestation (p.136-140) ☑

15) Name a gas that causes acid rain. Where does it come from? ☑
16) How does acid rain affect lakes and trees? ☑
17) How does the greenhouse effect work? ☑
18) What is the effect of increasing the concentration of greenhouse gases in the atmosphere? ☑
19) Give two man-made sources of nitrous oxide. ☑
20) Explain how fertilisers can cause eutrophication. ☑
21) Describe four effects of deforestation. ☑

Increasing Crop Yields

Growing plants outdoors can be <u>very difficult</u>, especially on a <u>large scale</u> — it's almost impossible to control the weather and other conditions. But there's a way around that...

The Rate of **Photosynthesis** Affects **Crop Yield**

1) A plant's <u>rate of photosynthesis</u> is affected by the amount of <u>light</u>, the amount of <u>carbon dioxide</u> (CO_2) and the <u>temperature</u> (see pages 33-34).

2) Since plants have to photosynthesise in order to make food for themselves and <u>grow</u>, these three factors need to be <u>carefully controlled</u> in order to <u>maximise crop yield</u>.

You Can **Create** the **Ideal Conditions** for **Photosynthesis**

Photosynthesis can be helped along by artificially creating the ideal conditions in <u>glasshouses</u> (big greenhouses to you and me) or <u>polytunnels</u> (big tube-like structures made from polythene).

1) Keeping plants <u>enclosed</u> in a glasshouse makes it easier to keep them free from <u>pests</u> and <u>diseases</u>.

2) It also helps farmers to control the <u>water supplied</u> to their crops.

3) Commercial farmers often supply <u>artificial light</u> after the Sun goes down to give their plants <u>more</u> time to <u>photosynthesise</u>.

4) Glasshouses <u>trap</u> the Sun's <u>heat</u> to keep the plants <u>warm</u>. In winter, a farmer might also use a <u>heater</u> to help keep the temperature at the ideal level.

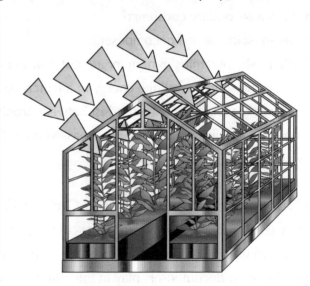

5) Farmers can also <u>increase</u> the level of <u>carbon dioxide</u> in glasshouses, e.g. by using a <u>paraffin heater</u> to heat the place. As the paraffin burns, it makes carbon dioxide as a <u>by-product</u>.

6) By <u>increasing</u> the <u>temperature</u> and <u>CO_2 concentration</u>, as well as the amount of <u>light available</u>, a farmer can <u>increase</u> the rate of <u>photosynthesis</u> for his or her plants. This means the plants will grow bigger and faster — and <u>crop yields</u> will be <u>higher</u>.

You can use glasshouses to control the growing environment

Farmers use <u>glasshouses</u> to make sure crops get the right amount of <u>carbon dioxide</u>, <u>light</u> and <u>heat</u>. They can alter the conditions using paraffin heaters (to supply extra CO_2 and warmth) and artificial light. This ensures nothing becomes a <u>limiting factor</u> for photosynthesis, which means a good crop is produced.

Increasing Crop Yields

As well as growing plants in glasshouses, there are other ways of increasing crop yields. Fertilisers are handy for giving plants the nutrients they need and pesticides can stop pesky pests from eating crops.

Fertilisers Are Used to Ensure the Crops Have Enough Minerals

1) Plants need certain minerals, e.g. nitrogen, potassium and phosphorus, so they can make important compounds like proteins.

2) If plants don't get enough of these minerals, their growth and life processes are affected.

3) Sometimes these minerals are missing from the soil because they've been used up by a previous crop.

4) Farmers use fertilisers to replace these missing minerals or provide more of them. This helps to increase the crop yield.

Pest Control Stops Pests Eating Crops

1) Pests include microorganisms, insects and mammals (e.g. rats). Pests that feed on crops are killed using various methods of pest control. This means fewer plants are damaged or destroyed, increasing crop yield.

2) Pesticides are a form of chemical pest control. They're often poisonous to humans, so they must be used carefully to keep the amount of pesticide in food below a safe level. Some pesticides also harm other wildlife.

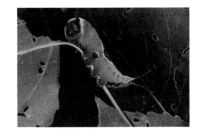

3) Biological control is an alternative to using pesticides. It means using other organisms to reduce the numbers of pests, either by encouraging wild organisms or adding new ones.

4) The helpful organisms could be predators (e.g. ladybirds eat aphids), parasites (e.g. some flies lay their eggs on slugs, eventually killing them), or disease-causing (e.g. bacteria that affect caterpillars).

5) Biological control can have a longer-lasting effect than spraying pesticides, and be less harmful to wildlife. But introducing new organisms can cause problems — e.g. cane toads were introduced to Australia to eat beetles, but they are now a major pest themselves because they poison the native species that eat them.

Reducing pest numbers can increase crop yield

In the exam, you might be asked to evaluate the methods of pest control. Each method has its advantages and disadvantages — so make sure you write about both sides.

Bacteria and Making Yoghurt

Lots of microorganisms are used to produce food, including <u>bacteria</u>. You need to know how <u>yoghurt</u> is produced, and that microorganisms can be grown in giant <u>fermenters</u> for use in industry.

Bacteria **Ferment Milk** to Produce **Yoghurt**

<u>Fermentation</u> is when <u>microorganisms</u> break sugars down to release energy — usually by <u>anaerobic respiration</u>. <u>Yoghurt</u> is basically <u>fermented milk</u>. Here's how it's made...

1) The <u>equipment</u> is <u>sterilised</u> to kill off any unwanted microorganisms.

2) The milk is <u>pasteurised</u> (heated up to 72 °C for 15 seconds) — again to kill any harmful microorganisms. Then the milk's <u>cooled</u>.

3) *Lactobacillus* bacteria are added, and the mixture is <u>incubated</u> (heated to about 40 °C) in a vessel called a <u>fermenter</u> (see below).

4) The bacteria ferment the <u>lactose sugar</u> in the milk to form <u>lactic acid</u>.

5) Lactic acid causes the milk to <u>clot</u>, and <u>solidify</u> into <u>yoghurt</u>.

6) Finally, <u>flavours</u> (e.g. fruit) and <u>colours</u> are sometimes added and the yoghurt is <u>packaged</u>.

Microorganisms are Grown in **Fermenters**

1) <u>Microorganisms</u> (like bacteria) can be used to make really <u>useful stuff</u>, e.g. penicillin or insulin (see p.153).

2) <u>In industry</u>, microorganisms are grown in large containers called <u>fermenters</u>. The fermenter is full of liquid '<u>culture medium</u>' in which microorganisms can grow and reproduce.

3) The conditions inside the fermentation vessels are kept at the <u>optimum</u> (best) levels <u>for growth</u> — this means the <u>yield</u> of <u>products</u> from the microorganisms can be <u>as big as possible</u>.

Lactobacillus bacteria ferment lactose to form lactic acid

Microorganisms are <u>really useful</u> — you can use them to make all sorts of stuff that other organisms can't. For starters, without microorganisms you couldn't make yoghurt. And that would be sad. But remember you can't just use any old bacteria for making yoghurt — first you have to kill off any harmful microorganisms in the milk and then you can add the useful ones, like *Lactobacillus*.

Growing Bacteria

In industry, if you want to grow lots of microorganisms, it's best to use a <u>fermenter</u>. Inside a fermenter you can make sure the <u>conditions</u> are just right, so you can get as much product as possible.

Fermenters Can Provide Optimum Conditions for Microorganisms

Here's a bit about how fermenters work:

The <u>pH</u> is monitored and kept at the <u>optimum level</u> for the microorganisms' <u>enzymes</u> to work <u>efficiently</u>. This keeps the <u>rate of reaction</u> and product yield as high as possible.

<u>Nutrients</u> needed by the microorganisms for <u>growth</u> are provided in the liquid <u>culture medium</u>.

Microorganisms are kept in <u>contact</u> with <u>fresh medium</u> by <u>paddles</u> that <u>circulate</u> (or <u>agitate</u>) the medium around the vessel. This <u>increases</u> the product yield because microorganisms can <u>always access</u> the <u>nutrients</u> needed for <u>growth</u>.

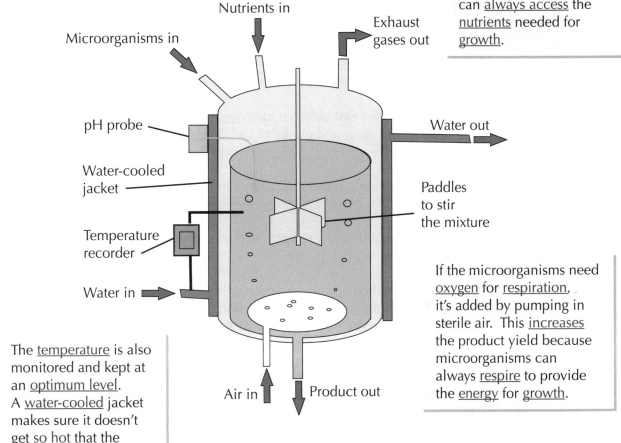

Microorganisms in
Nutrients in
Exhaust gases out
pH probe
Water out
Water-cooled jacket
Paddles to stir the mixture
Temperature recorder
Water in
Air in
Product out

If the microorganisms need <u>oxygen</u> for <u>respiration</u>, it's added by pumping in sterile air. This <u>increases</u> the product yield because microorganisms can always <u>respire</u> to provide the <u>energy</u> for <u>growth</u>.

The <u>temperature</u> is also monitored and kept at an <u>optimum level</u>. A <u>water-cooled</u> jacket makes sure it doesn't get <u>so hot</u> that the enzymes <u>denature</u>.

Vessels are <u>sterilised</u> between uses with <u>superheated steam</u> that kills <u>unwanted microbes</u>. Having <u>aseptic</u> conditions <u>increases</u> the product yield because the microorganisms <u>aren't competing</u> with other organisms. It also means that the product doesn't get <u>contaminated</u>.

Optimum conditions for microorganisms = high yield of product

Microorganisms will happily grow in a <u>fermenter</u> even when it's cold and <u>blowing a gale</u> outside. That's because inside a fermenter you can control all the conditions so they're perfect. The more microorganisms that grow, the more product you can make, so it's important to keep them happy.

Yeast and Making Bread

If you've ever made <u>bread</u>, you'll know that the finished product somehow ends up a lot <u>bigger</u> than the <u>dough</u> you make at the beginning. That's all thanks to a certain handy <u>microorganism</u>...

We Use **Yeast** for **Making Bread**

Yeast is a useful <u>microorganism</u>. When it respires <u>aerobically</u> (in the presence of <u>oxygen</u>), it breaks down <u>sugar</u> into CO_2 and <u>water</u>. It's used in baking, where it's mixed into dough to create bubbles of CO_2 that make the dough <u>rise</u>.

1) A bread dough is made by mixing <u>yeast</u> with <u>flour</u>, <u>water</u> and a bit of <u>sugar</u>.

2) The dough is then left in a warm place to <u>rise</u> — this happens with the help of the yeast.

3) Enzymes break down the carbohydrates in the flour into <u>sugars</u>.

4) The yeast then uses these sugars in aerobic respiration, producing <u>carbon dioxide</u>.

5) When the oxygen runs out, the yeast switches to <u>anaerobic</u> respiration. This is also known as <u>fermentation</u>, and produces <u>carbon dioxide</u> and alcohol (<u>ethanol</u>).

6) The carbon dioxide produced is <u>trapped</u> in bubbles in the dough.

7) These pockets of gas expand, and the dough begins to <u>rise</u>.

8) The dough is then <u>baked</u> in an oven, where the yeast continues to ferment until the <u>temperature</u> of the dough rises enough to <u>kill</u> the yeast. Any <u>alcohol</u> produced during anaerobic respiration is <u>boiled away</u>.

9) As the yeast dies, the bread <u>stops rising</u>, but pockets are left in the bread where the carbon dioxide was trapped.

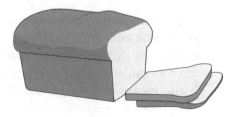

Respiration in yeast produces carbon dioxide, making bread rise

You might not have thought there was much of an overlap between <u>baking</u> and <u>biology</u>, but you thought wrong. Understanding how yeast works has allowed humans to make bread for <u>thousands of years</u>.

Investigating Yeast

The rate of respiration of yeast changes depending on the conditions it's in.

The **Respiration Rate** of **Yeast** Depends on its **Conditions**

You can do experiments to investigate how the rate of CO_2 production by yeast during anaerobic respiration changes under different conditions. Here's how to measure the effect of changing temperature:

1) Mix together some sugar, yeast and distilled water, then add the mixture to a test tube.
2) To create anaerobic conditions, add a layer of oil to the top of the yeast mixture. This will prevent oxygen from the air getting into the mixture.
3) Attach a bung with a tube leading to a second test tube of water.
4) Place the tube containing the yeast mixture in a water bath at a certain temperature.

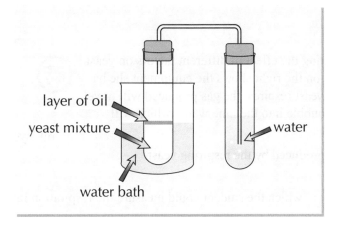

5) Leave the tube to warm up a bit and then count how many bubbles are produced in a given period of time (e.g. one minute).
6) Calculate the rate of CO_2 production by dividing the number of bubbles produced by the time taken for them to be produced in seconds. This gives an indication of respiration rate.
7) Repeat the experiment with the water bath set at different temperatures.
8) Respiration is controlled by enzymes — so as temperature increases, so should the rate of respiration (up until the optimum temperature, see page 10 for more).

You Can Also Test Other **Variables**

1) The example looks at how temperature affects the rate, but the basic idea would be the same whatever variable you were investigating.
2) For example, you could vary the concentration of sugar but keep the temperature of the water bath the same).
3) You could also alter the experiment to give more accurate results by replacing the second tube with a gas syringe — you'd measure the volume of gas produced instead.

The more bubbles produced, the faster the rate of respiration

Counting bubbles isn't an accurate way to measure the volume of gas produced, but it does allow you to compare the relative amounts of gas produced at different temperatures.

Warm-Up & Exam Questions

Now's your chance to practice some incredibly life-like exam questions, but do the warm-up first — you don't want to end up straining something.

Warm-Up Questions

1) Why do farmers use pest control?
2) Name the bacteria used to produce yoghurt from milk.
3) Give two conditions which need to be kept at an optimum level inside a fermenter.

Exam Questions

PRACTICAL

1   A student is investigating the effect of different factors on yeast growth. The diagram on the right shows the equipment she has set up so far. As the yeast respires, the gas produced will travel through the tube and bubble into the lime water, which will gradually turn cloudy.

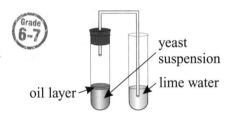

yeast suspension

lime water

oil layer

(a)   Identify the gas produced by the respiring yeast.

[1 mark]

(b)   Suggest **one** way in which the student could measure the respiration rate of the yeast.

[1 mark]

(c)   The student wants to investigate how temperature affects the rate of respiration.
   (i) Suggest how the student could alter the temperature of the yeast suspension.

[1 mark]

   (ii) Suggest how increasing the temperature from 20 °C to 25 °C would affect the rate of respiration.

[1 mark]

2   A farmer has three polythene tunnels which she uses to grow strawberries. She uses a different fertiliser (A, B or C) in each tunnel and records the strawberry yield for 5 years. Her results are shown in the table below.

Fertiliser	Strawberry yield each year (kg)				
	2008	2009	2010	2011	2012
A	592	615	580	632	599
B	600	601	566	604	587
C	575	630	599	661	612

(a)   Suggest why the farmer grows her strawberries in polythene tunnels. Explain your answer.

[3 marks]

(b)   (i) Which fertiliser, A-C, had the best effect on strawberry yield overall? Explain your answer.

[2 marks]

   (ii) Explain how fertilisers increase crop yield.

[3 marks]

Selective Breeding

'Selective breeding' sounds like it has the potential to be a tricky topic, but it's actually dead simple. You take the <u>best</u> plants or animals and breed them together to get the best possible <u>offspring</u>. That's it.

Selective Breeding is Mating the **Best Organisms** Together

Organisms are <u>selectively bred</u> to develop the <u>best features</u>, which are things like:

- <u>Maximum yield</u> of meat, milk, grain etc.
- <u>Good health</u> and <u>disease resistance</u>.
- In animals, other qualities like <u>temperament</u>, <u>speed</u>, <u>fertility</u>, <u>good mothering skills</u>, etc.
- In plants, other qualities like <u>attractive flowers</u>, <u>nice smell</u>, etc.

Selective breeding is also known as artificial selection.

This is the basic process involved in <u>selective breeding</u>:

1) From your <u>existing stock</u> select the ones which have the <u>best characteristics</u>.
2) <u>Breed them</u> with each other.
3) Select the <u>best</u> of the <u>offspring</u>, and <u>breed them together</u>.
4) Continue this process over <u>several generations</u>, and the desirable trait gets <u>stronger</u> and <u>stronger</u>. In farming, this will give the farmer gradually better and better <u>yields</u>.

Selective Breeding is Very **Useful**

Selective breeding can increase the **productivity** of **cows**

1) Cows can be <u>selectively bred</u> to produce offspring with, e.g. a <u>high meat yield</u>.
2) First, the animals with <u>characteristics</u> that will <u>increase meat yield</u> (e.g. the largest cows and bulls) are <u>selected</u> and <u>bred together</u>.
3) Next, the <u>offspring</u> with the best characteristics (e.g. the largest) are selected and <u>bred together</u>.
4) If this is continued over <u>several generations</u>, cows with <u>very large meat yields</u> can be produced.
5) Mating cows and bulls naturally can be difficult, so <u>artificial insemination</u> is often used. It's <u>safer</u> for the cow, and it's much quicker and cheaper to <u>transport</u> semen than bulls. The semen can also be used to impregnate <u>multiple</u> cows, and can be <u>stored</u> after the bull has died.

Selective breeding can increase the **number of offspring** in **sheep**

Farmers can selectively breed <u>sheep</u> to <u>increase</u> the number of <u>lambs born</u>. Female sheep (ewes) who produce large numbers of offspring are bred with rams whose mothers had large numbers of offspring. The <u>characteristic</u> of having large numbers of offspring is <u>passed on</u> to the next generation.

Selective breeding can increase **crop yield**

1) Selective breeding can be used to combine <u>two different desirable characteristics</u>.
2) <u>Tall wheat plants</u> have a good grain yield but are easily damaged by wind and rain. <u>Dwarf wheat plants</u> can resist wind and rain but have a lower grain yield.
3) These two types of wheat plant were <u>cross-bred</u>, and the best resulting wheat plants were cross-bred again. This resulted in a <u>new variety</u> of wheat <u>combining the good characteristics</u> — dwarf wheat plants which could <u>resist bad weather</u> and had a <u>high grain yield</u>.

Fish Farming

We're catching so many wild fish that, if we're not careful, there won't be many left.
A possible solution to this problem is <u>fish farms</u> — big <u>enclosures</u> or <u>tanks</u> where fish are raised for food.
<u>Fish farms</u> rear fish in a controlled way that's designed to produce <u>as many fish as possible</u>.

Fish Can Be Farmed in Cages in the Sea

<u>Salmon farming</u> in Scotland is a good example of this:

1) The fish are kept in <u>cages</u> in the <u>sea</u> to <u>stop them using as much energy</u> swimming about.

2) The cage also <u>protects</u> them from <u>interspecific predation</u> (being eaten by other animals like birds or seals).

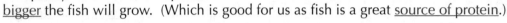

3) They're fed a <u>diet</u> of food pellets that's <u>carefully controlled</u> to <u>maximise</u> the amount of energy they get. The better the <u>quality</u> the food is, the <u>quicker</u> and <u>bigger</u> the fish will grow. (Which is good for us as fish is a great <u>source of protein</u>.)

4) Young fish are reared in <u>special tanks</u> to ensure as many survive as possible.

5) It's important to keep younger fish <u>separate</u> from <u>bigger fish</u>, and to provide <u>regular food</u> — this makes sure that the big fish <u>don't eat the little ones</u>. This is <u>intraspecific predation</u> — where organisms eat individuals of the same species.

6) Fish kept in cages are more prone to <u>disease</u> and <u>parasites</u>. One pest is <u>sea lice</u>, which can be treated with <u>pesticides</u> that kill them. To <u>avoid pollution</u> from chemical pesticides, <u>biological pest control</u> (see page 145) can be used instead, e.g. a small fish called a <u>wrasse</u> eats the lice off the backs of the salmon.

7) The fish can be <u>selectively bred</u> (see page 151) to produce <u>less aggressive</u>, <u>faster-growing</u> fish.

Fish Can Be Farmed in Tanks Too

Freshwater fish, e.g. <u>carp</u>, can be farmed in <u>ponds</u> or <u>indoors</u> in tanks where conditions can be <u>controlled</u>. This is especially useful for controlling the <u>water quality</u>.

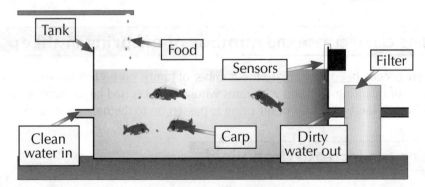

1) The <u>water</u> can be <u>monitored</u> to check that the <u>temperature</u>, <u>pH</u> and <u>oxygen level</u> is OK.

2) It's easy to control <u>how much food</u> is supplied and give <u>exactly the right sort</u> of food.

3) The water can be <u>removed</u> and <u>filtered</u> to get rid of <u>waste food</u> and <u>fish poo</u>. This keeps the water <u>clean</u> for the fish and avoids <u>pollution</u> wherever the water ends up.

Genetic Engineering

The idea of genetic engineering is to move <u>useful genes</u> from one organism's chromosomes into the cells of another. This sounds tricky, but people have found <u>enzymes</u> and <u>vectors</u> (carriers) that can do it.

Enzymes Can Be Used To **Cut Up DNA...**

...or **Join DNA Pieces** Together

1) <u>Restriction enzymes</u> recognise <u>specific sequences</u> of DNA and <u>cut the DNA</u> at these points.

2) <u>Ligase</u> enzymes are used to join <u>two pieces of DNA</u> together.

3) <u>Two different bits</u> of DNA stuck together are known as <u>recombinant DNA</u>.

Vectors Can Be Used To **Insert DNA** Into **Other Organisms**

A <u>vector</u> is something that's used to <u>transfer DNA</u> into a <u>cell</u>. There are two sorts — <u>plasmids</u> and <u>viruses</u>:

- Plasmids are <u>small</u>, <u>circular</u> molecules of DNA that can be <u>transferred</u> between <u>bacteria</u>.
- Viruses <u>insert</u> DNA into the organisms they <u>infect</u>.

Here's how genetic engineering works:

1) The <u>DNA</u> you want to <u>insert</u> (e.g. the gene for human insulin) is cut out with a <u>restriction enzyme</u>. The <u>vector DNA</u> is then cut open using the <u>same</u> restriction enzyme.

2) The vector DNA and the DNA you're inserting are <u>mixed together</u> with <u>ligase enzymes</u>.

3) The ligases <u>join</u> the two pieces of DNA together to produce <u>recombinant DNA</u>.

4) The recombinant DNA (i.e. the vector containing new DNA) is <u>inserted</u> into other cells, e.g. bacteria.

5) These cells can now <u>use the gene you inserted</u> to <u>make the protein</u> you want.
E.g. <u>bacteria</u> containing the gene for <u>human insulin</u> can be grown in huge numbers in a fermenter (see page 146) to produce <u>insulin</u> for people with <u>diabetes</u>.

6) Bacteria that contain the gene for human insulin are <u>transgenic</u> — this means that they contain <u>genes transferred from another species</u>. You can get transgenic animals and plants too.

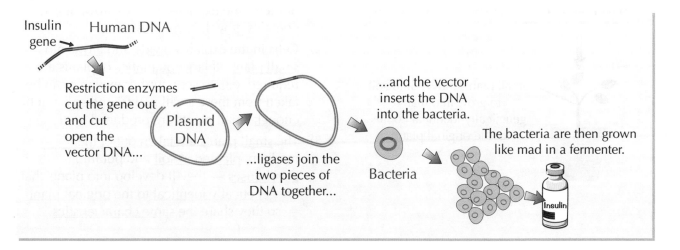

Insulin gene — Human DNA

Restriction enzymes cut the gene out and cut open the vector DNA...

Plasmid DNA

...ligases join the two pieces of DNA together...

...and the vector inserts the DNA into the bacteria.

Bacteria

The bacteria are then grown like mad in a fermenter.

Insulin

Genetic Engineering and Cloning Plants

You can use <u>genetic engineering</u> to produce plants with <u>desirable characteristics</u>, or you can use <u>cloning</u> to grow more of plants that already have desirable characteristics. Either way you can grow more food...

Genetically Modified Plants Can Improve Food Production

1) Crops can be <u>genetically modified</u> to increase <u>food production</u> in lots of different ways — one is to make them <u>resistant to insects</u>, another is to make them resistant to <u>herbicides</u> (chemicals that kill plants).

2) Making crops <u>insect-resistant</u> means farmers don't have to <u>spray as many pesticides</u> (see page 145) — so <u>wildlife</u> that doesn't eat the crop <u>isn't harmed</u>. It also <u>increases</u> crop <u>yield</u>, making more <u>food</u>.

3) Making crops <u>herbicide-resistant</u> means farmers can <u>spray</u> their crops to <u>kill weeds</u>, <u>without affecting</u> the <u>crop</u> itself. This can also increase crop yield.

4) There are concerns about growing genetically modified crops though. One is that <u>transplanted genes</u> may get out into the <u>environment</u>. For example, a herbicide resistance gene may be picked up by weeds, creating a new 'superweed' variety. Another concern is that genetically modified crops could adversely affect <u>food chains</u> — or even <u>human health</u>.

5) Some people are against <u>genetic engineering</u> altogether — they <u>worry</u> that changing an organism's genes might create unforeseen <u>problems</u> — which could then get passed on to <u>future generations</u>.

Micropropagation is Used to Clone Plants

Plants can be cloned from existing plants using a technique called <u>micropropagation</u> (tissue culture):

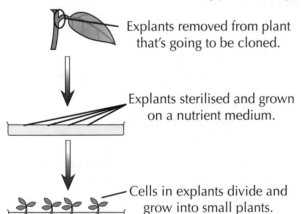

Explants removed from plant that's going to be cloned.

Explants sterilised and grown on a nutrient medium.

Cells in explants divide and grow into small plants.

Small plants moved into soil to grow into many genetically identical copies of the original plant.

1) A plant with <u>desirable characteristics</u> (e.g. large fruit or pretty flowers) is selected to be <u>cloned</u>. Small pieces (called <u>explants</u>) are taken from the <u>tips of the stems</u> and the <u>side shoots</u> of this plant.

2) The explants are <u>sterilised</u> to kill any <u>microorganisms</u>.

3) The explants are then grown <u>in vitro</u> — they're placed in a <u>petri dish</u> containing a <u>nutrient medium</u>. The medium has all the nutrients the explants need to grow. It also contains <u>growth hormones</u>.

4) Cells in the explants <u>divide</u> and <u>grow</u> into a <u>small plant</u>. If <u>large quantities</u> of plants are required (e.g. to sell), further explants can be taken from these small plants, and so on until <u>enough</u> small plants are produced.

5) The <u>small plants</u> are taken out of the medium, <u>planted in soil</u> and put into <u>glasshouses</u> — they'll develop into plants that are <u>genetically identical</u> to the <u>original plant</u> — so they share the <u>same characteristics</u>.

Paper 2

Paper 2

Cloning Animals

It's not just plants that can be cloned — <u>animals</u> can be <u>cloned</u> too. So if you have a particular favourite sheep, it's possible to create another one just like it. Keep reading to find out how...

Cloning a **Mammal** is Done by **Transplanting** a **Cell Nucleus**

The <u>first mammal</u> to be successfully cloned from a <u>mature (adult) cell</u> was a sheep called "Dolly" in 1996. This is the method that was used to produce Dolly:

1) The <u>nucleus</u> of a sheep's <u>egg cell</u> was removed, creating an <u>enucleated cell</u> (i.e. a cell without a nucleus).

2) A <u>diploid</u> nucleus (with a full set of paired chromosomes — see page 92) was <u>inserted</u> in its place. This was a nucleus from a mature udder cell of a <u>different sheep</u>.

3) The cell was <u>stimulated</u> (by an electric shock) so that it started <u>dividing by mitosis</u>, as if it was a normal <u>fertilised egg</u>.

4) The dividing cell was <u>implanted</u> into the <u>uterus</u> of another sheep to develop until it was ready to be born.

5) The result was <u>Dolly</u>, a <u>clone</u> of the sheep that the <u>udder cell</u> came from.

<u>Other animals</u> can also be cloned using this method.

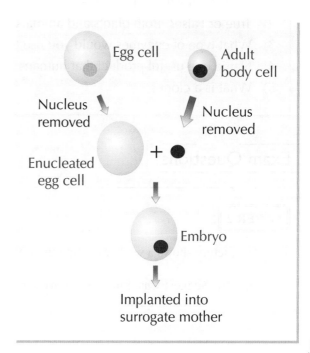

Egg cell

Adult body cell

Nucleus removed

Nucleus removed

Enucleated egg cell

Embryo

Implanted into surrogate mother

Cloned **Transgenic Animals** Can Produce **Human Proteins**

1) <u>Cows</u> and <u>sheep</u> make <u>protein</u> naturally in their milk. By transferring human genes into the cells of these animals, researchers have managed to get them to produce useful <u>human proteins</u> in their milk.

2) For example, they can produce <u>human antibodies</u> that can be used in therapy for illnesses like <u>arthritis</u>, some types of <u>cancer</u> and <u>multiple sclerosis</u>.

3) Transgenic <u>chickens</u> have also been engineered to produce human proteins in <u>egg white</u>.

4) These transgenic animals can then be <u>cloned</u> so that the useful genetic characteristic is <u>passed on</u> — this doesn't always happen with <u>breeding</u>.

Remember that genetic engineering and cloning are different things...

...though transgenic animals can be cloned. Look back to p.153 for a reminder of what 'transgenic' means.

Warm-Up & Exam Questions

Would you believe it, these are the last warm-up and exam questions in the book — not including the practice papers that is. Forget about them for now though and enjoy working your way through these.

Warm-Up Questions

1) How is selective breeding done?
2) True or False? Both plants and animals can be selectively bred.
3) What type of enzymes would you use to recognise and cut specific DNA sequences?
4) Name one useful product that humans have genetically modified bacteria to produce.
5) What is a clone?

Exam Questions

PAPER 2

1   The picture shows a worker treating the water at a fish farm.

   (a) (i) Suggest what must be removed from the water to maintain
             the water quality.

                                                                        [1 mark]

        (ii) Name **one** other factor that needs to be monitored
             to make sure the water quality is maintained.

                                                                        [1 mark]

   (b) Suggest why the fish tanks are covered over.

                                                                        [1 mark]

   (c) Explain what intraspecific predation is and give **one** way in which it can be avoided on a fish farm.

                                                                        [2 marks]

   (d) Name the process a fish farmer could use to produce fish
        with more desirable characteristics.

                                                                        [1 mark]

   (e) Fish can be farmed in cages in the sea or in indoor tanks. Describe an investigation
        to find out which of these methods results in the highest growth rate of fish.

                                                                        [6 marks]

2   The characteristics of two varieties of wheat plants are shown in the table below.

Variety	Grain yield	Resistance to bad weather
Tall stems	High	Low
Dwarf stems	Low	High

Describe how selective breeding could be used to create a wheat plant with a high grain yield
and high resistance to bad weather.

                                                                        [3 marks]

Exam Questions

3 Dolly the sheep was cloned by transplanting a cell nucleus.

(a) Which of the following describes the process used to clone Dolly?

◻ **A** A haploid nucleus from a sheep egg cell was inserted into an enucleated mature udder cell of the same sheep.

◻ **B** A diploid nucleus from a mature sheep udder cell was inserted into an enucleated egg cell of the same sheep.

◻ **C** A haploid nucleus from a sheep egg cell was inserted into an enucleated mature udder cell of a different sheep.

◻ **D** A diploid nucleus from a mature sheep udder cell was inserted into an enucleated egg cell of a different sheep.

[1 mark]

(b) (i) Plants can also be cloned. Describe how plants are cloned using micropropagation.

[4 marks]

(ii) Explain why micropropagation is beneficial for commercial farmers.

[1 mark]

4 Read the article below about GM crops and answer the questions that follow.

Recently some farmers took part in crop trials to see what effects growing herbicide-resistant GM crops might have on wildlife.
They used four kinds of crops in the trials. In each case, the farmer split one of their normal fields in half. They then grew a 'normal' crop
5 in one half and its GM equivalent in the other. With the GM crops, the farmers followed instructions about how much of which herbicides to use, and when to apply them. They applied herbicides to the 'normal' crop as they usually would. As the crops grew, the researchers monitored the populations of insects, slugs, spiders and other wildlife in each
10 environment.

The researchers found that with three kinds of crops, growing normal crops was better for wildlife — they found more butterflies and bees on the normal crops. With the fourth crop, the opposite seemed to be true — there were slightly more butterflies and bees around the GM crops.

a) i) Suggest why each field was divided in half rather than choosing separate fields for normal and GM crops (lines 3 and 4).

[2 marks]

ii) Suggest **one** thing the researchers may have done to improve the reliability of the trial.

[1 mark]

b) Some people are worried that growing GM crops will reduce the variety of wildlife in the environment. Do you think the results of the trial support this concern? Explain your answer.

[1 mark]

Revision Summary for Section 9

And that's the final section finished. Award yourself a gold star and take a look at these beautiful questions.

- Try these questions and <u>tick off each one</u> when you <u>get it right</u>.
- When you've done <u>all the questions</u> for a topic and are <u>completely happy</u> with it, tick off the topic.

Increasing Crop Yields (p.144-145) ☑

1) How can farmers create the ideal conditions for photosynthesis inside a glasshouse? ☑
2) Describe how biological control reduces pest numbers. ☑
3) Give one advantage and one disadvantage of using biological control instead of pesticides. ☑

Bacteria, Yoghurt, Yeast and Bread (p.146-149) ☑

4) Describe the process of making yoghurt. Don't forget to name the bacteria involved. ☑
5) Describe how yeast is used to make bread rise. ☑
6) Describe an experiment to measure carbon dioxide production by yeast during anaerobic respiration. ☑

Selective Breeding (p.151) ☑

7) What is selective breeding? ☑
8) Give three examples of the use of selective breeding. ☑

Fish Farming (p.152) ☑

9) Describe how fish farms reduce the following:
   a) interspecific predation,
   b) disease. ☑
10) What is interspecific predation? ☑
11) Why is feeding carefully controlled in fish farms? ☑

Genetic Engineering and Cloning (p.153-155) ☑

12) Describe the function of:
   a) a restriction enzyme,
   b) a ligase. ☑
13) What is a vector? ☑
14) Outline the important stages of genetically engineering a bacterium to produce the human insulin gene. ☑
15) What is a transgenic organism? ☑
16) Describe one way plants can be genetically modified to help improve food production. ☑
17) Give an advantage of producing cloned plants. ☑
18) Describe the process of cloning an animal from a mature cell (e.g. cloning a sheep). ☑
19) Describe how cloned transgenic animals can be used to produce human proteins. ☑

Experimental Know-How

Scientists need to know how to <u>plan</u> and <u>carry out scientific experiments</u>. Unfortunately, the examiners think <u>you</u> should be able to do the same. But don't worry — that's what this section's all about.

You Might Get Asked Questions on **Reliability** and **Validity**

1) <u>RELIABLE results</u> come from <u>experiments</u> that give the <u>same data</u>:

> - each time the experiment is <u>repeated</u> (by you),
> - each time the experiment is <u>reproduced</u> by <u>other scientists</u>.

2) <u>VALID results</u> are both <u>reliable</u> AND come from <u>experiments</u> that were designed to be a <u>fair test</u>.

In the exam, you could be asked to suggest ways to <u>improve</u> the <u>reliability</u> or <u>validity</u> of some <u>experimental results</u>. If so, there are a couple of things to think about:

Controlling Variables Improves **Validity**

1) A variable is something that has the potential to <u>change</u>, e.g. temperature.
   In a lab experiment you usually <u>change one variable</u> and <u>measure</u> how it affects <u>another variable</u>.

> <u>Example</u>: you might change <u>only</u> the temperature of an enzyme-controlled reaction and measure how it affects the rate of reaction.

2) To make it a <u>fair test</u>, <u>everything else</u> that could affect the results should <u>stay the same</u> — otherwise you can't tell if the thing you're changing is causing the results or not.

> <u>Example continued</u>: you need to keep the pH the same, otherwise you won't know if any change in the rate of reaction is caused by the change in temperature, or the change in pH.

3) The variable you <u>CHANGE</u> is called the <u>INDEPENDENT</u> variable.
4) The variable you <u>MEASURE</u> is called the <u>DEPENDENT</u> variable.
5) The variables that you <u>KEEP THE SAME</u> are called <u>CONTROL</u> variables.

> <u>Example continued</u>:
> Independent variable = temperature
> Dependent variable = rate of reaction
> Control variables = pH, volume of reactants, concentration of reactants, etc.

6) Because you can't always control all the variables, you often need to use a <u>CONTROL EXPERIMENT</u> — an experiment that's kept under the <u>same conditions</u> as the rest of the investigation, but doesn't have anything done to it. This is so that you can see what happens when you don't change anything at all.

Carrying Out Repeats Improves **Reliability**

1) To improve reliability you need to <u>repeat</u> any measurements you make and calculate the <u>mean</u> (average).
2) You need to repeat each measurement at least <u>three times</u>.

Getting reliable and valid results is very important

An exam question might <u>describe an experiment</u>, then ask <u>you to suggest</u> what variables need to be controlled. For example, you know that <u>enzymes</u> are affected by <u>temperature</u> and <u>pH</u>, so these variables need to be kept constant (providing you're not investigating one of them). You might also need to say <u>how</u> to control them, e.g. you could control temperature using a <u>water bath</u>.

More Experimental Know-How

You Might Have to **Suggest Ways** to Make an **Experiment Safer**

1) It's important that experiments are safe. If you're asked to suggest ways to make an experiment safer, you'll first need to identify what the <u>potential hazards</u> might be. Hazards include things like:

- <u>Microorganisms</u>, e.g. some bacteria can make you ill.
- <u>Chemicals</u>, e.g. hydrochloric acid can burn your skin and alcohols catch fire easily.
- <u>Fire</u>, e.g. an unattended Bunsen burner is a fire hazard.
- <u>Electricity</u>, e.g. faulty electrical equipment could give you a shock.

> You can find out about potential hazards by looking in textbooks, doing some internet research, or asking your teacher.

2) Then you'll need to suggest ways of <u>reducing</u> the <u>risks</u> involved with the hazard, e.g.

- If you're working with <u>hydrochloric acid</u>, always wear gloves and safety goggles. This will reduce the risk of the acid coming into contact with your skin and eyes.
- If you're using a <u>Bunsen burner</u>, stand it on a heat proof mat. This will reduce the risk of starting a fire.

You Could be Asked About **Accuracy**...

1) It's important that results are <u>accurate</u>. Accurate results are those that are <u>really close</u> to the <u>true answer</u>.
2) The accuracy of your results usually depends on your <u>method</u>.

> E.g. say you wanted to measure the <u>rate</u> of an <u>enzyme-controlled reaction</u> that releases a <u>gas</u> as a product. The rate of the reaction would be the <u>amount of gas produced per unit time</u>. You could <u>estimate</u> how much gas is produced by <u>counting</u> the number of <u>bubbles</u> that are released. But the bubbles could be <u>different sizes</u>, and if they're produced really quickly you might <u>miss some</u> when counting. It would be more accurate to <u>collect the gas</u> (e.g. in a gas cylinder) and <u>measure</u> its <u>volume</u>.

To make sure your results are as <u>accurate</u> as possible, you need to make sure you're measuring the <u>right thing</u> and that you <u>don't miss</u> anything or <u>include</u> anything that shouldn't be included in the measurements.

> E.g. if you want to know the <u>length</u> of a <u>potato chip</u>, you need to <u>start measuring</u> from '<u>0 cm</u>' on the ruler, <u>not</u> the <u>very end</u> of the ruler (or your measurement will be a few mm too short).

...And **Precision**

Results also need to be <u>precise</u>. Precise results are the ones where the data is <u>all really close</u> to the <u>mean</u> (average) of your repeated results (i.e. not spread out).

> Sometimes, results are described as precise if they've been taken using sensitive instruments that can measure in small increments, e.g. using a ruler with a millimetre scale gives more precise data than a ruler with a scale in centimetres.

Repeat	Data set 1	Data set 2
1	12	11
2	14	17
3	13	14
Mean	13	14

Data set 1 is more precise than data set 2.

Safety first — goggles on before you read this book...

You might be asked to <u>describe</u> how you'd carry out your <u>own experiment</u> in the exam. All this stuff about accuracy and what not will apply then too. So make sure you learn it and write it down.

Sampling and Ethics

You need to be able to carry out <u>sampling</u> that'll give you <u>non-biased results</u>. First up <u>why</u>, then <u>how</u>...

Sampling Should be **Random**

1) When you're investigating a population, it's generally <u>not possible</u> to study <u>every single organism</u> in the population. This means that you need to take <u>samples</u> of the population you're interested in.

2) The sample data will be used to <u>draw conclusions</u> about the <u>whole</u> population, so it's important that it <u>accurately</u> represents the <u>whole population</u>.

If a sample doesn't represent the population as a whole, it's said to be biased.

3) To make sure a sample represents the population, it should be <u>random</u>.

Organisms Should Be Sampled At **Random Sites** in an Area

1) If you're interested in the <u>distribution</u> of an organism in an area, or its <u>population size</u>, you can take population samples in the area you're interested in using <u>quadrats</u> or <u>transects</u> (see p.127-128).

2) If you only take samples from <u>one part</u> of the area, your results will be <u>biased</u> — they may not give an <u>accurate representation</u> of the <u>whole area</u>.

3) To make sure that your sampling isn't biased, you need to use a method of <u>choosing sampling sites</u> in which every site has an <u>equal chance</u> of being chosen. For example:

> If you're looking at plant species in a field...
> 1) <u>Divide</u> the field into a <u>grid</u>.
> 2) <u>Label the grid</u> along the bottom and up the side with numbers.
> 3) Use a <u>random number generator</u> (on a computer or calculator) to select coordinates, e.g. (2,6).
> 4) Take your samples at these coordinates.
>
> Non-random sampling
> Only looks at a small part of the field.
>
> Random sampling
> Randomly selects squares from all over the field.

You Need to Think About **Ethical Issues** In Your Experiments

1) Any <u>organisms</u> involved in your investigations need to be treated <u>safely</u> and <u>ethically</u>.

2) <u>Animals</u> need to be treated <u>humanely</u> — they should be <u>handled carefully</u> and any wild animals captured for studying (e.g. during an investigation of the distribution of an organism) should be <u>returned to their original habitat</u>.

3) Any animals kept in the lab should also be <u>cared for</u> in a humane way, e.g. they should not be kept in <u>overcrowded conditions</u>.

4) If you are carrying out an experiment involving other <u>students</u> (e.g. investigating the effect of exercise on breathing rate), they should not be forced to participate <u>against their will</u> or feel <u>pressured</u> to take part.

Processing Data

Processing your data means doing some <u>calculations</u> with it to make it <u>more useful</u>.

You Should Be Able to Identify **Anomalous Results**

1) Most results vary a bit, but any that are <u>totally different</u> are called <u>anomalous results</u>.

2) They're <u>caused</u> by <u>human errors</u>, e.g. by a mistake made when measuring or by not setting up a piece of equipment properly.

3) You could be asked to <u>identify</u> an anomalous result in the exam and suggest what <u>caused</u> it — just look for a result that <u>doesn't fit in</u> with the rest (e.g. it's <u>too high</u> or <u>too low</u>) then try to figure out what could have <u>gone wrong</u> with the experiment to have caused it.

4) If you're calculating an <u>average</u>, you can <u>ignore</u> any anomalous results.

You Might Have to **Process Your Data**

1) When you've done repeats of an experiment you should always calculate the <u>mean</u> (a type of average). To do this <u>add together</u> all the data values and <u>divide</u> by the total number of values in the sample.

2) You might also need to calculate the <u>range</u> (how spread out the data is). To do this find the <u>largest</u> number and <u>subtract</u> the <u>smallest</u> number from it.

Ignore anomalous results when calculating these.

Example: The results of an experiment to find the volume of gas produced in an enzyme-controlled reaction are shown below. Calculate the mean volume and the range.

Repeat 1 (cm³)	Repeat 2 (cm³)	Repeat 3 (cm³)	Mean (cm³)	Range (cm³)
28	37	32	(28 + 37 + 32) ÷ 3 = 32	37 − 28 = 9

3) You might also need to calculate the <u>median</u> or <u>mode</u> (two more types of average). To calculate the <u>median</u>, put all your data in <u>numerical order</u> — the median is the <u>middle value</u>. The number that appears <u>most often</u> in a data set is the <u>mode</u>.

If you have an even number of values, the median is halfway between the middle two values.

E.g. If you have the data set: 1 2 1 1 3 4 2
The <u>median</u> is: 1 1 1 <u>2</u> 2 3 4. The <u>mode</u> is <u>1</u> because 1 appears most often.

EXAM TIP

Don't forget your calculator...

In the exam you could be given some <u>data</u> and be expected to <u>process it</u> in some way. Even if it looks easy enough to do in your head, it's always worth checking on a calculator just to be sure.

Drawing Graphs

Once you've processed your data, e.g. by calculating the mean, you can present your results in a nice chart or graph. This will help you to spot any patterns in your data.

Bar Charts can be Used to Show Different Types of Data

Bar charts are used to display:

1) Categoric data — data that comes in distinct categories, e.g. flower colour, blood group.

2) Discrete data — data that can be counted in chunks, where there's no in-between value, e.g. number of bacteria is discrete because you can't have half a bacterium.

3) Continuous data — numerical data that can have any value in a range, e.g. length, volume, temperature.

There are some golden rules you need to follow for drawing bar charts:

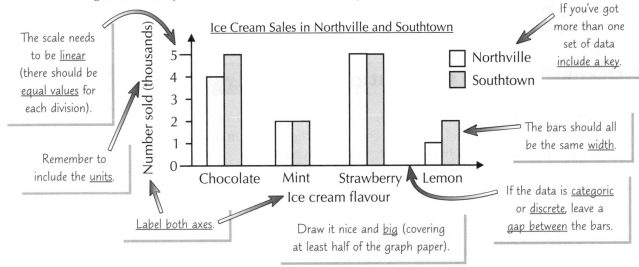

Graphs can be Used to Plot Continuous Data

1) If both variables are continuous you should use a graph to display the data.

2) Here are the rules for plotting points on a graph:

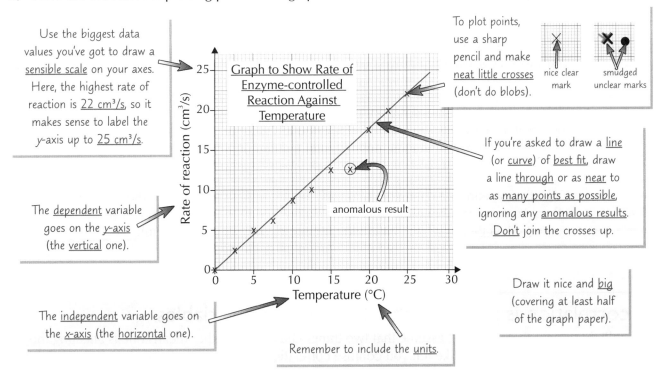

Describing Experiments

Interpreting Results

Graphs aren't just fun to plot, they're also really useful for showing <u>trends</u> in your data.

You Need to be Able to **Interpret** Graphs

1) A graph is used to show the <u>relationship</u> between two variables — you need to be able to look at a graph and <u>describe</u> this relationship.

> *A relationship is directly proportional if one variable increases at the same rate as the other variable. E.g. if one variable doubles, the other also doubles. This is only true if the line is straight and goes through the origin (O,O).*

> <u>Example</u>: The graph on the previous page shows that as <u>temperature increases</u>, <u>so does rate of reaction</u>.

2) You also need to be able to <u>read information</u> off a graph. In the example on the previous page, to find what the rate of reaction was at <u>11 °C</u>, you'd draw a <u>vertical line up</u> to the graph line from the *x*-axis at 11 °C and a <u>horizontal line across</u> to the *y*-axis. This would tell you that the rate of reaction at 11 °C was around <u>9.7 cm³/s</u>.

Graphs Show the **Correlation** Between Two Variables

1) You can get <u>three</u> types of <u>correlation</u> (relationship) between variables:

2) Just because there's correlation, it doesn't mean the change in one variable is <u>causing</u> the change in the other — there might be <u>other factors</u> involved.

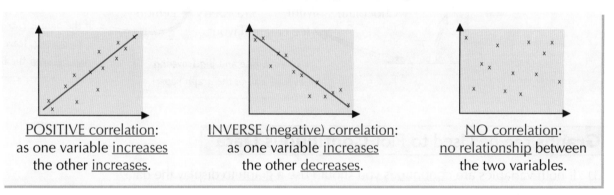

<u>POSITIVE correlation</u>: as one variable <u>increases</u> the other <u>increases</u>.

<u>INVERSE (negative) correlation</u>: as one variable <u>increases</u> the other <u>decreases</u>.

<u>NO correlation</u>: <u>no relationship</u> between the two variables.

3) There are three possible reasons for a correlation:

- <u>CHANCE</u>: It might seem strange, but two things can show a correlation purely due to <u>chance</u>.

- <u>LINKED BY A 3RD VARIABLE</u>: A lot of the time it may <u>look</u> as if a change in one variable is causing a change in the other, but it <u>isn't</u> — a <u>third variable links</u> the two things.

- <u>CAUSE</u>: Sometimes a change in one variable does <u>cause</u> a change in the other. You can only conclude that a correlation is due to cause when you've <u>controlled all the variables</u> that could, just could, be affecting the result.

A correlation is a relationship between two variables

It's <u>really important</u> that you don't assume that two things changing together means one is affecting the other — examiners really won't like it if you confuse <u>correlation</u> with <u>causation</u>, so always stop and think.

Planning Experiments

In the exam, you could be asked to plan or describe how you'd carry out an experiment. It might be one you've already come across or you might be asked to come up with an experiment of your own.

You Need to Be Able to Plan a **Good Experiment**

Here are some general tips on what to include when planning an experiment:

1) Say what you're measuring (i.e. what the dependent variable is going to be).

2) Say what you're changing (i.e. what the independent variable is going to be) and describe how you're going to change it.

3) Describe the method and the apparatus you'd use (e.g. to measure the variables).

4) Describe what variables you're keeping constant — and how you're going to do it.

5) Say that you need to repeat the experiment at least three times, to make the results more reliable.

6) Say whether you're using a control or not.

> Even if you can't remember all the details of an experimental method you've learned about, you could still get marks for describing things like the independent and dependent variables.

Here's an idea of the sort of thing you might be asked in the exam and what you might write as an answer...

Exam-style Question:

1   Describe an investigation to find out what effect temperature has on the rate of photosynthesis in Canadian pondweed.   (6 marks)

Example Answer:

Set up a test tube containing a measured amount of Canadian pondweed, water and sodium hydrogencarbonate. Connect the test tube up to a capillary tube containing water and a syringe, then place it in a water bath in front of a source of white light.

Leave the pondweed to photosynthesise for a set amount of time. As it photosynthesises, the oxygen released will collect in the capillary tube. At the end of the experiment, use the syringe to draw the gas bubble in the tube up alongside a ruler and measure the length of the gas bubble. This is proportional to the volume of O_2 produced. Repeat the experiment with the water bath set to different temperatures (e.g. 10 °C, 20 °C, 30 °C and 40 °C).

The pondweed should be left to photosynthesise for the same amount of time at each temperature (monitored using a stopwatch). The test tubes should also be set up the same distance away from the light source (measured using a ruler) and the same mass of pondweed should be used in each test tube (measured using a balance).

A control should also be set up at each temperature. This should be a test tube containing water and boiled pondweed (so that it can't photosynthesise).

Repeat the experiment three times at each temperature. Use the results to find an average rate of photosynthesis at each temperature. This will make the results more reliable.

Experiments Test **Hypotheses**

1) A hypothesis is a possible explanation for something that you've observed.

2) You can use experiments to test whether a hypothesis might be right or not. This involves making a prediction based on the hypothesis and testing it by gathering evidence (i.e. data) from investigations. If evidence from experiments backs up a prediction, you're a step closer to figuring out if the hypothesis is true.

Conclusions

Once you've carried out an experiment and processed your data, it's time to work out <u>what it shows</u>.

You Can **Only Conclude** What the Data Shows and **NO MORE**

1) Drawing conclusions might seem pretty straightforward — you just <u>look at your data</u> and <u>say what pattern or relationship you see</u> between the dependent and independent variables.

> The table below shows the heights of pea plant seedlings grown for three weeks with <u>different fertilisers</u>.
>
> | Fertiliser | Mean growth / mm |
> |:---:|:---:|
> | A | 13.5 |
> | B | 19.5 |
> | No fertiliser | 5.5 |
>
> <u>CONCLUSION</u>:
> Fertiliser <u>B</u> makes <u>pea plant</u> seedlings grow taller over a <u>three week</u> period than fertiliser A.

2) But you've got to be really careful that your conclusion <u>matches the data</u> you've got and <u>doesn't go any further</u>.

> You <u>can't</u> conclude that fertiliser B makes <u>any other type of plant</u> grow taller than fertiliser A — the results could be totally different.

3) You also need to be able to <u>use your results</u> to <u>justify your conclusion</u> (i.e. back up your conclusion with some specific data).

> Over the three week period, fertiliser B made the pea plants grow <u>6 mm more</u> on average than fertiliser A.

4) When writing a conclusion you need to <u>refer back</u> to the original hypothesis and say whether the data <u>supports it</u> or not:

> The <u>hypothesis</u> for this experiment might have been that adding fertiliser would <u>increase the growth</u> of plants because it would provide plants with <u>nutrients</u>. The <u>prediction</u> may have been that fertiliser B contained more nutrients and so would <u>increase growth more</u> than fertiliser A. If so, the data <u>increases confidence</u> in the hypothesis.

Your conclusions have to be consistent with your evidence

That means you have to be <u>careful</u> you're only writing things based on your experiment's results — you need to be able to <u>back up</u> anything you say using your data. And remember, your data might not match the original hypothesis. That's fine — just point this out in your <u>conclusion</u>.

Evaluations

Hurrah! The end of another investigation. Well, now you have to work out all the things you did <u>wrong</u>. That's what <u>evaluations</u> are all about I'm afraid. Best get cracking with this page...

Evaluations — Describe **How** Investigations Could be **Improved**

An evaluation is a <u>critical analysis</u> of the whole investigation.

1) You should comment on the <u>method</u> — was it <u>valid</u>?
   Did you control all the other variables to make it a <u>fair test</u>?

2) Comment on the <u>quality</u> of the <u>results</u> — was there <u>enough evidence</u> to reach a valid <u>conclusion</u>? Were the results <u>reliable</u>, <u>valid</u>, <u>accurate</u> and <u>precise</u>?

3) Were there any <u>anomalous</u> results? If there were <u>none</u> then <u>say so</u>.
   If there were any, try to <u>explain</u> them — were they caused by <u>errors</u> in measurement?
   Were there any other <u>variables</u> that could have <u>affected</u> the results?

4) All this analysis will allow you to say how <u>confident</u> you are that your conclusion is <u>right</u>.

5) Then you can suggest any <u>changes</u> to the <u>method</u> that would <u>improve</u> the quality of the results, so that you could have <u>more confidence</u> in your conclusion. For example, you might suggest <u>changing</u> the way you controlled a variable, or <u>increasing</u> the number of <u>measurements</u> you took. Taking more measurements at <u>narrower intervals</u> could give you a <u>more accurate result</u>. For example:

> <u>Enzymes</u> have an <u>optimum temperature</u> (a temperature at which they <u>work best</u>). Say you do an experiment to find an enzyme's optimum temperature and take measurements at 10 °C, 20 °C, 30 °C, 40 °C and 50 °C. The results of this experiment tell you the optimum is <u>40 °C</u>. You could then <u>repeat</u> the experiment, taking <u>more measurements around 40 °C</u> to get a <u>more accurate</u> value for the optimum.

6) You could also make more <u>predictions</u> based on your conclusion, then <u>further experiments</u> could be carried out to test them.

When suggesting improvements to the investigation, always make sure that you say why you think this would make the results better.

Always look for ways to improve your investigations

Around <u>20% of the available marks</u> in the exam will come from being able to describe experiments, and analysing and evaluating data and methods in an appropriate way. So, make sure you're happy with everything in this section. Best of luck.

Candidate Surname		Candidate Forename(s)	

Centre Number	Candidate Number

Edexcel
International GCSE

Biology
Paper 1B

Practice Paper
Time allowed: 2 hours

You must have:
- A ruler.
- A calculator.

Total marks:

Instructions to candidates
- Use **black** ink to write your answers.
- Write your name and other details in the spaces provided above.
- Answer **all** questions in the spaces provided.
- In calculations, show clearly how you worked out your answers.
- You will need to answer some questions by placing a cross in a box, like this: ☒
  To change your answer, draw a line through the box like this: ☒
  Then mark your new answer as normal.

Information for candidates
- The marks available are given in brackets at the end of each question.
- There are 110 marks available for this paper.

Advice for candidates
- Read all the questions carefully.
- Write your answers as clearly and neatly as possible.
- Keep in mind how much time you have left.

Answer **all** questions

1   The diagram below shows the human male and female reproductive systems.

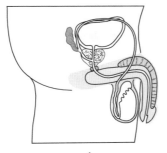 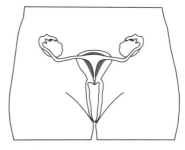

male
reproductive system

female
reproductive system

(a)   Cells in the reproductive systems undergo cell division to produce gametes.
Gametes contain half the usual number of chromosomes.

Sex cell sperm/egg

(i)   Give the word that describes cells that contain half the usual number of chromosomes.

haploid cells ✓

[1]

(ii)   In humans, how many chromosomes does one gamete contain?

☐ **A** 12

☒ **B** 23 ✓

☐ **C** 32

☐ **D** 46

[1]

(iii)   Which of the following structures in the human male reproductive system is the site of gamete production?

☐ **A** vas deferens

☒ **B** testes ✓

☐ **C** urethra

☐ **D** erectile tissue

[1]

(b)   An embryo develops in the female reproductive system.
Describe how a human embryo is formed.

to form a zygote

After the sperm fuses with the egg, it starts ✓
to ~~gess ust~~ produce cells through mitosis. This
means that the embryo ~~keeps~~ *produces* ✓ ~~splittin~~ 2 daughter cells.

[3]

[Total 6 marks]

5 marks

Turn over ▶

2 Some pondweed was used to investigate how the amount of light available affects the rate of photosynthesis.

The apparatus that was used for this experiment is shown below.

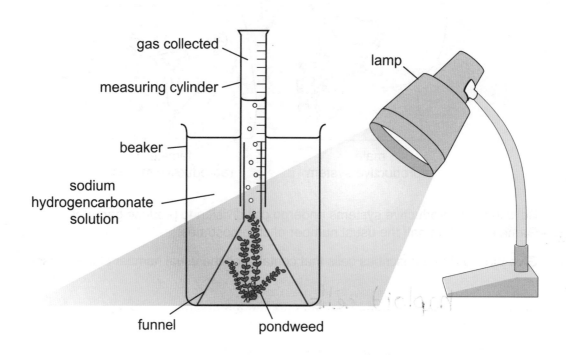

gas collected

measuring cylinder

lamp

beaker

sodium hydrogencarbonate solution

funnel

pondweed

(a) Name the gas that is being collected in the measuring cylinder.

Oxygen ✓

[1]

(b) Explain what would happen to the volume of gas collected if the investigation was repeated with the lamp turned off.

The volume of gas would decrease as light is needed ~~to~~ for photosynthesis to occur however ~~the~~ as there is less light less photosynthesis would occur so less CO_2 is produced ✓ [3]

(c) Sodium hydrogencarbonate dissolves in water and releases carbon dioxide.
Suggest why sodium hydrogencarbonate was added to the water in this experiment.

CO_2 is needed for photosynthesis
Sodium hydrogencarbonate was added to the water to ensure that ~~CO_2~~ is being produced not a limiting factor
If the sodium hydrogen carbonate turns yellow the concentra
tion of CO_2 has increased. [2]
~~is high~~
NOT NEEDED
0 marks

(d) Explain how temperature affects the rate of photosynthesis, and suggest how temperature could be controlled in the experiment.

Temperature can affect the rate of photosynthesis. As the temperature rises and gets closer to the optimum temperature of the enzymes the rate of photosynthesis increases. If the temperature gets too high or too low the enzymes will denature and the rate of photosynthesis will decrease. In this experiment a thermometer could be placed in the beaker to ensure the measure temperature stays the same and placing it in a water bath would keep the temperature constant. **[3]**

After the experiment was conducted, a leaf from the pondweed was tested for starch.

(e) (i) Which of the following is **not** a stage in testing a leaf for starch?

- [ ] **A** Boil the leaf to stop any chemical reactions happening.
- [X] **B** Dry the leaf in an oven to remove water.
- [ ] **C** Heat the leaf with ethanol to remove chlorophyll.
- [ ] **D** Add a few drops of iodine solution.

[1]

(ii) Would you expect the test to produce a positive result? Explain your answer.

Yes you would expect a positive result as photosynthesis produces glucose which plants store as starch.

[1]

[Total 11 marks]

9 marks

3   The diagram below shows nutrients being absorbed from the gut into the blood.

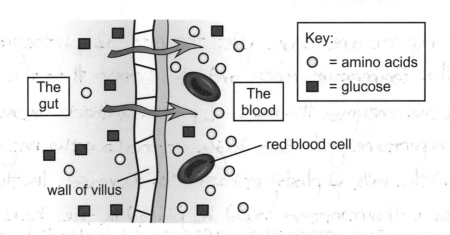

Key:
○ = amino acids
■ = glucose

The gut

The blood

red blood cell

wall of villus

(a)   Describe **three** ways that villi are adapted to absorb the products of digestion.

Villi have a very high surface area to volume ratio. This *which increases the rate of diffusion* allows for a very high conc. They also have a ~~large~~ good blood supply *due to having* with a lot of capillaries. Villi have microvilli *for a high concentration gradient* which have are 1 cell thick walls for a *short* ~~shortd~~ diffusion pathway.

[3]

(b)   The diagram shows glucose being absorbed into the blood by diffusion.
Describe how the amino acids are absorbed into the blood.

Amino acids are absorbed through active transport as they have to travel against a concentration gradient from an area of ~~high~~ *low* concentration *in the gut* to an area of high concentration in the ~~blood~~ blood.*

[2]

(c)   The diagram shows red blood cells in the blood.

(i)   State the function of red blood cells.

Red blood cells ~~are so~~ *carry* ~~transport~~ ~~blood~~ *oxygen* around the body.
improve ← *from our lungs*

[1]

✱ (ii)   Explain how red blood cells are adapted to their function.

Red blood cells do not have a nucleus, this allows for more space for haemoglobin to carry more oxygen. The concave shape of red blood cells allows for a much higher ~~surface~~ *surface area* to ~~volume ratio which~~ ~~surface area~~ that allows for a faster diffusion rate of oxygen and carbon dioxide.

[3]

[Total 9 marks]

They contain a large amount of haemoglobin which combines reversibly with oxygen to form oxyhaemoglobin

4   A student grew three plants in a windowsill tray. This is shown in Diagram 1.

He then put the plants in a cardboard box with a cut-out hole. This is shown in Diagram 2.

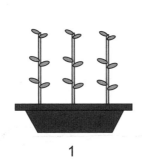 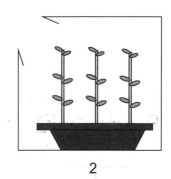

1   2

(a) (i)   Draw a diagram to show how you would expect the plants in the box to look after 3 days.

[1]

(ii)   Explain what caused the plants' response.

positive

The plant uses ~~phototropism~~ to grow towards ~~the~~ light from the box.
A growth harmone called auxin gathers in the
shaded part of the stem. The auxin stimulates cell *faster*
growth in the part of the stem in the shade. This
causes the plant to ~~grow and~~ bend away from
the shade and grow towards the light

[4]

(b)   Which of the following responses is shown by the plants in this experiment?

☒ **A**   positive phototropism

☐ **B**   negative phototropism

☐ **C**   positive geotropism

☐ **D**   negative geotropism

[1]

[Total 6 marks]

Turn over ▶

174

5   Cystic fibrosis is a genetic disorder caused by a recessive allele.

A couple have a baby boy. The doctor tells them that the baby has inherited cystic fibrosis. Neither parent shows signs of the disorder.

(a) (i)   In the space below, construct a diagram to show how the baby inherited cystic fibrosis.

Your diagram should show the genotypes of both parents, the genotypes of their gametes, and all the possible genotypes of their offspring.

Use **F** to represent the dominant allele and **f** to represent the recessive allele.

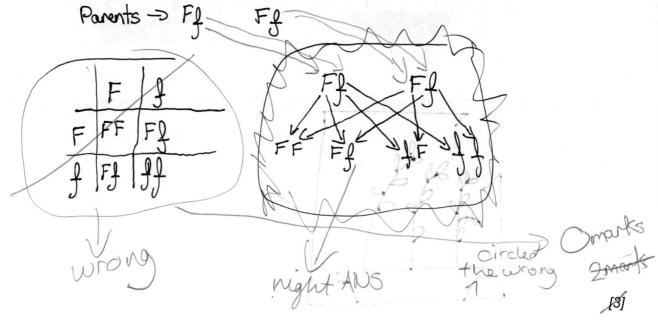

Parents → Ff   Ff

	F	f
F	FF	Ff
f	Ff	ff

wrong

right ANS

circled the wrong 1

0 marks

2 marks

[3]

(ii)   Is the baby homozygous or heterozygous for this condition?
Explain your answer.

The baby is homozygous because Cystic fibrosis is recessive so you must have 2 cystic fibrosis genotypes for it to be the phenotype

[1]

(b)   The doctor tells the parents that if they have another child, the fetus can be tested to see if it will have cystic fibrosis.

State the probability that the couple's next baby will have cystic fibrosis.

25%

[1]

The family pedigree below shows a family with a history of cystic fibrosis.

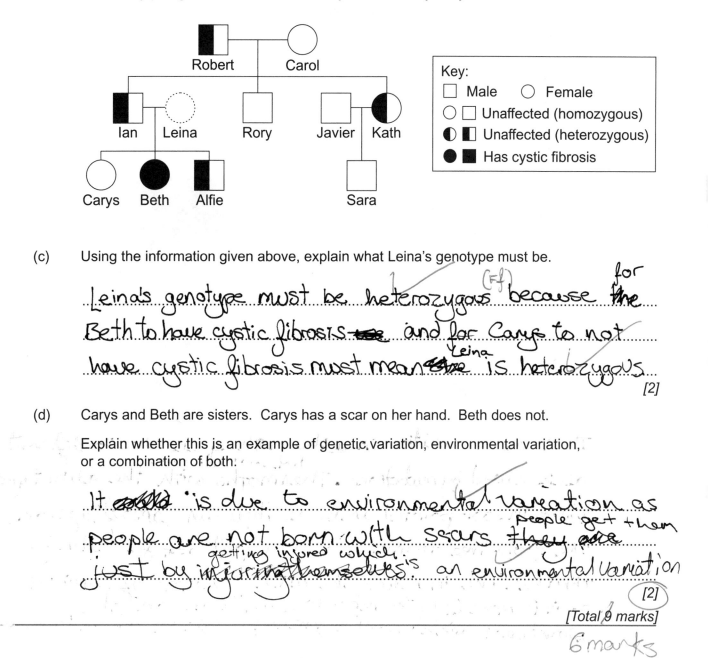

(c) Using the information given above, explain what Leina's genotype must be.

Leina's genotype must be heterozygous (Ff) because for
Beth to have cystic fibrosis and for Carys to not
have cystic fibrosis must mean Leina is heterozygous

[2]

(d) Carys and Beth are sisters. Carys has a scar on her hand. Beth does not.

Explain whether this is an example of genetic variation, environmental variation, or a combination of both.

It is due to environmental variation as
people are not born with scars they are people get them
just by injuring themselves getting injured which is an environmental variation

[2]

[Total 9 marks]

6 marks

Turn over ▶

6 The peppered moth is an insect that lives on the trunks of trees in Britain.
The moths are prey for birds such as thrushes.

The peppered moth exists in two varieties:

1. A light-coloured variety — they are
better camouflaged on tree trunks in
unpolluted areas.

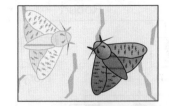

2. A dark-coloured variety — they are
better camouflaged on sooty
tree trunks in badly polluted areas.

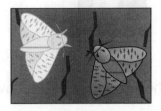

The dark variety of the moth was first recorded in the north of England in 1848.
It became increasingly common in polluted areas until the 1960s, when the number
of soot-covered trees declined because of the introduction of new laws.

(a) Using the idea of natural selection, explain why the dark variety of moth became more
common in soot-polluted areas.

There was a variation in ~~ex~~ the moth species due to different
alleles ~~caused~~ by mutations. The ~~moths~~ <u>dark coloured</u> moths <u>have</u> with the advantageous
allele in soot-polluted areas as they can camouflage on
the sooty tree trunks so they don't ~~kett~~ get eaten by
thrushes. This increases the moths chances of survival
so it is more likely to reproduce and pass on the [4]
advantageous allele. So the frequency of the allele increases.

The following bar charts show the percentages of dark- and light-coloured peppered moths in two different towns.

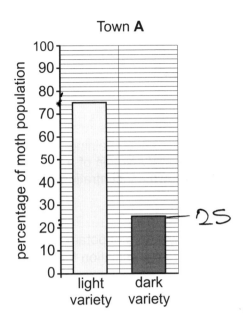

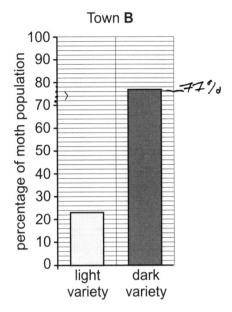

(b) State which town, **A** or **B**, is the most polluted. Give a reason for your answer.

B as there are more dark moths which prosper in ~~such~~ polluted areas

[1]

(c) Calculate the difference in percentage between the dark-coloured moth population in Town **A** and Town **B**. Show your working.

$$77 - 25 = 52\%$$

52 %

[2]

[Total 7 marks]

7   A student carried out an experiment to investigate osmosis.

The student cut cylinders out of potatoes and placed them into different concentrations of sugar solution, as shown in the diagram below.

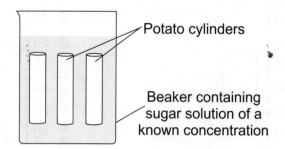

Potato cylinders

Beaker containing sugar solution of a known concentration

The student then measured the mass of the cylinders of potato before and after they had been placed in different concentrations of sugar solution for 20 minutes. The student's results are shown below.

Concentration of sugar solution (M)	Change in mass (g)			Mean change in mass (g)
	Potato cylinder 1	Potato cylinder 2	Potato cylinder 3	
0.0	+0.67	+0.65	+0.69	+0.67
0.2	+0.30	+0.31	+0.33	+0.31
0.4	+0.02	−0.02	+0.01	0
0.6	−0.27	−0.31	−0.25	−0.28
0.8	−0.48	−0.50	−0.47	−0.48
1.0	−0.71	−0.65	−0.72	−0.69
1.2	−0.78	−0.81	−0.82	−0.80

0.7

-1.5

-0.8

(a)   Calculate the mean change in mass in a 1.2 M sugar solution. Show your working.

$$\frac{(-0.78) + (-0.81) + (-0.82)}{3} = -0.80$$

.... −0.80 g

[2]

(b) Draw a graph of the concentration of sugar solution against the mean change in mass on the grid below. Use straight lines to join the points.

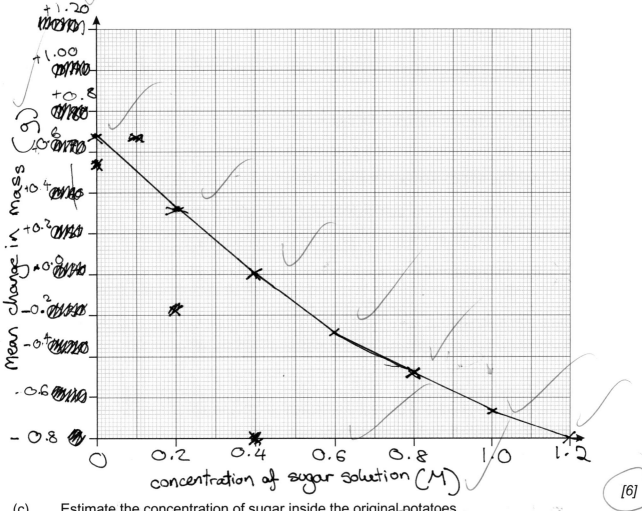

concentration of sugar solution (M)

Mean change in mass (g)

[6]

(c) Estimate the concentration of sugar inside the original potatoes. Explain your answer.

The concentration of sugar inside the original potatoes was around 0.4 M as there was no change in mass so no diffusion took place.

osmosis

[2]

(d) Suggest why the student used three potato cylinders in each concentration of sugar solution, and took a mean of the results.

To make his experiment more reliable

[1]

[Total 11 marks]

10 marks

Turn over ▶

8   The diagram below shows the amount of energy contained within an area of plants.
It shows how much energy from the plants is transferred to each trophic level in
a food chain.

plants	→	grasshoppers	→	mice	→	snakes
11 000 J		1100 J		130 J		12 J

(a) (i)   Plants are the producers in this food chain.

Which of the following statements describes a producer?

☐ **A**   The first consumer in the food chain.

☐ **B**   An organism that gets its food from other organisms.

☐ **C**   An organism that gets eaten by tertiary consumers.

☒ **D**   An organism that makes its own food using energy from the Sun.

[1]

(ii)   State how much energy is available to the tertiary consumers in this food chain.

.... 12J × 130J ....

[1]

(iii)   In the area, the population of bluebirds increases. The bluebirds feed on the grasshoppers,
causing the population of grasshoppers to decrease.

Suggest **one** way that the change in grasshopper population may affect the population of
another organism in this food chain. Explain your answer.

A decrease in the grasshopper population may
decrease the mouse population as they would have
less grasshoppers to feed on.

[2]

Four pyramids of biomass are shown below.

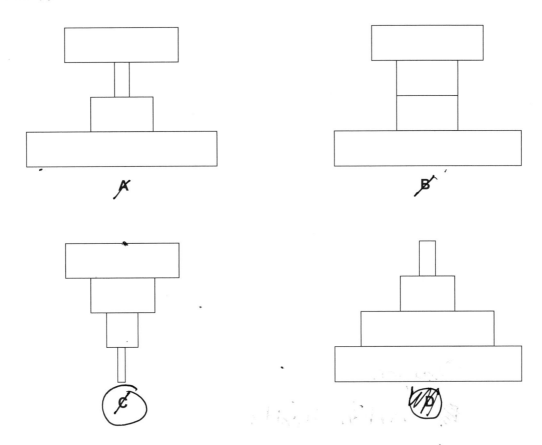

A   B

C   D

(b)   Explain which pyramid of biomass (**A**, **B**, **C** or **D**) represents this food chain.

~~[1]~~ C D Pyramid of biomass ~~B~~ represents this food chain
because
as the biomass of ~~grass~~ the organisms is the smallest and it ~~increases~~ decreases
as you go up the food chain .   [2]

(c)   Calculate the percentage of energy in the grasshoppers that is transferred to the mice.
Show your working.

$$\frac{130}{1100} \times 100 = 11.8$$

                                                            ✓

..............11.8.............. %
                                                            [2]

(d)   This food chain has four trophic levels.
Most food chains have no more than five trophic levels.

Suggest why the length of food chains is limited in this way.

As you go up the food chain the amount of
~~eat~~ energy transferred between trophic levels decreases so after 5
trophic levels there is too little energy transferred.
                                                            [2]

[Total 10 marks]

7 marks

Turn over ▶

182

9   The diagram below shows an alveolus and a blood capillary.

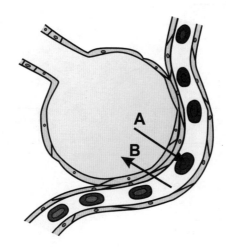

(a)   The arrows on the diagram show the net movement of two gases, **A** and **B**.

Name gases **A** and **B**.

Gas **A** ...Oxygen...

Gas **B** ... Carbon dioxide...

[2]

(b)   Explain **three** ways that alveoli are adapted for gas exchange.

~~Capill~~ Alveoli have a ~~circular~~ spherical shape to have a
high surface area to volume ~~see~~ ratio. Alveoli have a ~~two~~ lot of
capilaries for good blood supply for a high concentration
gradient. Alveoli walls are 1 cell thick to have a
short diffusion pathway.

[3]

(c)   Ventilation allows air to enter and leave the lungs.

Describe the process that results in air leaving the lungs.

The diaphragm relaxes causing it to move upwards.
The intercostal muscles relax which pulls in the ribcage. This
~~de~~ increases pressure in the lungs causing air to
be pushed out of the lungs.

[4]

[Total 9 marks]

✱ 10   Describe an investigation to find out if lettuces grown in a polythene tunnel have a faster growth rate than those grown outside.

I will change whether the lettuces are grown in a polythene tunnel or grown outside a polythene tunnel. I will use 10 lettuces per batch living inside and 10 lettuces living outside. I will use lettuces of the same species. I will measure their height and width each day for 2 weeks. I will use a ruler and I will measure in millimetres. I will water the plants 0.5L of water every 2 days and I will use insecticide once a week to stop insects from eating them. I will use the same fertiliser in the soil for both the lettuces in the polythene tunnel and outside the polythene tunnel.

[Total 6 marks]

11 Two students carried out an experiment to investigate the effects of different minerals on plant growth. Their teacher gave them three pea plants of the same species, all of a similar height. The method they used is described below.

> 1. Measure the height of the three pea plants.
> 2. Add a solution containing minerals to three beakers as follows:
>   Beaker A: solution high in magnesium and nitrates.
>   Beaker B: solution high in magnesium and low in nitrates.
>   Beaker C: solution low in magnesium and high in nitrates.
> 3. Place a pea plant in each of the beakers, A, B and C.
> 4. Leave the plants to grow for one week.
> 5. Measure the height of each of the plants at the end of the week.

The results of the experiment are shown below.

Beaker	Height at start (cm)	Height at end (cm)	Change in height (cm)
A	4	9	5
B	5	7	2
C	4	8	4

(a) Explain why the growth in beaker B was poor.

Because nitrates are needed in plants for *as they are used to make amino acids or protein* increased growth and since beaker B *the plant* had low nitrates it couldn't grow as much.

2 [3]

(b) Describe how you would expect the pea plant in beaker C, which was low in magnesium, to look at the end of the week. Explain your answer.

It should look pale as it wouldn't be able to produce chlorophyll in its chloroplasts

[2]

(c) State **two** factors that the students would have had to keep the same in each beaker to make the experiment a fair test.

1 Temperature ✓

2 Oxygen levels ✓

[2]

[Total 7 marks]

6 mark

12   A study collected data from a sample of male British doctors.
      It compared the death rate from coronary heart disease per 1000 men
      per year to the number of cigarettes smoked each day.

      The results are shown in the graph below.

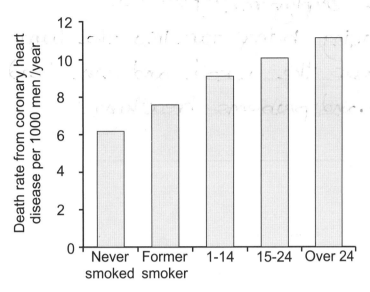

      Number of cigarettes smoked per day

(a) (i)   What conclusions can you draw from this graph?

The number of cigarettes smoked per day
is directly 'proportional to the deathrate of
coronary heart disease per 1000men/year. I know this
          who smoked 7-14 cigarettes
because a person when 8/1000 men per year die   a day
                    per year   per year
from coronary heart disease where as ~~12~~ 11/1000 men who
smoked over 24 cigarettes a day die from coronary heart disease per   [3]
year.

(ii) A scientist hypothesises that anyone who smokes is more likely to die from
      coronary heart disease.

      Suggest **one** change you could make to the study above to test this hypothesis.

~~Incude~~ Include women in the study.

      [1]

186

(b)   Describe and explain **two** effects of smoking on the lungs.

1 ~~Dame~~ Smoking damages the cilia in the trachea
so it increases the amount of mucus in the lungs and
causes ~~emphysema~~ emphysema bronchitis

2 Smoking brings ~~tar~~ smoke into the lungs which
damages the alveoli and can lead to ~~popcorn~~ emphysema
lungs ~~and problems breathing~~

[4]

[Total 8 marks]

8 marks

13   A student is investigating how his heart rate changes during and after exercise.
      He measures his heart rate using a portable heart rate monitor. He takes his
      resting heart rate then immediately runs around a running track for two minutes.
      Then he rests again. His results are shown on the graph below.

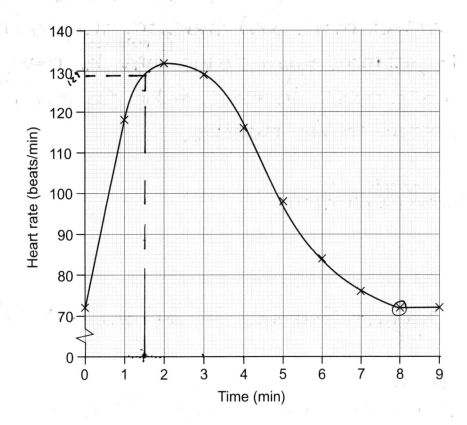

(a)   Give the independent variable in the student's experiment.

      Whether he is exercising

                                                                              [1]

(b)   Use the graph to estimate the student's heart rate after 90 seconds.

      129

                                                                              [1]

(c)   The student stopped running two minutes after taking his first heart rate measurement.
      How long did it take for his heart rate to return to normal after he stopped running?

      6 minutes

                                                                              [1]

188

(d)   Explain how the student's heart rate changes with exercise.

The students heart rate increases with exercise. This
is because ~~more~~ during exercise his muscles
contract more and therefore they need more oxygen.*
To get more oxygen to his ~~lungs~~ his ~~must~~ heart
rate must increase ~~so he~~ to pump blood
faster to his muscles

                                                                    more

* aerobic
  ~~for~~ respiration

                                                                    [5]

(e)   When the student first starts running he respires aerobically.

(i)   Write the word equation for aerobic respiration.

Oxygen + Glucose → Carbon Dioxide + Water (+ energy)

                                                                    [2]

(ii) Give **one** advantage of aerobic respiration over anaerobic respiration.

Aerobic respiration
        ~~It~~ releases more energy than anaerobic
respiration.

                                                                    [1]

                                                    [Total 11 marks]

                                            [Total for paper 110 marks]

                                                    95/110

                                                    86%

Practice Paper 1B

Candidate Surname		Candidate Forename(s)	

Centre Number	Candidate Number

Edexcel
International GCSE

Biology
Paper 2B

Practice Paper
Time allowed: 1 hour 15 minutes

You must have:
- A ruler.
- A calculator.

Total marks:

Instructions to candidates
- Use **black** ink to write your answers.
- Write your name and other details in the spaces provided above.
- Answer **all** questions in the spaces provided.
- In calculations, show clearly how you worked out your answers.
- You will need to answer some questions by placing a cross in a box, like this: ☒
  To change your answer, draw a line through the box like this: ☒
  Then mark your new answer as normal.

Information for candidates
- The marks available are given in brackets at the end of each question.
- There are 70 marks available for this paper.

Advice for candidates
- Read all the questions carefully.
- Write your answers as clearly and neatly as possible.
- Keep in mind how much time you have left.

Answer **all** questions

1   Read the passage below, then answer the questions that follow.

Genetically modified crops — Golden Rice

Vitamin A deficiency is a major health problem across the world — particularly in developing countries in South Asia and parts of Africa. A lack of dietary vitamin A makes people more vulnerable to disease and more likely to die from infections. It's also a primary cause of preventable blindness in children, and can contribute to women dying during
5   pregnancy or shortly after childbirth.

To try to address this problem, scientists from across the world have worked together to develop a type of transgenic rice, named Golden Rice. The rice has been genetically engineered to contain a gene from a maize plant and a gene from a soil bacterium, which together allow the rice to synthesise a compound known as beta-carotene.

10   Beta-carotene is an orange pigment which occurs naturally in a range of different plants and fruits. It is also known as provitamin A. In the body it is an early component of the chemical pathway that leads to the production of vitamin A, so a larger amount of beta-carotene in the diet allows the production of a larger amount of vitamin A.

Rice is widely eaten in many areas where vitamin A deficiency is a problem. However,
15   normal rice does not contain any beta-carotene and is therefore not a source of vitamin A. In contrast, it is estimated that an adult would only need to eat around 150 g (uncooked) of Golden Rice per day in order to obtain the estimated average daily requirement (EAR) of vitamin A.

Eating a small amount of Golden Rice is a simple solution to the problem of insufficient
20   dietary vitamin A. Farmers in the developing world can grow their own Golden Rice and protect themselves and others from the negative health impacts of vitamin A deficiency, without having to rely on dietary supplements such as vitamin tablets.

(a) Unlike in many developing countries (lines 1-2), vitamin A deficiency is not a major health problem in developed countries such as the UK.

Suggest **one** reason why this is the case.

In developed countries people have access to good food and healthcare

[1]

(b) (i) Apart from Golden Rice, name a food that is a good source of vitamin A.

Carrots

[1]

(ii) Which of the following is a function of vitamin A in the human body?

☐ **A** making haemoglobin

☐ **B** providing energy

☒ **C** maintaining a healthy visual system

☐ **D** aiding the movement of food through the gut

[1]

(c) Golden Rice is a **transgenic organism** (line 7).
Explain what this means with reference to the passage.

This means it has genetics from 2 ~~plots~~ organisms, the maize plant & a gene from a soil bacterium

[1]

(d) Suggest why beta-carotene is also known as provitamin A (line 11).

It leads to the production of vitamin A

[1]

(e) Golden Rice has been genetically modified to increase its nutrient content (line 9).
Describe **two** other ways in which organisms can be genetically modified to benefit humans.

1 They can be genetically modified to increase resistance to disease

2 It can be genetically modified to ~~increase~~ make it last longer.

[2]

Turn over ▶

192

(f) There are different ways of estimating how much vitamin A a person needs in their diet. EAR is one. Recommended daily allowance (RDA) is another.

The EAR for vitamin A (lines 16-17) is around 70% of the RDA.

Calculate how much Golden Rice an adult would need to eat to obtain 100% of the RDA of vitamin A. Show your working.

.... g

[2]

(g) Suggest and explain why farmers who grow Golden Rice to supply their dietary vitamin A may be financially better off than if they regularly bought vitamin A tablets.

....

....

....

[2]

(h) With some genetically modified crop plants, farmers are not allowed to save seeds at the end of a growing season and replant them the following year. The project behind Golden Rice does allow farmers in the developing world to save seed from Golden Rice plants.

Suggest why this is beneficial to farmers in the developing world.

....

....

....

[2]

[Total 13 marks]

2   The diagram below shows the nitrogen cycle.
        The labels **A-D** represent different stages of the cycle.

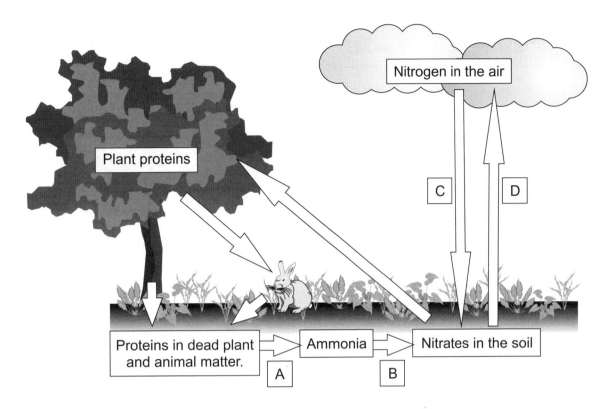

(a)   Complete the table by writing in the types of bacteria that are involved
        at each of the stages **A-D**. The first one has been done for you.

Stage	Type of Bacteria
A	Decomposers
B	Nitrogen fixing
C	.
D	Nitrogen fixing

[3]

(b)   Decomposers also play a role in the carbon cycle.
        Explain the role of decomposers in the carbon cycle.

....

....

....

[2]

[Total 5 marks]

Turn over ▶

3   Environmental officers studied a river that was polluted by sewage.

They measured the amount of dissolved oxygen in the river at different points along its length. The flow of water is from point 1 towards point 15.

The graph shows their results.

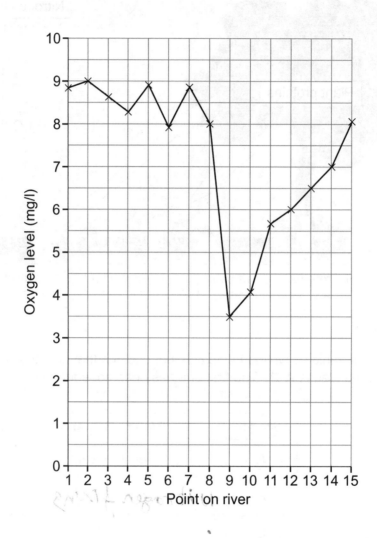

(a)   Using the information in the graph, state where the source of pollution is located.
Give a reason for your answer.

....

....

[2]

(b)   The larvae of an insect known as a mayfly can be used to estimate pollution levels in water. Mayfly larvae cannot survive in polluted water.

Suggest how the population size of mayfly larvae at **point 1** would differ from the population size at **point 10**.

....

....

[1]

(c) Explain how the pollution of water by sewage affects the oxygen level in the water.

....

....

....

....

....

....

....

[4]

(d) A survey was carried out into the number of birds feeding along the river.

Although fairly common elsewhere, few herons were spotted feeding near the source of the pollution.

Suggest an explanation for this.

....

....

....

[2]

(e) Calculate the range of the dissolved oxygen concentration measured along the length of the river.

.... mg/l

[1]

[10 marks]

Turn over ▶

4   An experiment was carried out to discover the best growth medium for the tissue culture of a certain species of plant. Four different growth media, 1 - 4, were used.

The scientists weighed ten blocks of stem tissue, each measuring 1 mm × 1 mm × 1 mm. These were placed onto growth medium 1, as shown in the diagram.

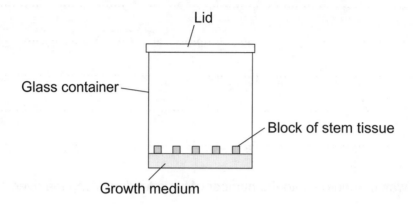

The container was then incubated at 35 °C for two days. At the end of that time, the blocks were taken out and weighed again to see how much they had grown.

This was repeated with the other three growth media.

The whole experiment was repeated again, using root tissue instead of stem tissue.

The results of the experiments are shown in the table.

Growth medium	Average % increase in mass	
	Stem tissue	Root tissue
1	120	77
2	85	62
3	65	58
4	98	102

(a)   Draw a bar chart to represent the average percentage increase in mass for stem and
        root tissue in each growth medium.

[5]

(b)   Which combination of plant tissue and growth medium produced the best results?
        Explain your answer.

        ....

        ....

[2]

(c)   Give **two** variables that needed to be controlled in this experiment.

        1 ....

        2 ....

[2]

Turn over ▶

(d)   Which of the following is another name for tissue culture?

☐ **A**   selective breeding

☐ **B**   genetic engineering

☐ **C**   differentiation

☐ **D**   micropropagation

[1]

(e)   Tissue culture is an example of asexual reproduction.

Give **three** differences between asexual and sexual reproduction.

1 ....

....

....

2 ....

....

....

3 ....

....

....

[3]

[Total 13 marks]

5 The menstrual cycle is controlled by the hormones FSH, oestrogen, LH and progesterone.

(a) Name the part of the body where the hormone FSH is produced.

....

[1]

(b) Describe the roles of the hormones involved in the menstrual cycle.

....

....

....

....

....

....

....

....

....

....

[6]

[Total 7 marks]

Turn over ▶

6   The diagram below shows the structure of a DNA double-stranded helix.
The two strands are held together by cross-linking between their bases.

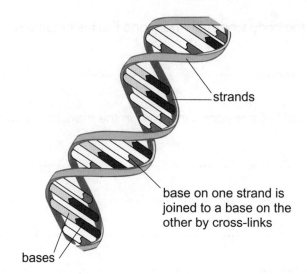

strands

base on one strand is
joined to a base on the
other by cross-links

bases

(a)   Explain why there will always be equal amounts of bases A and T in a molecule of DNA.

....

....

[1]

(b)   Name the part of a cell where strands of human DNA are found.

....

[1]

A sequence of bases in a section of DNA is shown below.

A T C A G G C T A G T T

(c)   State the number of amino acids that the base sequence would code for.

....

[1]

A mutation occurs in the base sequence of the section of DNA.
The mutation is shown in the diagram below.

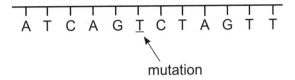

mutation

The mutation does not result in a change of phenotype.

(d) (i) Which of the following describes the term phenotype?

☐ **A** The combination of alleles that an individual has.

☐ **B** Having two alleles that are the same.

☐ **C** The characteristics produced by alleles.

☐ **D** Having two different dominant alleles.

[1]

(ii) Suggest **two** reasons why the mutation does not have an affect on phenotype.

....

....

....

....

[2]

[Total 6 marks]

202

7   A student did an experiment to investigate the effect of pH on the action of the enzyme amylase. The method used is shown below.

> 1. Add a set quantity of starch solution to a test tube and the same quantity of amylase solution to another.
> 2. Add a set quantity of a buffer solution with a pH of 5 to the tube containing starch solution.
> 3. Place the test tubes in a water bath at 35 °C.
> 4. Allow the starch and amylase solutions to reach the temperature of the water bath, then mix them together and return the mixture to the water bath.
> 5. Take a small sample of the mixture every minute and test for starch.
> 6. Stop the experiment when starch is no longer present in the sample, or after 30 minutes (whichever is sooner).
> 7. Repeat the experiment using buffer solutions of different pH values.

(a)   Describe what happens to the starch solution during the experiment.

....
[1]

(b)   Explain why a set quantity of starch solution was used for each repeat in the experiment.

....

....
[1]

The graph below shows the student's results.

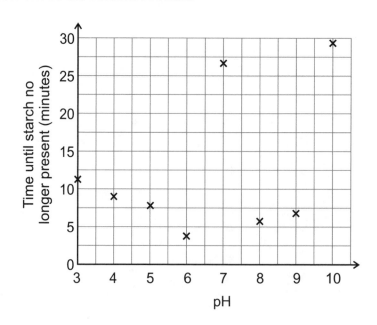

(c) Explain the results between **pH 9** and **pH 10**.

....

....

....

....

....
[3]

(d) (i) The student thinks that one of the results shown on the graph is likely to be anomalous. Identify the anomalous result and give a reason for your answer.

....

....
[2]

(ii) Suggest what the student might have done to cause this anomalous result.

....

....
[1]

[Total 8 marks]

8 The kidneys play a crucial role in filtering the blood.
The diagram shows a kidney nephron and the blood vessels associated with it.

(a) Label the glomerulus and the loop of Henle on the diagram.

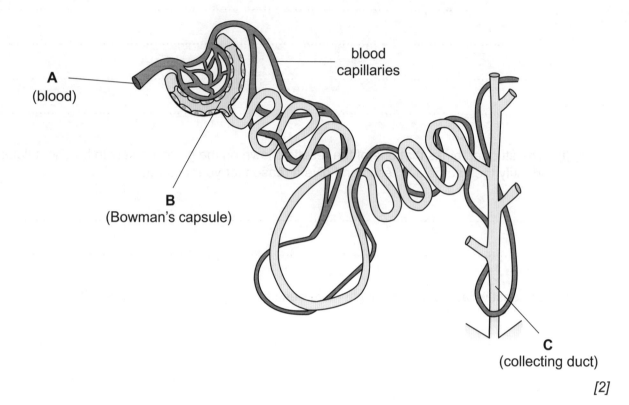

[2]

(b) Many different proteins are found in the blood at point **A** on the diagram,
but hardly any are found at point **B**.

Explain why there is almost no protein at point **B**.

....

....

[1]

(c) (i) The concentration of urea is greatest at point **C**. Explain why.

....

....

[1]

(ii) Explain how the concentration of sugar at point **C** would compare to the concentration at point **B**.

....

....

....

[2]

(d) Describe the effect of ADH on the kidney nephron.

....

....

[2]

[Total 8 marks]

[Total for paper 70 marks]

Section 1 — The Nature and Variety of Organisms

Pages 7-8
Warm-Up Questions

1) Similarities — any two from: e.g. both an animal cell and a plant cell have a cell membrane. / Both an animal cell and a plant cell have a nucleus. / Both an animal cell and a plant cell have cytoplasm.
   Differences — any two from: e.g. an animal cell doesn't have a vacuole, but a plant cell does. / An animal cell doesn't have a cell wall, but a plant cell does. / An animal cell doesn't contain chloroplasts, but a plant cell does.
2) It is made up of thread-like structures called hyphae, which contain lots of nuclei.
3) a) e.g. *Chlorella*
   b) e.g. *Amoeba*
4) *Plasmodium.* A protactist.

Exam Questions

1 B *[1 mark]*
2 a) It is an organelle surrounded by its own membrane *[1 mark]*. It contains genetic material *[1 mark]*.
  b) i) Chloroplasts are the site of photosynthesis *[1 mark]*.
     ii) The vacuole helps to support the cell *[1 mark]*.
  c) Tissues, organs, organ systems *[2 marks for correct answers in correct order, otherwise 1 mark for correct answers]*.
3 a) i) A, because *Lactobacillus bulgaricus* is rod-shaped *[1 mark]*. *Pneumococcus bacteria are spherical (like the bacteria in diagram B).*
     ii) It can be used to produce yoghurt from milk *[1 mark]*.
  b) A pathogen is an organism that can cause disease *[1 mark]*.
  c) By feeding off other (living or dead) organisms *[1 mark]*.
  d) Any three from: e.g. it has a cell wall. / It has a cell membrane. / It has cytoplasm. / It has plasmids. / It has a circular chromosome of DNA. / It doesn't have a nucleus. *[3 marks]*
4 a) It is made up of thread-like structures called hyphae *[1 mark]*, which contain lots of nuclei *[1 mark]*.
  b) B *[1 mark]*
5 a) The tobacco mosaic virus *[1 mark]* discolours the leaves of tobacco plants by stopping them from producing chloroplasts *[1 mark]*.
  b) E.g. the influenza virus *[1 mark]* causes 'flu' *[1 mark]*. The HIV virus *[1 mark]* causes AIDS *[1 mark]*.
6 Any three from: e.g. they feed, which means they require nutrition. / They are sensitive to chemicals in the water, allowing them to detect food. This shows they can respond to changes in their environment. / They are able to travel towards food, showing that they can move. / They release eggs/sperm, which suggests they reproduce. *[3 marks]*

Page 13
Warm-Up Questions

1 active site
2 For an enzyme to work, a substrate has to be the correct shape to fit the enzyme's active site. The substrate fits into the enzyme just like a key fits into a lock.
3 The enzymes and substrate don't have much energy at cold temperatures, so they don't move about as much. This means they're less likely to collide and form enzyme-substrate complexes.

Exam Questions

1 A *[1 mark]*
2 a) 36 °C, as this was the temperature at which the iodine solution stopped turning blue-black first *[1 mark]*, meaning the starch had been broken down the fastest *[1 mark]*.
  b) E.g. the amylase was denatured by the high temperature, so the starch was not broken down *[1 mark]*.
  c) Any two from: e.g. the concentration of starch solution / the concentration of amylase / the volume of starch and amylase solution added to the iodine / the volume of iodine solution in the wells / the pH of the starch and amylase solution *[2 marks]*.
  d) E.g. test the solutions more frequently (e.g. every 10 seconds) *[1 mark]*. / Do more repeats of the experiment at 36 °C and at 37 °C *[1 mark]*.

Pages 20-21
Warm-Up Questions

1) Osmosis is the net movement of water molecules across a partially permeable membrane from a region of higher water concentration to a region of lower water concentration.
2) Cells are surrounded by tissue fluid, which usually has a different concentration to the fluid inside a cell. If the tissue fluid is more dilute than the fluid inside the cell, water will move into the cell by osmosis. If the tissue fluid is more concentrated than the water inside the cell, water will move out of the cell by osmosis.
3) respiration

Exam Questions

1) a) D *[1 mark]*
   b) Diffusion will cause the oxygen concentration in the cell to decrease *[1 mark]*.
2 a) partially permeable membrane *[1 mark]*
Remember that osmosis always takes place across a partially permeable membrane.
  b) The liquid level on side B will fall *[1 mark]*, because water will flow from the region of higher water concentration on side B to the region of lower water concentration on side A *[1 mark]*.
3 a) diffusion (1 mark)
  b) $(835 + 825 + 842 + 838) \div 4 = 835$ s
     [2 marks for correct answer, otherwise 1 mark for adding together 4 values and dividing by 4]
  c) As the size of the gelatine cube increases, the time taken for the cube to become yellow increases *[1 mark]*. This is because the bigger cubes have a smaller surface area to volume ratio *[1 mark]*, which decreases the rate of diffusion *[1 mark]*.
4 a) Seedling A because there is more energy at higher temperatures *[1 mark]* so the potassium ions move faster, resulting in a faster rate of uptake *[1 mark]*.
  b) It would have no effect *[1 mark]*.
Increasing a concentration gradient increases the rate of diffusion and osmosis but has no effect on the rate of active transport.

Section 2 — Human Nutrition

Pages 30-31
Warm-Up Questions

1) a) Lipids are made up of glycerol and fatty acids.
   b) Proteins are made up of amino acids.
2) Add 3 drops of Sudan III stain solution to the sample and gently shake it. If lipids are present, a separate red layer will form at the top of the liquid.
3) That starch is present in the sample.

Exam Questions

1)

Enzyme	Function
proteases	convert proteins into amino acids
amylase	converts starch into maltose
maltase	converts maltose into glucose
lipases	convert lipids into fatty acids and glycerol

[5 marks]

2) B *[1 mark]*

3) a) He should add some Benedict's solution to each test tube using a pipette *[1 mark]*. He should then place the test tubes in a water bath set at 75 °C and leave them for 5 minutes *[1 mark]*. He should look out for a colour change and note which of a range of colours the solutions become *[1 mark]*.

b)

	Tube 1	Tube 2	Tube 3	Tube 4
substance observed	yellow precipitate	blue solution	red precipitate	green precipitate
glucose concentration (M)	0.1	0	1	0.02

[1 mark]

The higher the concentration of glucose in the solution, the further the colour change goes along the following scale: blue — green — yellow — brick red. If no precipitate forms then there are no glucose molecules in the solution.

4) a) The mass of the dried bean *[1 mark]*, the temperature of the water *[1 mark]*.

b) The change in temperature of the water *[1 mark]*.

c) Energy = 20 × 21 × 4.2 = 1764 J *[1 mark]*

d) 1764 ÷ 0.7 = 2520 J/g *[1 mark. Allow carry through of any answer from part b).]*

e) E.g. not all of the energy used to heat the water is retained by the water *[1 mark]* because it is lost to the surroundings instead *[1 mark]*.

f) E.g. she could insulate the boiling tube (to reduce heat loss) *[1 mark]*.

5) Bacterial species B because the clear zone around the bacteria indicates there is no lipid present in this area *[1 mark]*. This is because the lipase produced by the bacterial cells has broken it down into fatty acids and glycerol *[1 mark]*.

Section 3 — Plant Nutrition and Transport

Pages 38-39
Warm-Up Questions

1) A limiting factor is something that stops photosynthesis happening any faster.

2) If the temperature's too high (over about 45 °C), the plant's enzymes will be denatured, so the rate of photosynthesis rapidly decreases.

3) Put a plant in a sealed bell jar with some soda lime. The soda lime will absorb the carbon dioxide out of the air in the jar. Leave the jar under a light for a while and then test a leaf for starch using the iodine test. If the leaf doesn't turn blue-black it shows that carbon dioxide is needed for photosynthesis.

4) oxygen production

Exam Questions

1) delivers water and nutrients to every part of the leaf — E *[1 mark]*
helps to reduce water loss by evaporation — A *[1 mark]*
where most of the chloroplasts in the leaf are located, to maximise the amount of light they receive — B *[1 mark]*
allows carbon dioxide to diffuse directly into the leaf — D *[1 mark]*

2) a) Photosynthesis involves the conversion of light energy to chemical energy *[1 mark]*, which is stored in glucose *[1 mark]*.

b) i) carbon dioxide + water → glucose + oxygen
[1 mark for carbon dioxide + water on the left-hand side of the equation, 1 mark for glucose + oxygen on the right.]

ii) $6CO_2 + 6H_2O \rightarrow C_6H_{12}O_6 + 6O_2$
[1 mark for $6CO_2 + 6H_2O$ on the left-hand side of the equation, 1 mark for $C_6H_{12}O_6 + 6O_2$ on the right. Allow 1 mark if the correct symbols are used, but the equation isn't correctly balanced.]

3) a) At low light intensities, increasing the CO_2 concentration has no effect *[1 mark]*, but at higher light intensities, increasing the concentration of CO_2 increases the maximum rate of photosynthesis *[1 mark]*.

b) The rate of photosynthesis does not continue to increase because temperature or the level of carbon dioxide becomes the limiting factor *[1 mark]*.

4) a) The chlorophyll was removed from the leaf *[1 mark]*.

b) That starch is present in the leaf *[1 mark]*.

c) I would expect the green parts of the leaf to turn blue-black *[1 mark]* and the white part of the leaf to turn brown *[1 mark]*. This is because the green parts of the leaf contain chlorophyll and so they will be able to photosynthesise and produce starch *[1 mark]*. The white part of the leaf does not contain chlorophyll, so it will not be able to photosynthesise or produce starch *[1 mark]*.

Remember: photosynthesis produces glucose, which is stored in the leaves as starch.

5) E.g. take two plants of the same type. Grow one plant without any light for 48 hours (e.g. in a dark cupboard). Grow the other plant in bright light for 48 hours (e.g. in a cupboard under artificial lights). Keep both plants at the same temperature and give them the same amount of water. Keep the carbon dioxide concentration for both plants the same too. After 48 hours, take a leaf from each plant and test it for starch using iodine solution. Record the results. Repeat the experiment at least twice.
[1 mark for stating that one plant will be grown without light and one will be grown with light, 1 mark for stating that both plants should be the same type, 1 mark for describing one control variable, e.g. temperature, 1 mark for describing a second control variable, e.g. water, 1 mark for stating what will be measured, e.g. starch production, 1 mark for stating how it will be measured, e.g. using the iodine test, 1 mark for stating that repeats should be carried out. Maximum 6 marks available.]

208

Pages 46-47
Warm-Up Questions
1) making amino acids and proteins
2) In unicellular organisms, substances can diffuse directly into and out of the cell (across the cell membrane). The rate of diffusion is quick because of the short distances substances have to travel. But in multicellular organisms, diffusion across the outer surface would be too slow to reach every cell in the organism's body. So multicellular organisms need transport systems to move substances to and from individual cells quickly.
3) light intensity, temperature, wind speed, humidity

Exam Questions
1) C *[1 mark]*
2 a) Osmosis *[1 mark]*. Water moves from a higher concentration in the soil to a lower concentration in the root hair cell *[1 mark]*.
   b) E.g. they have a large surface area *[1 mark]*.
3 a) The plants are lacking in magnesium and magnesium is needed to make chlorophyll (the pigment that makes plant leaves green) *[1 mark]*.
   b) i) The magnesium-deficient plants had a lower total dry mass than those grown with a complete mineral supply *[1 mark]*.
      ii) The magnesium-deficient plants are unable to produce chlorophyll, which is needed for photosynthesis *[1 mark]*. If photosynthesis is reduced, plant growth will also be reduced *(1 mark)* and the plants will gain less mass *[1 mark]*.
4 a) E.g. the evaporation (and diffusion) of water from a plant's surface *[1 mark]*.
   b) 9 a.m. *[1 mark]*
   c) Any one from: e.g. day 2 was colder, so the water evaporated/ diffused more slowly. / Day 2 was less windy, so the water vapour was carried away more slowly. / Day 2 was wetter/ more humid, so there was a smaller diffusion gradient, so the water diffused more slowly. / The light intensity was lower on day 2, so fewer stomata were open to allow water vapour to escape. *[1 mark for reason, 1 mark for explanation]*
   d) At night the light intensity is low *[1 mark]* so the stomata close, allowing less water vapour to escape *[1 mark]*.
5 a) $10 + 11 + 9 = 30 \div 3 =$ **10%** *[2 marks for correct answer, otherwise 1 mark for adding together 3 percentages and dividing by 3]*
   b) The movement of air from the fan sweeps away water vapour, maintaining a low concentration of water outside the leaf *[1 mark]* and increasing the rate at which water is lost through diffusion *[1 mark]*. This means that the plants next to the fan would lose more water (and therefore more mass) than the plants in a still room in the same amount of time *[1 mark]*.
   c) The rate of transpiration would be slower *[1 mark]* since most water loss occurs through the stomata, which are on the underside of the leaves *[1 mark]*.
   d) E.g. you could put a new group of 3 basil plants in a separate room *[1 mark]* and increase the humidity in the room by misting/spraying the air with water *[1 mark]*.

If you've thought of another __sensible__ way to increase or decrease the humidity around the plants, you'd still get the mark in the exam.

Section 4 — Respiration and Gas Exchange

Pages 55-56
Warm-Up Questions
1) ATP
2) glucose $\rightarrow$ lactic acid (+ energy)
3) ethanol, carbon dioxide/CO_2
4) false (plants respire all the time)

Exam Questions
1 a) To transfer energy from glucose. / To produce ATP which provides energy for cells *[1 mark]*.
   b) Any two from: e.g. aerobic respiration uses oxygen, anaerobic respiration does not. / Glucose is only partially broken down during anaerobic respiration, but is broken down fully during aerobic respiration. / Anaerobic respiration produces lactic acid, aerobic respiration does not. / Anaerobic respiration transfers less energy/ produces less ATP than aerobic respiration. *[2 marks]*
   c) B *[1 mark]*
2 a) i) A: oxygen / water vapour *[1 mark]*
         B: carbon dioxide *[1 mark]*
      ii) diffusion *[1 mark]*
   b) i) photosynthesis *[1 mark]*
      ii) respiration *[1 mark]*
3 a) Tube A: the bromothymol blue indicator has changed colour from green to yellow *[1 mark]*. This is because the beetle has respired and produced carbon dioxide *[1 mark]*.
       Tube B: the bromothymol blue indicator has not changed colour/is still green *[1 mark]* because no respiration has taken place, so no carbon dioxide has been produced *[1 mark]*.
   b) To act as a control / to show that the colour change in the indicator solution only happened in the presence of a living/respiring organism *[1 mark]*.
4 a) To prevent gas exchange with the surrounding air *[1 mark]*.
   b) To make sure that any change in the hydrogen-carbonate indicator is due to processes occurring in the leaves *[1 mark]*.
   c) Tube A: no/little change in colour of the hydrogen-carbonate indicator *[1 mark]*. Some light is available, so the rates of photosynthesis and respiration roughly balance and the CO_2 concentration in the tube remains the same/similar *[1 mark]*.
       Tube B: hydrogen-carbonate indicator turns yellow *[1 mark]*. Foil blocks out all light, so the CO_2 produced by respiration is not used up in photosynthesis. This means that the CO_2 concentration in the tube increases *[1 mark]*.
       Tube C: hydrogen-carbonate indicator turns purple *[1 mark]*. The rate of photosynthesis will be high because of the bright light, so the leaf takes up more CO_2 than it produces through respiration and the CO_2 concentration in the tube decreases *[1 mark]*.

To answer this question, you need to think about how the amount of light entering each tube will affect the rate of photosynthesis in the leaf — and whether there'll be a net gain or loss of CO_2 in the tube as a result. Then you need to decide how this will affect the colour of the indicator.

Page 62

Warm-Up Questions

1) Around/surrounding the lungs
2) true
3) The intercostal muscles and the diaphragm.

Exam Questions

1 a) E.g.

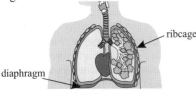

ribcage

diaphragm

[1 mark for a label pointing to the diaphragm,
1 mark for a label pointing to the ribcage].

b) bronchiole *[1 mark]*
c) the alveoli *[1 mark]*

2

Event	Order
Pressure in the lungs decreases	3
Intercostal muscles and diaphragm contract	1
Air is drawn into the lungs	4
Thorax volume increases	2

[3 marks for all answers in the correct order,
2 marks for three answers in the correct order,
1 mark for two answers in the correct order.]

3 E.g. the person being tested should first sit still for 5 minutes. The number of breaths they take in one minute should then be recorded. These time periods should be measured with a stopwatch. The same person should then run on a treadmill for 4 minutes. The number of breaths they take in one minute should then be recorded immediately. Repeats should be carried out using the same time periods, the same intensity of exercise (e.g. by setting the same speed on the treadmill), and at the same temperature.
[1 mark for including a control (i.e. recording the breathing rate at rest), 1 mark for stating that the same person should do the rest and exercise tests, 1 mark for stating that the breathing rate should be measured, 1 mark for saying how the breathing rate should be measured, 1 mark for stating that the investigation should be repeated, 1 mark for controlling one variable (e.g. length of rest/ exercise periods / intensity of exercise / temperature at which experiment takes place), 1 mark for controlling a second variable. Maximum of 6 marks available.]

4 a) The blood in the capillary has just returned to the lungs from the rest of the body, so contains a low concentration of oxygen *[1 mark]*. The alveolus contains air that has just been breathed in, so it has a high concentration of oxygen *[1 mark]*. So oxygen diffuses out of the alveolus and into the capillary *[1 mark]*.

b) Any two from: e.g. they have thin outer walls *[1 mark]* so gases don't have to diffuse far/there's a short diffusion pathway *[1 mark]*. / They have a moist lining *[1 mark]* which gases can dissolve in *[1 mark]*. / They have a good blood supply *[1 mark]* to maintain a high concentration gradient *[1 mark]*. / They have permeable walls *[1 mark]* to allow gases to diffuse easily *[1 mark]*.

Section 5 — Blood and Organs

Pages 70-71

Warm-Up Questions

1) red blood cells, white blood cells and platelets
2) antigens
3) false
It's arteries that carry blood away from the heart — veins carry it back to the heart.
4) the bicuspid valve

Exam Questions

1

Structure	Letter
pulmonary artery	B
hepatic artery	F
vena cava	C
kidneys	H
aorta	E
hepatic portal vein	G

[1 mark for each correct answer]

2 a) It is biconcave *[1 mark]* which gives it a large surface area for absorbing and releasing oxygen *[1 mark]*.

b) E.g. it contains haemoglobin *[1 mark]* which reacts with oxygen so red blood cells can carry it around the body *[1 mark]*. / It has no nucleus *[1 mark]* so there is space for more haemoglobin and so more oxygen *[1 mark]*.

3 a) Some white blood cells/phagocytes can engulf pathogens *[1 mark]* and digest them *[1 mark]*.

b) Antibodies are produced by certain white blood cells/ lymphocytes *[1 mark]*. They attach to specific antigens on the surface of the pathogen *[1 mark]* and mark the pathogen for destruction by other white blood cells *[1 mark]*.

4 a) Any two from, e.g. some food molecules, oxygen, carbon dioxide *[2 marks]*

b) E.g. capillaries are very small *[1 mark]* so they can carry blood close to any cell *[1 mark]*. They have permeable walls *[1 mark]* so substances can diffuse in and out of them *[1 mark]*. Their walls are only one cell thick *[1 mark]* to increase the rate of diffusion by decreasing the distance over which it happens *[1 mark]*.

5 a) E.g. smoking increases blood pressure, which can cause damage to the inside of the coronary arteries / chemicals in cigarette smoke can cause damage to the inside of the coronary arteries *[1 mark]*. The damage makes it more likely that fatty deposits will form, which cause a narrowing of the coronary arteries *[1 mark]*.

b) E.g. cut down on foods high in saturated fat *[1 mark]* / exercise regularly *[1 mark]*.

6 a) The cat felt threatened by the dog so its adrenal glands secreted adrenaline *[1 mark]*. Adrenaline binds to specific receptors in the heart *[1 mark]* causing the cardiac muscle to contract more frequently and with more force, so the cat's heart rate increased *[1 mark]*.

b) By increasing the oxygen supply to the tissues *[1 mark]*.

7 When vaccinated, child A was given dead or inactive rubella pathogens *[1 mark]*. These would have had antigens on their surface and so would cause lymphocytes to start producing antibodies *[1 mark]*. Some of these lymphocytes remained in the blood as memory cells *[1 mark]*. When child A was exposed to the virus, the memory cells made the specific antibodies more quickly/in greater quantities, so child A didn't become ill *[1 mark]*. Child B did not have these memory cells, so when they were infected by the virus they became ill *[1 mark]*.

Page 75
Warm-Up Questions
1)   In the liver.
2)   high pressure
3)   bladder

Exam Questions
1 a)   E.g. the maintenance of a balance between water coming
        into the body and water going out of the body *[1 mark]*.
  b)   urine *[1 mark]*.
  c) i) B *[1 mark]*
    ii) pituitary gland *[1 mark]*
2 a)   Bowman's capsule *[1 mark]*
  b) i) As the blood flows from the renal artery into the glomerulus
        [1 mark] a high pressure builds up *[1 mark]*, which
        squeezes/filters small molecules out of the blood into the
        Bowman's capsule to form the glomerular filtrate *[1 mark]*.
    ii) C *[1 mark]*
3   As the runner ran, she sweated, resulting in water loss and
        less water in her blood *[1 mark]*. Her brain detected the
        decreased water content of her blood *[1 mark]* and instructed
        the pituitary gland to release ADH (anti-diuretic hormone)
        into the blood *[1 mark]*. The ADH made the collecting ducts
        of the nephrons more permeable *[1 mark]* so that more water
        could be reabsorbed back into the blood *[1 mark]*, resulting
        in less water being released in her urine, so her urine was
        more concentrated and appeared darker in colour *[1 mark]*.

Section 6 — Coordination and Response

Pages 81-82
Warm-Up Questions
1)   eyes, ears, nose, tongue and skin
2)   brain and spinal cord
3)   electrical impulses
4)   E.g. they can reduce your chances of getting injured.
5)   E.g. the iris reflex (in response to bright light) /
        accommodation of the eye / withdrawing your hand from a
        painful stimulus / release of adrenaline in response to shock.

Exam Questions
1 a)   E.g. so they can respond to the changes in order to avoid
        danger/increase their chances of survival *[1 mark]*.
  b)   receptors *[1 mark]*
  c)   Stimulus: sight of food *[1 mark]*
        Sense organ: the eye *[1 mark]*
        Effectors: muscle cells *[1 mark]*
  d)   hormonal system *[1 mark]*
2 a)   X: sensory neurone *[1 mark]*
        Y: relay neurone *[1 mark]*
        Z: motor neurone *[1 mark]*
  b)   a synapse *[1 mark]*
  c)   The effectors are muscle cells *[1 mark]* and they respond
        by contracting (which causes the man to drop the plate)
        [1 mark].
3 a)   A: cornea *[1 mark]*
        B: pupil *[1 mark]*
  b)   To control the diameter of the pupil/the amount
        of light entering the eye *[1 mark]*.
  c) i) rods *[1 mark]*, cones *[1 mark]*
    ii) the fovea *[1 mark]*
  d)   Information is sent using impulses *[1 mark]*,
        via the optic nerve *[1 mark]*.

4 a)   The ciliary muscles relax *[1 mark]* allowing the suspensory
        ligaments to pull tight *[1 mark]*, which results in the
        lens becoming thinner/less rounded *[1 mark]*.
  b)   If the lens cannot form a rounded shape, light from
        nearby objects won't be bent enough to be focused on the
        retina *[1 mark]*. This means that people with presbyopia
        will be unable to focus on nearby objects *[1 mark]*.
5 a)   B, because the pupil has contracted in this eye *[1 mark]*
        to stop too much light entering the eye *[1 mark]*.
  b) i) Reflex responses happen very quickly/are automatic
        [1 mark] so the eye can adjust quickly to prevent the
        retina being damaged by bright light *[1 mark]*.
    ii) Light receptor cells detect the bright light *[1 mark]* and
        send electrical impulses along sensory neurones to the
        brain/central nervous system *[1 mark]*. The impulse then
        passes along a relay neurone *[1 mark]* to a motor neurone
        [1 mark] and then to effectors/the circular muscles in the
        iris, which contract, making the pupil smaller *[1 mark]*.

Pages 89-90
Warm-Up Questions
1) a)   ovaries
   b)   ovaries
   c)   adrenal glands
2)   adrenaline
3)   It increases the permeability of the kidney tubules to water.
4)   It's the optimum temperature for enzymes in the human body.
5)   Plant hormones which control growth at the tips
        of shoots and roots. / Plant growth hormones.

Exam Questions
1 a)   The maintenance of a constant internal
        environment *[1 mark]*.
  b) i) Through his skin as sweat *[1 mark]*.
        Via the lungs in his breath *[1 mark]*.
    ii) It is very concentrated *[1 mark]* because he has lost a lot of
        water in his sweat/breath, so loses less in his urine *[1 mark]*.
  c)   E.g. it is a cooler day so he sweats less. / He drank
        more water before/during the ride *[1 mark]*.
2 a) i) A growth response away from gravity *[1 mark]*.
    ii) The shoot *[1 mark]*.
  b) i) The root will grow down again *[1 mark]*.
    ii) D *[1 mark]*
3 a) i) vasoconstriction *[1 mark]*
    ii) It means that less blood flows near the surface *[1 mark]*,
        so less energy is transferred to the surroundings,
        which helps to keep the body warm *[1 mark]*.
  b)   Sweat glands respond by producing very little sweat
        [1 mark], because sweat transfers heat from the body
        to the environment when it evaporates *[1 mark]*.
4   Nervous responses are very fast and hormonal
        responses are slower *[1 mark]*. Nerves use electrical
        impulses/signals, while hormones use chemical
        signals *[1 mark]*. Nervous responses usually act for
        a short time while hormonal responses last for longer
        [1 mark]. Nerves act on a very precise area whereas
        hormones act on a more general area *[1 mark]*.

5 a)   the tip *[1 mark]*

  b)   Shoot B grew straight upwards / did not bend *[1 mark]*. This is because the tip of the shoot was not exposed to light *[1 mark]*, which is the stimulus needed for phototropism to occur *[1 mark]*.

  c)   Any two from: e.g. the shoots should have been from the same type of plant. / Each shoot should have been the same distance from the light source. / The light source should have been the same intensity for each shoot. / Each shoot should have been exposed to the light stimulus for the same amount of time. / Each shoot should have been left to grow at the same temperature. / Each shoot should have been given the same amount of nutrients/water. *[2 marks]*

  d)   E.g. it's likely that none of the shoots would have bent / all of the shoots would have grown straight up *[1 mark]* as auxin/the hormone responsible for the response is produced in the tips *[1 mark]*.

Section 7 — Reproduction and Inheritance

Pages 99-100
Warm-Up Questions

1)   A chromosome is a long length of DNA coiled up.
2)   thymine
3)   mitosis
4)   one
5)   two

Exam Questions

1 a)   the nucleus *[1 mark]*

  b) i)   They have two copies of each chromosome *[1 mark]*.

    ii)   46 *[1 mark]*

2 a)   C *[1 mark]*

mRNA contains almost the same bases as DNA. The only difference is T (thymine) is replaced by U (uracil).

  b)   B *[1 mark]*

  c)   nucleus *[1 mark]*

  d)   (complementary) base pairing *[1 mark]*

  e)   To bring amino acids to the ribosome in the correct order *[1 mark]*.

  f)   To carry the coding information from DNA in the nucleus *[1 mark]*, to the ribosomes in the cytoplasm (where protein synthesis takes place) *[1 mark]*.

3 a)   Each gene codes for a specific protein *[1 mark]*, and proteins determine inherited characteristics *[1 mark]*.

  b)   There are different/alternative versions of the same gene, called alleles *[1 mark]*, that give different versions of a characteristic *[1 mark]*. The two kittens must have different versions/alleles of the gene for fur length, meaning one is long-haired and the other is short-haired *[1 mark]*.

4 a)   The amount of DNA is doubling *[1 mark]* because each new cell needs to have a complete set of chromosomes *[1 mark]*.

  b)   The two new cells separate *[1 mark]*.

  c)   two *[1 mark]*

5   RNA polymerase binds to the region of non-coding DNA in front of the gene *[1 mark]*. The two DNA strands unzip and the RNA polymerase moves along one of the strands, using the coding DNA in the gene as a template to make mRNA *[1 mark]*. Base pairing ensures that the mRNA is complementary to the gene *[1 mark]*. Once made, the mRNA molecule moves out of the nucleus and joins to a ribosome in the cytoplasm *[1 mark]*. tRNA molecules bring amino acids to the ribosome — anticodons on the tRNA pair up with complementary codons in the mRNA to ensure that amino acids are brought to the ribosome in the correct order *[1 mark]*. The ribosome joins the amino acids together to make a protein *[1 mark]*.

Pages 106-107
Warm-Up Questions

1)   anther, filament
2) a)   The end part of the carpel, which pollen grains attach to.
  b)   The rod-like section that supports the stigma.
3)   When seeds start to grow.
4)   enough water, enough oxygen, a suitable temperature

Exam Questions

1 a)   Pollen grains from an anther *[1 mark]* are transferred to a stigma *[1 mark]*, so that male gametes can fertilise female gametes *[1 mark]*.

  b)   Sexual reproduction involving only one plant / the transfer of pollen from an anther to a stigma on the same plant *[1 mark]*.

2 a)   X: Filament *[1 mark]*. It supports the anther *[1 mark]*. Y: Ovary *[1 mark]*. It contains the female gametes/eggs *[1 mark]*.

  b)   Flower B because e.g. long filaments hang the anthers outside the flower *[1 mark]*, so that a lot of pollen gets blown away *[1 mark]* / the large, feathery stigmas *[1 mark]* are efficient at catching pollen drifting past in the air *[1 mark]*.

  c)   Any two from: e.g. brightly coloured petals to attract insects / scented flowers/nectaries/produce nectar to attract insects / large, sticky pollen grains that stick easily to insects / a sticky stigma to collect pollen from insects *[2 marks]*.

3 a)   Runners are rapidly growing stems that grow sideways from the plant above ground *[1 mark]*. The runners take root, producing new plants that begin to grow *[1 mark]*.

  b)   Because the strawberry plant's offspring are clones of the parent plant/genetically identical to the parent *[1 mark]*.

4 a)   E.g. she wants to ensure that the offspring will have exactly the same characteristics as the parent plants *[1 mark]*, which they wouldn't if she allowed the parent plants to reproduce sexually *[1 mark]*.

  b)   E.g. taking cuttings *[1 mark]*

5 a)   Because oxygen is needed for germination *[1 mark]* and oxygen was removed from the air in flask A by the sodium pyrogallate solution *[1 mark]*.

  b)   From food reserves stored within the seeds *[1 mark]*.

  c)   E.g. normally, after seeds have produced green leaves, they can start to obtain energy through photosynthesis *[1 mark]*. But in flask B, sodium hydroxide has removed the carbon dioxide from the air, so photosynthesis can't occur *[1 mark]*. The seedlings have used up their food reserves, so there is no energy available for growth *[1 mark]*.

Page 111
Warm-Up Questions

1)   To make sperm.
The other function of the testes is to produce testosterone.
2)   To carry the sperm from the testis towards the urethra.
3)   testosterone
4)   Extra hair on underarms and pubic area. Widening of hips. Development of breasts. Ovum release and start of periods.

Exam Questions

1   D *[1 mark]*

2 a)   To allow food, oxygen and waste substances to be exchanged between mother and fetus *[1 mark]*.

  b)   It protects the fetus against knocks/bumps *[1 mark]*.

3 a)   A, because a rise in the level of oestrogen results in the release of an egg *[1 mark]*.

  b)   The uterus lining is thickest during the second half of the cycle/after the egg is released/between days 14 and 28 *[1 mark]*. This is because the uterus is preparing to receive a fertilised egg/zygote *[1 mark]*.

Pages 117-118
Warm-Up Questions
1) Different versions of the same gene.
2) Which alleles something has.
3) dominant alleles
4) The Y chromosome.

Exam Questions
1 a) They have brown hair *[1 mark]*.
  b) heterozygous *[1 mark]*

2 a)
Genotypes of parents: Rr Rr

Genotypes of gametes: R r R r

Genotypes of offspring: RR Rr Rr rr

Phenotypes of offspring: red eyes red eyes red eyes white eyes

[1 mark for correct genotypes of the parents, 1 mark for correct genotypes of gametes, 1 mark for correct genotypes and phenotypes of offspring]

  b) i) 1 in 4 / 25% / 0.25 / ¼ *[1 mark]*
    ii) 75% of the offspring are likely to have red eyes
    $(75 \div 100) \times 60 = 45$ *[2 marks for the correct answer, otherwise 1 mark for 75 ÷ 100, 75%, ¾ or 0.75]*

3 Dd *[1 mark]*. Polydactyly is a dominant disorder, so if she was DD all of her children would be affected *[1 mark]*.

4 a) E.g.
Genotypes of parents: aa Aa

Genotypes of gametes: a a A a

Genotypes of offspring: Aa Aa aa aa

Phenotypes of offspring: no albinism, no albinism, albinism, albinism

[1 mark for correct genotypes of both parents, 1 mark for correct genotypes of gametes, 1 mark for correct genotypes of offspring, 1 mark for correct phenotypes of offspring]

  b) 50% *[1 mark]*
  c) Fertilisation is random/the genetic diagram only shows the probability of the outcome, so the numbers of offspring produced will not always be exactly in those proportions *[1 mark]*.

5 a)
Chromosomes of parents: female XX, male XY

Chromosomes of gametes: X X X Y

Chromosomes of offspring: XX XX XY XY

Sex of offspring: female female male male

[1 mark for correct chromosomes in parents, 1 mark for correct chromosomes in gametes, 1 mark for correct chromosomes in offspring, 1 mark for correct sex of offspring]

  b) Male children will not inherit the colour blindness allele because they don't inherit an X chromosome from their father *[1 mark]*.
  c) 0 / 0% *[1 mark]*

A daughter of this couple would inherit the recessive colour blindness allele from her father, but also a dominant allele from her mother, so she would not be colour blind.

6 a) Codominant *[1 mark]*, because the spotted flowers display both red and white characteristics *[1 mark]*.
  b)
Parent 1 RW
Parent 2 RW

	R	W
R	RR	RW
W	RW	WW

[1 mark for correct genotypes of both parents, 1 mark for correct genotypes of gametes (shown in grey boxes), 1 mark for correct genotypes of offspring]

  c) 1 : 2 : 1 (red : spotted : white flowers) *[1 mark]*

Pages 123-124
Warm-Up Questions
1) E.g. sunlight, moisture level, temperature, mineral content of soil.
2) Life began as simple organisms from which more complex organisms evolved (rather than just popping into existence).
3) A rare, random change in an organism's DNA that can be inherited.
4) E.g. X-rays, gamma rays, ultraviolet light. It can cause mutations.
5) E.g. tobacco.

Exam Questions
1 Mutations change the sequence of DNA bases *[1 mark]*, which can change the protein produced by a gene *[1 mark]* and lead to a different phenotype, increasing variation *[1 mark]*.

2 a) natural selection *[1 mark]*
  b)

Stage	Order
The gene for methicillin resistance became more common in the population over time.	4
Individual bacteria with the mutated genes were more likely to survive and reproduce in a host being treated with methicillin.	2
Random mutations in the DNA of *Staphylococcus aureus* led to it being less affected by methicillin.	1
The gene for methicillin resistance was passed on to lots of offspring, who also survived and reproduced.	3

[2 marks for all answers in the correct order, otherwise 1 mark for two or more answers in the correct order.]

3 a) No, because hair colour is controlled by genes *[1 mark]* and identical twins have the same genes *[1 mark]*.
  b) The difference in weight must be caused by the environment *[1 mark]*, because the twins have exactly the same genes *[1 mark]*.

In this case, the environment can mean the amount of food each twin eats or the amount of exercise they each do.

  c) No, because if they were caused by genes both twins should have the birthmark *[1 mark]*.

4 There is no guarantee that the foal will be a successful racehorse *[1 mark]* because sexual reproduction results in a random combination of genes in the offspring *[1 mark]*, meaning that the foal might not be genetically suited to racing *[1 mark]*. In addition, environmental conditions contribute to how successful the foal is and these cannot be exactly replicated/completely controlled *[1 mark]*.

5   E.g. ancestors of the modern buff tip moth showed variation in their appearance *[1 mark]*. The moths that looked more like broken twigs were less likely to be seen and eaten by predators/more likely to survive *[1 mark]* and so were more likely to reproduce *[1 mark]*. As a result, the alleles that caused the moths to look more like broken twigs were more likely to be passed on to the next generation *[1 mark]*, meaning that over time these genes became increasingly widespread in the population and eventually all buff tip moths resembled a broken twig *[1 mark]*.

6   After the storm, there will be fewer larger seeds available on the island *[1 mark]*. Birds with larger beaks will be less able to get food and seed size will become a selection pressure *[1 mark]*. Small seeds will still be available, so birds with smaller beaks will be better adapted to their environment than the birds with larger beaks *[1 mark]*. This makes birds with smaller beaks more likely to survive and reproduce than birds with larger beaks *[1 mark]*. In turn, this means that the alleles responsible for small beaks are more likely to be passed on to the next generation than the alleles for larger beaks *[1 mark]*. The alleles for smaller beaks will become more common in the population over time and eventually, all the finches in the population will have smaller beaks *[1 mark]*.

Section 8 — Ecology and the Environment

Pages 132-133
Warm-Up Questions
1) a)   a community
   b)   an ecosystem
2)   A producer is an organism that makes its own food using energy from the Sun. A consumer is an organism that eats other organisms.
3)   A stage/feeding level in a food chain.

Exam Questions
1 a)   4 *[1 mark]*
  b)   crab *[1 mark]*
  c)   decomposers *[1 mark]*
2 a)   E.g. they could have placed quadrats at regular intervals *[1 mark]* in a straight line from the wood to the opposite side of the field *[1 mark],* and counted the dandelions in each quadrat *[1 mark]*.
  b)   The number of dandelions increases with distance from the wood *[1 mark]*.
3 a)   2070 ÷ 10 = 207 kJ available to the second trophic level *[1 mark]*
       207 − (90 + 100) = **17 kJ** available to Animal A *[1 mark]*
  b)   Any two from: e.g. respiration / transfer of energy to the surroundings by heat / loss in waste/faeces *[1 mark for each correct answer]*
  c)   Because energy is lost at each trophic level *[1 mark]* so there's not enough energy to support more levels *[1 mark]*.
4   E.g. the weevils eat platte thistles so could decrease this population, reducing the food available for honeybees *[1 mark]*. If the honeybee population decreases, the amount of wild honey produced will decrease *[1 mark]*.
5 a)   The concentration of DDT in organisms increases as you go up the trophic levels *[1 mark]*.
  b)   13.8 ÷ 0.04 = **345 times**
       [2 marks for correct answer, otherwise 1 mark for using 13.8 and 0.04 in calculation]
  c)   E.g. because DDT is stored in the tissues of animals and a pyramid of biomass represents the mass of the living tissues *[1 mark]*.

Pages 141-142
Warm-Up Questions
1)   E.g. it's a poisonous gas. / If carbon monoxide combines with haemoglobin in red blood cells, it prevents them from carrying oxygen.
2)   Sources of 'man-made' methane are on the increase, for example rice-growing and cattle rearing.
3)   E.g. aerosols and fridges

Exam Questions
1 a) i)   photosynthesis *[1 mark]*
     ii)   carbon dioxide *[1 mark]*
  b)   respiration *[1 mark]*
  c)   Microorganisms break down/decompose material from dead organisms *[1 mark]* and return carbon to the air as carbon dioxide through respiration *[1 mark]*.
  d) i)   Fossil fuels are formed from dead animals and/or plants which contain carbon *[1 mark]*.
     ii)   Carbon is released into the atmosphere as carbon dioxide when fossil fuels are burnt *[1 mark]*.
2   C *[1 mark]*
3 a)   Greenhouse gases absorb heat that is radiated away from the Earth *[1 mark]* and re-radiate it in all directions, including back to Earth *[1 mark]*.
  b)   E.g. it would be very cold at night *[1 mark]*.
  c)   Increasing levels of greenhouse gases in the atmosphere *[1 mark]* have enhanced the greenhouse effect *[1 mark]* causing the Earth to warm up, which is global warming *[1 mark]*.
  d)   E.g. melting ice caps/glaciers *[1 mark]* could lead to flooding of human towns/settlements *[1 mark]*. / Changing rainfall patterns *[1 mark]* could lead to changing crop growth patterns/less food being grown *[1 mark]*.
4   The number of microorganisms increases downstream of the sewage pipe *[1 mark]*. The sewage provides extra nutrients causing rapid algal growth *[1 mark]*. The algae block out light from plants causing them to die *[1 mark]*. The dead plants provide food for microorganisms, causing the number of microorganisms to increase *[1 mark]*.
5 a)   When forests are cut down, less carbon dioxide is removed from the atmosphere by photosynthesising trees *[1 mark]*. The trees that are cut down are often burnt to clear the land, which releases carbon dioxide into the atmosphere *[1 mark]*. Any trees that aren't burned are decomposed by microorganisms, which release carbon dioxide through respiration *[1 mark]*. All of these processes increase the level of carbon dioxide (a greenhouse gas) in the atmosphere, which contributes to global warming *[1 mark]*.
  b)   When trees are cut down, evapotranspiration is reduced *[1 mark]*. This results in a reduction in precipitation/rainfall, which leads to a drier climate *[1 mark]*.
  c)   Tree roots help hold the soil together *[1 mark]*. When trees are removed soil can be eroded/washed away by rain *[1 mark]*.
  d)   Trees take up nutrients from the soil and return them when fallen leaves decay/the trees die *[1 mark]*. When trees are removed, the nutrients are washed out of/leached from the soil by rain and are not replaced, leaving infertile soil *[1 mark]*.

Section 9 — Use of Biological Resources

Page 150
Warm-Up Questions
1)   To reduce the number of plants being damaged or destroyed by pests, increasing crop yield.
2)   *Lactobacillus* bacteria
3)   Any two from, e.g. temperature / pH / oxygen level

Exam Questions

1 a) carbon dioxide *[1 mark]*
   b) E.g. by counting the bubbles of carbon dioxide produced over a certain amount of time *[1 mark]*.
   c) i) E.g. she could stand the test tube containing the yeast suspension in a water bath *[1 mark]*.
      ii) It would increase the rate of respiration *[1 mark]*.
2 a) To increase her crop yield *[1 mark]* as she can create the ideal conditions for photosynthesis inside a polythene tunnel *[1 mark]* and it's easier to keep her plants free from diseases/pests *[1 mark]*.
   b) i) Fertiliser C *[1 mark]* because strawberry yield was highest with this fertiliser for 4 out of the 5 years/in total over the 5 years/on average over the five years *[1 mark]*.
      ii) Fertilisers contain some of the elements that crops need in order to grow and to carry out life processes *[1 mark]*. These elements may be missing from the soil, so fertilisers are used to replace them *[1 mark]* or to add more to the soil *[1 mark]*.

Pages 156-157
Warm-Up Questions

1) Organisms with the best characteristics are selected and bred with each other. The best of their offspring are then selected and bred. This process is repeated over several generations.
2) True
3) restriction enzymes
4) E.g. insulin.
5) A clone is an organism that is genetically identical to another organism.

Exam Questions

1 a) i) E.g. wasted food / excrement / parasites *[1 mark]*
      ii) E.g. pH / temperature / oxygen level *[1 mark]*
   b) E.g. to protect the fish from predatory birds / interspecific predation *[1 mark]*.
   c) Intraspecific predation is where organisms eat individuals of the same species *[1 mark]*. It can be avoided on a fish farm by keeping small fish separate from big fish / providing regular food *[1 mark]*.
   d) selective breeding *[1 mark]*
   e) E.g. rear some fish in cages in the sea and some in tanks. Use the same species and age of fish in both places. Make sure the fish in both places have the same access to and type of food and the same protection from predators. Measure the mass of the fish in each place at the start of the experiment and again after three months. Repeat the experiment at least three times and calculate the mean change in mass in each place.
   [1 mark for stating that some fish will be raised in cages in the sea and some in tanks, 1 mark for stating that all the fish used will be the same age and species, 1 mark for describing a control variable that needs to be kept the same (e.g. type of food used), 1 mark for describing a second control variable (e.g. same protection from predators), 1 mark for stating how long the fish will be allowed to grow for (e.g. three months), 1 mark for stating what will be measured (e.g. the mass of the fish), 1 mark for stating that repeats should be carried out. Maximum 6 marks available.]
   Have a look at the Describing Experiments section for more tips on what you need to include when you're answering this type of question.
2 The tall and dwarf wheat plants could be cross-bred *[1 mark]*. The best of the offspring/the offspring with the highest grain yield and highest bad weather resistance could then be cross-bred *[1 mark]*, and this process repeated over several generations *[1 mark]*.

3 a) D *[1 mark]*
   b) i) Small pieces of a plant/explants are taken from the tips of the plant's stems and side shoots *[1 mark]*. The small pieces of plant/explants are sterilised and grown in vitro *[1 mark]* on nutrient medium *[1 mark]*. Cells in the small pieces of plant/explants divide and grow into a plant *[1 mark]*.
      ii) E.g. lots of plants with desirable characteristics can be grown *[1 mark]*.
4 a) i) So that both types of crop experienced the same conditions *[1 mark]*, meaning it was a fair test *[1 mark]*.
      ii) E.g. the researchers could carry out a large number of repeats *[1 mark]*.
   b) E.g. yes, because for three out of the four kinds of crop grown, more butterflies and bees were found on the normal crops compared to the GM crops *[1 mark]*.

Practice Paper 1B

1 a) i) haploid *[1 mark]*
      ii) B *[1 mark]*
      iii) B *[1 mark]*
   b) At fertilisation a male gamete fuses with a female gamete *[1 mark]* to form a zygote *[1 mark]*. The zygote then undergoes cell division and develops into an embryo *[1 mark]*.
2 a) oxygen *[1 mark]*
   Remember, plants give off oxygen when they photosynthesise.
   b) The volume of gas collected would decrease *[1 mark]* because when the lamp is turned off the light intensity will decrease *[1 mark]*, so the rate of photosynthesis will decrease too *[1 mark]*.
   c) Carbon dioxide is needed for photosynthesis *[1 mark]*, so adding it to the water ensures that the rate of photosynthesis is not limited by a lack of carbon dioxide *[1 mark]*.
   d) The enzymes needed for photosynthesis work more slowly at low temperatures, so the rate of photosynthesis will be slower at low temperatures *[1 mark]*. But if the temperature is too high, the enzymes are denatured so photosynthesis won't happen *[1 mark]*. The temperature could be controlled, for example, by putting the beaker into a warm water bath to keep the temperature constant *[1 mark]*.
   e) i) B *[1 mark]*
      ii) Yes. The pondweed has been photosynthesising, so it will have produced glucose, which is stored as starch *[1 mark]*.
3 a) Any three from: they provide a large surface area so that digested food is absorbed into the blood quickly. / They have a single permeable layer of surface cells to assist quick absorption. / They have a very good blood supply to assist quick absorption. / They have a lacteal for absorbing fats *[3 marks]*.
   b) Amino acids are absorbed into the blood by active transport *[1 mark]*. They are absorbed against the concentration gradient using energy (transferred from respiration) *[1 mark]*.
   The diagram shows more amino acids in the blood than in the gut, so they must be absorbed by active transport.
   c) i) To carry oxygen from the lungs to the cells *[1 mark]*.
      ii) They have a large surface area for absorbing oxygen *[1 mark]*. They don't have a nucleus, so they have more room to carry oxygen *[1 mark]*. They contain lots of haemoglobin, which combines reversibly with oxygen in the lungs to become oxyhaemoglobin *[1 mark]*.

4 a) i)

[1 mark for drawing the plant shoots growing towards the hole in the box]

   ii) Light coming through the hole in the box *[1 mark]* caused more auxin to accumulate on the shaded sides of the shoots *[1 mark]*. This made the cells on the shaded sides of the plants grow/elongate faster *[1 mark]*, so the shoots bent towards the light *[1 mark]*.

b)   A *[1 mark]*

5 a) i) E.g.

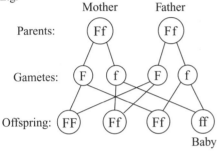

[1 mark for showing that the parents both have the Ff genotype, 1 mark for showing the gametes' genotypes as F or f, 1 mark for correctly showing all three possible genotypes of the couple's offspring.]

The parents must both have one copy of the recessive allele for cystic fibrosis — so they're both Ff.

In a question like this, the marks are allocated for the correct genotypes of the parents, gametes and offspring. It doesn't matter what type of genetic diagram you draw as long as it shows this information — so you could have drawn a Punnett square.

   ii) Homozygous, because he has two alleles the same/ both of his alleles are recessive *[1 mark]*.

b)   1 in 4 / 25% *[1 mark]*

c)   Ff *[1 mark]*. Ian has the genotype Ff, so Leina must also have the genotype Ff in order for her children to inherit the genotypes: FF (Carys), ff (Beth) and Ff (Alfie) *[1 mark]*.

d)   Environmental variation *[1 mark]*. The scar would have been caused by an environmental factor rather than being determined by genes *[1 mark]*.

6 a)   The dark variety is better camouflaged in soot-polluted areas, so it is less likely to be eaten by predators *[1 mark]*. This means more dark moths survive to breed *[1 mark]* and pass the gene(s) for this characteristic on to the next generation *[1 mark]*. As this process continues over time, the dark variety of moth becomes more common *[1 mark]*.

It makes sense that if an organism blends in with its background it'll be harder for predators to spot it.

b)   Town B is the most polluted because it contains a higher percentage of dark moths *[1 mark]*.

c)   77% – 25% = 52%
[2 marks for correct answer, otherwise 1 mark for correctly reading 77% and 25% off the graph]

7 a)   Mean change in mass = (–0.78 + –0.81 + –0.82) ÷ 3
                = –0.80 g
[2 marks for correct answer, otherwise 1 mark for adding together 3 values and dividing by 3]

b)

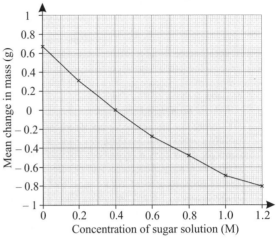

[1 mark for choosing a suitable scale, 1 mark for using straight lines to join the points, 1 mark for having axes labelled correctly (with correct units), 1 mark for having the axes the correct way round, 2 marks for all points plotted correctly (or 1 mark for at least 5 points plotted correctly). Plotting marks may still be given if an incorrect answer to 7 a) has been plotted correctly.]

c)   The concentration of sugar inside the original potatoes was approximately 0.4 M *[1 mark]*. This is the point where there was no change in weight of the potato cylinders, therefore no net movement of water, because the concentrations on both sides of the (partially permeable) membrane were the same *[1 mark]*.

d)   To give more reliable results *[1 mark]*.

Repeating an experiment also means that you should be able to spot any glaring errors — like reading the balance wrongly in this experiment.

8 a) i) D *[1 mark]*

   ii) 130 J *[1 mark]*

Tertiary consumers are the third consumers in a food chain — so in this case the tertiary consumers are the snakes.

   iii) E.g. the population of plants may increase *[1 mark]* because there are fewer grasshoppers to feed on them *[1 mark]*. / The population of mice may decrease *[1 mark]* because there is less food available for them *[1 mark]*.

b)   D, because the biomass of the organisms decreases at each trophic level *[1 mark]* and the bars on this pyramid get smaller at each trophic level *[1 mark]*.

c)   (130 ÷ 1100) × 100% = 11.8%
[2 marks for correct answer, otherwise 1 mark for using 130 ÷ 1100 in working]

d)   Energy is lost at each level of a food chain *[1 mark]*. After about five levels the amount of energy being passed on is not sufficient to support another level of organisms *[1 mark]*.

9 a)   Gas A = oxygen *[1 mark]*, Gas B = carbon dioxide *[1 mark]*

b)   Any three from: they provide a large surface area for diffusion to occur across. / They have a moist lining for gases to dissolve in. / They have thin walls, so gases only have to diffuse a short distance. / They have permeable walls so gases can diffuse across easily. / They have a good blood supply to maintain a high concentration gradient *[3 marks]*.

c)   The intercostal muscles and diaphragm relax *[1 mark]*. This causes the volume of the thorax to decrease *[1 mark]*, which increases the pressure in the lungs *[1 mark]*, so air is forced out *[1 mark]*.

10 E.g. plant some lettuce seeds outside and some under a polythene tunnel. Ensure that the lettuce seeds are of the same variety and plant them in compost taken from the same batch. Allow the lettuces to grow for 28 days, making sure that the lettuces in both environments receive the same amount of water and fertiliser during this time. After 28 days take three lettuces from outside and three lettuces from the polythene tunnel and measure the mass of each lettuce using a balance. Calculate the average mass of the lettuces grown outside and compare it to the average mass of those grown under the polythene tunnel. *[1 mark for stating that some lettuces will be grown in a polythene tunnel and some will be grown outside, 1 mark for stating that the lettuce seeds should be of the same variety, 1 mark for describing one control variable, 1 mark for describing a second control variable, 1 mark for stating how long the lettuces will be allowed to grow for, 1 mark for stating what will be measured (e.g. the mass of the lettuces), 1 mark for stating that repeats should be carried out (e.g. by measuring the mass of three lettuces from each environment). Maximum 6 marks available.]*

You're not expected to know exactly how to do this investigation or to have done it before. This type of question is designed to test your knowledge of experimental skills, even when the scenario is unfamiliar to you.

11 a) Beaker B was low in nitrates *[1 mark]*. Nitrates are needed for making amino acids/proteins *[1 mark]*, which are essential for growth *[1 mark]*.

b) It would have yellow leaves *[1 mark]* because without magnesium, plants can't make the chlorophyll that gives them their green colour *[1 mark]*.

c) Any two from: e.g. the amount of light shining on each beaker / the level of other substances in the mineral solution / the size of the beakers / the amount of air available / the amount of water available / the temperature of the beakers *[2 marks]*.

12 a) i) E.g. the graph suggests that the more cigarettes male doctors smoke per day, the more likely they are to die from coronary heart disease *[1 mark]*. The male doctors who give up smoking are less likely to die from coronary heart disease than those who do smoke *[1 mark]*. The male doctors who have never smoked are the least likely to die from coronary heart disease *[1 mark]*.

ii) E.g. you could include women as well as men in the study. / You could use a sample of people from several different professions *[1 mark]*.

b) Any two from: e.g. smoking damages the walls inside the alveoli *[1 mark]*, reducing the surface area for gas exchange/leading to diseases like emphysema *[1 mark]*. / The tar in cigarettes damages the cilia in the lungs/ trachea *[1 mark]*, leading to the build-up of mucus/ increasing the risk of chest infections *[1 mark]*. / Tar irritates the bronchi and bronchioles, *[1 mark]* leading to excess mucus/a smoker's cough/chronic bronchitis *[1 mark]*. / Tobacco smoke contains carcinogens *[1 mark]*, which can lead to lung cancer *[1 mark]*.

13 a) amount/rate of exercise *[1 mark]*

b) 129 beats/min (accept 128-130 beats/min) *[1 mark]*

c) 8 − 2 = 6 minutes *[1 mark]*

d) The student's heart rate increases during exercise *[1 mark]*. This is because when he exercises he needs more energy, so he respires more *[1 mark]*. Respiration increases the amount of carbon dioxide in his blood *[1 mark]*, which is detected by receptors (in his aorta and carotid artery) *[1 mark]*. The receptors send signals to his brain, which signals for his heart rate to increase *[1 mark]*.

e) i) glucose + oxygen → carbon dioxide + water (+ energy) *[1 mark for glucose + oxygen on the left-hand side of the equation, 1 mark for carbon dioxide + water (+ energy) on the right.]*

ii) E.g. aerobic respiration releases more energy than anaerobic respiration. / Aerobic respiration doesn't cause lactic acid to build up in the muscles, but anaerobic respiration does. / Aerobic respiration produces lots/32 molecules of ATP per molecule of glucose, whereas anaerobic respiration produces much fewer/2 molecules of ATP *[1 mark]*.

Practice Paper 2B

1 a) E.g. in developed countries people generally have a diet containing enough of the vitamins they need. / Sources of dietary vitamin A are affordable to a majority of people in developed countries. / Farming is more reliable, so the availability of foods containing vitamin A is likely to be more constant. / Healthcare is more widely available, so a lack of dietary vitamin A is more likely to be treated. *[1 mark]*

b) i) E.g. liver *[1 mark]*

ii) C *[1 mark]*

c) E.g. it contains genes transferred from other species — a maize plant and a soil bacterium *[1 mark]*.

d) E.g. because it is a substance/compound which is converted into vitamin A inside the body. / Because it is a substance/compound which is needed early on in the chemical pathway that produces vitamin A. / Because it is a precursor to vitamin A. *[1 mark]*

e) Any two from: e.g. bacteria can be genetically modified to produce insulin. / Crops can be genetically modified to be resistant to insect pests/herbicides. / Animals can be genetically modified to produce human proteins/antibodies (in their milk). *[2 marks]*

f) 150 ÷ 70 = 2.14...
2.14... × 100 = 214 g *[2 marks for the correct answer, otherwise 1 mark for using 2.14... in calculation]*

g) E.g. by growing Golden Rice, farmers grow their own source of vitamin A and they can earn money by selling any surplus rice *[1 mark]*, whereas regularly buying tablets is likely to be more expensive and no income can be made *[1 mark]*.

h) E.g. they don't have to buy new seed at the start of a growing season *[1 mark]* so it reduces their costs *[1 mark]*.

2 a) B — nitrifying bacteria *[1 mark]*
C — nitrogen-fixing bacteria *[1 mark]*
D — denitrifying bacteria *[1 mark]*

b) They decompose/break down dead plant and animal matter/waste, releasing carbon dioxide back into the atmosphere *[1 mark]* as they respire *[1 mark]*.

3 a) At point 9/Between points 8 and 9 *[1 mark]* because the oxygen level is lowest at point 9 *[1 mark]*.

b) The population size at point 1 would be larger than at point 10 *[1 mark]*.

c) The sewage provides extra nutrients, causing rapid algal growth *[1 mark]*. The algae block out the light, causing plants below to die *[1 mark]*. The dead plants provide food for microorganisms, causing the number of microorganisms to increase *[1 mark]*. The microorganisms then deplete/use up the oxygen in the water *[1 mark]*.

d) E.g. oxygen-depletion near the source of the pollution has caused the death of fish and other animals in the water *[1 mark]*. This means there's little/nothing for the herons to feed on in this area *[1 mark]*.

e) 9 − 3.5 = 5.5 mg/l *[1 mark]*

4 a) E.g.

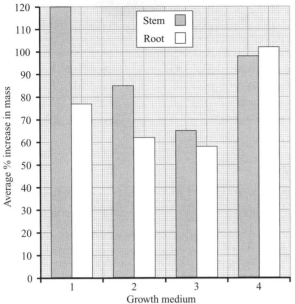

[1 mark for a bar chart covering at least half of the grid, 1 mark for correctly labelling the axes, including units, 1 mark for correctly labelling stem and root columns or including a key, 1 mark for plotting the points by using bars drawn with straight lines, 1 mark for correctly plotted points]

b) The combination of stem tissue and growth medium number 1 gave the best results *[1 mark]*, as this combination had the highest average percentage increase in tissue mass *[1 mark]*.

c) Any two from: e.g. the temperature in the incubator *[1 mark]* / the size of the tissue samples/blocks *[1 mark]* / the volume of growth medium used *[1 mark]*.

d) D *[1 mark]*

e) Any three from: sexual reproduction involves the fusion of male and female gametes, asexual reproduction doesn't *[1 mark]*. / Sexual reproduction involves two parents, asexual reproduction involves one parent *[1 mark]*. / There is mixing of genetic information in sexual reproduction, but not in asexual reproduction *[1 mark]*. / Asexual reproduction produces clones of the parents, sexual reproduction doesn't *[1 mark]*.

5 a) pituitary gland *[1 mark]*

b) FSH causes an egg to mature in one of the ovaries *[1 mark]*. It also stimulates the ovaries to produce oestrogen *[1 mark]*. Oestrogen causes the lining of the uterus to grow, and stimulates the release of LH / inhibits the release of FSH *[1 mark]*. LH stimulates the release of an egg/ovulation *[1 mark]*. Progesterone maintains the lining of the uterus during the second half of the menstrual cycle *[1 mark]*. The production of progesterone inhibits the release of LH and FSH *[1 mark]*.

6 a) Because the A and T bases in a DNA molecule always pair up with each other (complementary base-pairing) *[1 mark]*.

b) nucleus *[1 mark]*

c) four *[1 mark]*

d) i) C *[1 mark]*

ii) Any two from: e.g. the mutation may have occurred in an unimportant region of DNA. / The mutated codon may still code for the same amino acid so the structure and function of the protein is not affected. / The mutation may have occurred in a recessive allele. *[2 marks]*

7 a) The starch is broken down into sugars/maltose *[1 mark]*.

b) To make the experiment a fair test *[1 mark]*.

c) The time taken for the reaction to complete increases dramatically (from around 7 minutes to 29 minutes) *[1 mark]*. This is because the increasing pH causes the enzyme to change shape/denature *[1 mark]*. This means that the active site no longer matches the shape of the starch, so cannot catalyse its breakdown, and the reaction slows down *[1 mark]*.

d) i) The result for pH 7 is anomalous *[1 mark]* because the time taken until starch is no longer present is much slower than expected *[1 mark]*.

ii) E.g. the student may not have used the correct volume of starch solution. / The student may have used a buffer solution with the wrong pH. / The student may have carried out the experiment at a different temperature. / The student may have started timing the experiment too early *[1 mark]*.

8 a)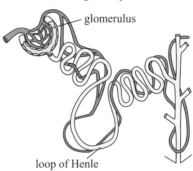

[1 mark for each correct label]

b) The blood is filtered in the Bowman's capsule and proteins are too big to pass through the membranes *[1 mark]*.

c) i) Urea is not reabsorbed into the blood, so its concentration increases through the nephron as water is reabsorbed *[1 mark]*.

ii) The concentration of sugar at point B would be high and there would be no sugar at point C *[1 mark]*, as all sugar is reabsorbed back into the blood in the proximal convoluted tubule/first part of the nephron *[1 mark]*.

d) ADH increases the permeability of the collecting duct of the nephron *[1 mark]*, causing more water to be reabsorbed into the blood *[1 mark]*.

Index

Index

Index